A Fruitful Season

A Fruitful Season

Barbara B. Smith

Bookcraft

SALT LAKE CITY, UTAH

Library of Congress Catalog Card Number: 88-72241

ISBN 0-88494-652-5

First Printing, 1988

Printed in the United States of America

Contents

Preface

Unique and challenging experiences were mine for nearly a decade as I served as the general president of the Relief Society of The Church of Jesus Christ of Latter-day Saints. Those experiences forever changed my outlook on the women of the Church and the women of the world. Now, in retrospect, I am aware that in many ways I am not the same woman who assumed that office by sacred call in the fall of 1974.

This book has been written to capture, in some measure, the experiences and insights I gleaned during my presidency and to share the abundance of that harvest—a harvest made more fruitful because of all with whom I was privileged to associate as we served in the Lord's vineyard.

Thrust in Your Sickle

Thrust in your sickle with
all your soul.
—D&C 31:5

October 5, 1974

Yesterday I was sustained as the general president of the Relief Society of The Church of Jesus Christ of Latter-day Saints. Since the prophet of the Lord, President Spencer W. Kimball, recently came to my home and asked me to serve in that capacity, a prayer has been in my heart.

I have been concerned that the release of Sister Belle S. Spafford, our wise and capable administrator of Relief Society for nearly the last thirty years, would come as a shock and cause dismay among the sisters of the Church. That which I feared happened yesterday. A gasp of surprise rippled audibly through the Salt Lake Tabernacle when the announcement was made. Then, as my name was presented to the membership for a sustaining vote, I instinctively looked to Sister Spafford who, without any hesitation, raised her hand high in support of my new calling. Her sensitivity to my great need for advocacy at that moment caused me to love and respect her more than ever before.

As I approached the Tabernacle podium to publicly respond to the sustaining vote by the Relief Society membership, my throat was dry and tears streamed down my cheeks. Humbled by the faith of the Saints and reassured by the spiritual confirmation I have recently received, I was still acutely aware of how much I need to continue to rely on the

Lord if I am to prove acceptable as a late laborer in his vineyard. The nine valiant women who have preceded me as the general Relief Society presidents thrust in their sickles and labored long and diligently to establish and develop the Relief Society organization to its present stature.

As I looked out over that vast audience yesterday, my commitment was firm and it remains so. I will trust in the Lord. I will try to bring together in proper perspective all of the experiences and lessons he has given me in preparation for this sacred calling. I will do all I can to be of assistance to the leaders of the Church in preparing for the time of harvest in the kingdom.

Gratitude filled my heart for my counselors, Janath R. Cannon and Marian R. Boyer, as well as for Mayola R. Miltenberger, our secretary-treasurer, and the members of the general board—all noble women with strong testimonies of the Lord Jesus Christ and of the influence for good Relief Society can be in the lives of the women of the Church. And there will be so many others I will need. I was comforted, for I knew the Lord would provide. There came to me the words of the song: "I'll strengthen thee, help thee, and cause thee to stand, upheld by my righteous, omnipotent hand." The mantle of presidency had fallen on me.

Part 1

Sowing the Seed

And the Lord was with
us; and we did prosper
exceedingly; for we did
sow seed, and we did reap
again in abundance.
—2 Nephi 5:11

That a Seed May Be Planted in Your Heart

If ye give place, that a seed may be planted in your heart, behold, if it be a true seed, or a good seed . . . ye will begin to say . . . it beginneth to enlarge my soul . . . to enlighten my understanding, yea, it beginneth to be delicious to me.
—Alma 32:28

There may have been a time when I had no idea what the Relief Society was, but I cannot remember it. From the very beginning of my conscious memory, Relief Society, my mother, and other women are intertwined. The faces of the women were familiar to me and I can still recall many of them clearly—one especially.

In fact, I believe my first introduction to the power of Relief Society is associated with that face; I can recall vividly that it was round, with blue eyes that twinkled. It belonged to a heavy-set woman with a broad English accent—Sister Barnes. She had red hair, and I remember that when she laughed her face crinkled up—at least that's how it looked to me as a little girl.

However, Sister Barnes wasn't always happy. She was from England, and Salt Lake City sometimes seemed a long way from home. At those times she looked sad. I feel certain that my mother, who was then her Relief Society president, knew that Sister Barnes felt lonely, being away from her homeland and the people there who were familiar to her. I believe my mother understood that the strangeness of this new country, even among the Saints, was hard for Sister Barnes.

One day Mother asked Sister Barnes to come to our home to cook her English specialty, fish and chips, for a meeting of the ward Relief Society presidency. They were marvelously delicious and the Relief Society officers asked Sister Barnes if she thought she could cook fish and chips for the bazaar. In those years, before the change in ward budgeting procedures, Relief Societies used to hold bazaars. They were a major event on every ward calendar and the Relief Society's key money-raising effort of the year. The sisters made many items to be sold, including food that always sold very well.

Sister Barnes was obviously pleased when they asked her to cook fish and chips for the bazaar. She said she knew she could do it if she had some women to help her. The presidency assured her that they would supply all the helpers she needed and would furnish the ingredients as well. I don't know how I happened to be in the room at the time that decision was made, but I remember the moment well and remember, too, how happy it made Sister Barnes. I was also at the bazaar, and I recall how Sister Barnes came early and was in the kitchen during the whole evening cooking her delicious fish and chips. Everybody bought some and then came back for more. I think Sister Barnes actually surpassed herself that night, for the fish and chips seemed even better than the first time I'd tasted them.

After that bazaar, Sister Barnes quickly became known in our area. Her fish and chips were in great demand, and so was Sister Barnes. The members of the ward came to value her not only as a capable cook, but as a fun-loving person. Everybody liked her. They just needed to get to know her. The Relief Society and Mother helped bring about that great change. I'm sure Sister Barnes never forgot her native country, but through Relief Society she found new friends and her face acquired a settled happiness.

I thought then, as a young girl, that it was because the fish and chips were so delicious that Mother and her officers had been inspired to ask that capable English woman to make them for the whole ward. Now I know that the inspiration actually came to provide a way of focusing on a wonderful individual and of helping her realize her own worth. Far more important than providing fish and chips for the ward bazaar, the work of Relief Society lay in confirming the gospel teaching that nothing is more important in the heavenly scheme of things than the individual soul. This was an insight I would need in the years ahead. Even as a child, my recognition of the great good that comes from Relief Society began to "enlarge my soul."

If the bazaars were a big job for Mother, she never showed it. She made them great fun for everyone who came. I liked to watch her take various ward members around from booth to booth, pointing out the items she thought would interest them. As she toured she would often smile at me, which I loved. The women also loved to see her smile; there was something wondrous in that smile. I really believe Mother's smile was a major feature in the success of many a bazaar.

After I had watched her through a number of bazaars, I became aware that it was my mother who saw to it that items really needed by struggling families in our ward were priced so that they could afford them. I also realized that my mother wanted to be certain that every item made for the bazaar was sold, so that every woman would know her efforts were appreciated and her handwork wanted by others. She circulated constantly and when the hour began to grow late, she would slash prices. If that didn't clear the item, she would go out among the crowd to find buyers for each remaining piece. I could tell that she was not satisfied until the last item in each booth found its way to a new owner.

I'm not sure if my mother always understood what made these events successful, but I believe that one of the great blessings of her Relief Society service, and certainly of my own, is that when a woman is willing to give prayerfully and unstintingly in response to her calling, she will realize continual growth in the ability to organize and carry out plans and projects. I think it is calculated in the plan of the Lord that we have the opportunity to learn these skills which have such importance to us now and eternally.

I cannot be certain about the chronological order, but I have many other happy Relief Society memories from that early period of my childhood. For me, all that bore the name of Relief Society also involved my mother. She was always there, and the charity that characterized her labors was apparent in her face. She had deep dimples which usually showed because she frequently smiled. The glasses she wore because of her nearsightedness did not veil the gentleness of her eyes. I thought her face was very beautiful: her skin was smooth, and she wore her brown hair in soft waves.

I remember Mother bringing home money from every Relief Society meeting. Mostly it was money from the dues the women had paid or collected when they went on their visiting teaching routes. (Relief Society is funded now by budget allocations, but in those days the women financed it by contributing handmade items to sell at bazaars, paying dues, and making charitable donations as well.) I can still see my mother sitting at the kitchen table after supper, carefully counting the money and getting it ready to be deposited in the bank the next day.

It was much harder to count the money after a bazaar. That was the big fund-raiser, so there was a lot more money to count. Mother would help plan and prepare for the bazaars and then work all day putting up displays. She continued her efforts throughout the evening to ensure the success of each bazaar, and finally had the laborious task, late at night, of counting the money. Meticulously, she counted and recounted piles of bills and stacks of coins to be certain there would be no mistake. Putting pennies, nickels, dimes, and quarters into paper wrappers, she then counted the paper money, bound it with an elastic, recorded the total on a piece of paper, and slipped it under the elastic. Mother always worried about the Relief Society money, so to safeguard it she somehow acquired a coffee can (a thing hard to come by in a Mormon home) and carefully hid the money in the can before retiring at night, thinking the coffee can a safe place because nobody would think of looking for Relief Society money there. The next morning the money was transferred to a very old handbag—again as a safety measure, because it wouldn't look as if it contained much money—and taken straight to the bank.

Mother loved the sisters and, as Relief Society president, she felt the importance of every woman's participation. It was a weekly ritual for her to call various women in the ward and make arrangements to take them to the Relief Society meetings. In this way, she managed to introduce a new or recently activated sister to all the other sisters in the ward. She made it possible for those sisters to visit and enjoy each other before the meetings, participate during the class periods, and visit again after the meetings concluded. Then she would take them back home again, renewed in spirit and warmed by the growing circle of friends they were making.

It was this whole mosaic of happy faces, of happy sounds, of laughter, and of a caring, sharing sisterhood that was planted in my heart as I became aware of Relief Society. I soon came to understand, however, that there was a great deal more to the Relief Society than I had observed as a child.

"Said Jesus, 'Ye shall do the work, which ye see me do.' " (*History of the Church*, vol. 5, p. 20). Those grand key words shaped the Relief Society work in our ward as it was directed by Mother and her associates. And as she labored to follow the Savior's injunction, the words shaped my mother's life as well. Not only did compassionate service assignments come to her formally as a part of her calling, but such service filled her personal life.

Very often a resolute look in Mother's face told me she was thinking about someone who needed her help. Mother's eyes would twinkle and her smile would deepen the dimples in her cheeks as she set about seeing what she could do about that need. It never seemed to be a problem for her to do for others. She would just get up a little earlier in the morning and work a little faster. She always tended to the needs of her own household: her husband, her children, her mother, and other family members came first. Then, before we knew it, she was out giving of herself to others.

Our home was clean, neat, and orderly; meals were prepared on time, and more often than not, both home and meals were shared with others. I think my mother thought that what she learned in Relief Society was intended to be used daily, including the scriptural counsel that pure religion is to care for the homeless, the poor, those in need, the sick, and those in pain. I know she believed that there was always room for one more. Our home was always open.

I remember when Aunt Elsie came to stay. Mother was so happy to include her that we children thought it must be a treat to have her there, even though we had to double up and sleep two or three in a bed. We had been to Aunt Elsie's home in Lonetree, Wyoming, many times. She was mother's older sister. It was always a great adventure to go and visit her. There we rode old Flax, the horse, and did other things we could only do on a ranch.

One time Aunt Elsie came to our house in Salt Lake City to have her baby when it was due. That was exciting; in the morning there was only Aunt Elsie, but when we came home in the afternoon there was a beautiful new baby. Mother was there tending to her sister's needs, thoughtfully, carefully, willingly. Through her I saw compassion every day and I loved the warm feelings that came with it.

When Aunt Bernice came to stay with us, it was the same. There she was, right in the middle of the activity of our home, where all of us could visit with her. Aunt Bernice was my father's cousin. She looked like she was going to have a baby just as Aunt Elsie did. Actually, the medical problem that brought Aunt Bernice from Lyman, Wyoming, to our house was a very different one. She had dropsy. She would tease us and say she was sure she was going to have at least triplets; when the water that had collected in her abdomen was withdrawn, she would laugh and say, "No such luck."

She was there at our house for months, almost until she died. She had to have a doctor's care, and Mother tenderly nursed her as well. I don't recall the work, but I fondly remember that sweet association with Aunt Bernice. She was comfortable there at our house. It was the way Mother made everyone feel, as if they really belonged and enhanced the happiness we all enjoyed.

Mother didn't act as though the additional work was too much for her. She just did it, then spent time talking and laughing with our much-loved house guests. She didn't make compassionate service seem a burden. As a result of her attitude, we all felt it was a privilege to have guests in our home. Now, when I consider all the meals Mother served to those who were confined to bed at our house, I marvel. I remember, too, the times Mother would adjust and plump a pillow between the knees, or rub backs to make our ailing guests more comfortable. Nothing took too much time or was too hard for Mother.

It was not just my parents' family members who found welcome in our home. Once, the parents of my sister's friend were having marital troubles and their daughter came to stay with us. It was as if I immediately had a new sister. We laughed and talked together and our family loved her as though she was one of us.

Then Jimmy came to stay. He was the son of one of my father's customers. When his parents were able to take him back into their home they did, but in the meantime he was treated like one of the boys in our family—not as an additional mouth to feed on a very meager income, but as a blessing to all of us, and as a friend we would enjoy more each day.

Whenever Nana, my maternal grandmother, came down from Wyoming, we all piled into the car and did all of her errands that needed to be done while she was in Salt Lake City. Then we went to visit her friends and family. It was a wonderful outing and a very special part of our lives.

It never even occurred to me, as a child, that Mother might have difficulty keeping up with this demanding schedule of civic, church, and family responsibilities. I didn't consider how difficult it must have been for her to take the boys on their weekly paper routes through the downtown businesses. I didn't realize she had to find time, in between, to complete the school census she helped take each year.

Then there was the vacuum-cleaner salesman who came to demonstrate the cleaning power of a certain vacuum to Mother. He gave her his usual halfhearted, lackluster demonstation, and afterward told her than he was very discouraged with selling. In her jovial way she encouraged him: "Unless you have a positive attitude, you will never sell your product."

So he tried again, and just to encourage him, she bought a vacuum. He left so happy that we all were pleased for him, but Mother didn't stop there. When she went to Relief Society, she told some of the sisters privately about him and the wonderful new cleaning tool, and suggested they call him. He came back many times to thank her for making it possible for him and his family to survive during that difficult time. It never dawned on me then that Relief Society had taught her that she must reach out even to strangers within her gate; but I saw her do it.

During those times when Mother was serving as secretary and then as president of Relief Society, in order to not leave us children home when she made calls she had us all get into the car and go with her. We would wait in the car while she would go into a home to give her encouraging words and help. She would come out and express sympathy for the people she had visited and gratitude for her own health and strength and for that of her family.

Once she went to visit the mother of a little child who was hydrocephalic, suffering from what was then termed "water on the brain." Her heart ached for both the child and its mother. She went frequently to help with the work that needed to be done in that home. On those nights she held us more tenderly as she tucked us in bed, and her prayers were given with a special tone of thanksgiving.

It seemed to me that no one was ever sick in our ward but that Mother was right there to see if there was anything she could do. It was never a one-time visit, but rather she returned again and again, until the crisis was over. Even then, she would call and pick up the sister and take her to her meetings or to complete her errands.

Mother did a lot of telephoning to accomplish the work of Relief Society. No matter who needed her, my mother had time to listen. I remember how frequently I would see her standing there at the wall phone, talking. (I have often wondered if Mother made the original proposal for the long telephone cord so that she could continue her work during those lengthy conversations.) Many people wanted to tell Mother their problems. She always listened and she always responded.

They apparently felt better when they could share their troubles with her.

I could not give a full account of all the people my mother helped, nor could I recount all the names of those who found comfort in our home for a night, a few days, weeks, or months. But without knowing it, I was learning the joy of giving service, and somehow, without any explanation, I became aware that this sharing of people's burdens was linked to Relief Society. Mother had gently planted the seed of Relief Society and consistently nurtured it throughout my early years.

As I reflect back on the years of my childhood, I know that I felt a great love for Relief Society because my mother loved it and served in it for so many years. I was shown, though never told, that Relief Society teaches important principles that should become a guide to personal behavior. One of those principles was compassionate service. I later recognized several scriptures regarding that service by which Mother lived: "I was a stranger, and ye took me in: Naked, and ye clothed me: I was sick, and ye visited me" (Matthew 25:35–36); "Bear ye one another's burdens" (Galatians 6:2); "Comfort those that stand in need of comfort" (Mosiah 18:9); "Inasmuch as ye have done it unto one of the least . . . ye have done it unto me" (Matthew 25:40). As I matured, that knowledge and awareness began to "enlighten my understanding" of the magnitude of Relief Society in the development of the women of the Church. Then, too, I was Mother's child and therefore enjoyed the rewards of love and kindness that flowed back to our household because of Mother's seeds of loving service. Relief Society began to enlighten my understanding and "to be delicious to me"; I could hardly wait until I could become a member, too.

Seek a
Godly Seed

Yet had he the residue of
the spirit. . . . That he
might seek a godly seed.
Therefore take heed to
your spirit.
—Malachi 2:15

Relief Society faces seemed to change when I married. Perhaps it was because I was no longer on the outside looking in. I marveled that I so comfortably became one of them.

The first time I went to Relief Society as an adult was in March of 1942. The Relief Society was celebrating its one hundredth anniversary, and Mother took me with her to the Whittier Ward in Salt Lake City. As we went into the Relief Society room she introduced me to some of the newer sisters with whom I was not acquainted. We had lived in the Whittier Ward for thirteen years, so I had known most of the women as I grew up. I had looked into their faces when I stood to give two-and-a-half-minute talks in Sunday School. Some had been my Sunday School teachers; others had taught me in Primary. I met them also when I was with Mother as she drove our family car, a big black Packard, to pick them up. (Mother always stopped and gave sisters rides if they were waiting for a bus.) But it was different now, sitting there beside them, looking directly into their eyes and talking to them woman to woman. Although they were not my age, they were very friendly and interested in my expected first baby, due any time. They freely shared the details of their first births and of the anxieties they

had felt then. I was fascinated. Their eyes shone as they re-
lived their experiences.

Soon the meeting was called to order. The Whittier Ward
sisters had prepared a historical vignette to tell the story of the
beginning of Relief Society. I remember it well. The first scene
depicted Sarah Melissa Granger Kimball talking to her seamstress, Miss Cook. As they discussed their pleasure in the newly
organized Church and how happy they were to be part of it,
their talk turned to the building of the Nauvoo Temple. Miss
Cook said, "I don't suppose there is anything specific I can do
to be of help. I have skills, but I don't have any money."

Sarah Kimball, realizing that she had means, but lacked
the skills of a seamstress, responded quickly, "Why don't we
combine our resources? I will furnish material if you will make
shirts for the workmen."

That happy thought was the beginning, and their enthusiasm grew as the scenario continued. They decided to invite
those sisters living near the Kimball home to a meeting to see if
any others would be interested in joining them. I remember
very clearly the excitement the women projected as they reen-
acted this scene.

The next scene was of a room full of sisters discussing what
they might do to move the new Church forward. At length,
they decided to form an organization of sisters and then find
what they, in their united strength, might do to be helpful to
the Brethren. They determined that to formalize the organization, they needed a constitution and bylaws. They agreed that
they should invite Eliza R. Snow to write these and then
should take them to the Prophet Joseph Smith, asking his approval for a women's organization in the new Church. Sarah
Kimball willingly accepted the responsibility of contacting
Eliza R. Snow.

The scene changed again and we saw Eliza R. Snow in
conversation with the Prophet Joseph Smith. His words have
been often repeated; he said that "the constitution and bylaws
were the best he had ever seen. Tell the sisters their offering is
accepted of the Lord, and he has something better for them

than a written constitution. Invite them all to meet me in the Masonic Hall over my store next Thursday afternoon, and I will organize the sisters under the priesthood after a pattern of the priesthood." The Prophet further said, "The Church was never perfectly organized until the women were thus organized." ("Story of the Organization of the Relief Society," *Relief Society Magazine*, March 1919, p. 129.)

The final scene presented at that anniversary meeting showed the Prophet organizing the women, proposing that the sisters elect a presiding officer, and that she "choose two counselors to assist in the duties of her office." He then said that he would give them counsel from time to time: "Let this presidency serve as a constitution—all their decisions considered law, and acted upon as such. If any officers are wanted to carry out the design of the institution let them be appointed and set apart. . . . The minutes of your meetings will be precedent for you to act upon—your constitution and law."

I still remember the thrill I experienced when the person portraying the Prophet said, "I now declare this society organized with president and counselors etc., according to parliamentary usages." (*A Centenary of Relief Society* [Salt Lake City: General Board of Relief Society, 1942], p. 15.) I don't know who the actor was, but when he spoke my heart responded and I knew those words were of the Lord. I wanted to be a part of Relief Society, for I knew it was God-given.

Mother saw me wiping away a tear. She came over to sit with me and asked if I were feeling all right. She might have been thinking of my pregnancy, but I believe that, mother-like, her concern was more far reaching. Perhaps she hoped that I had caught the vision that would lead me to enjoy all the blessings the Lord intended for women through the Relief Society organization. I told her that I had been touched by the presentation. I only wished that every woman could have such a persuasive introduction to Relief Society.

This feeling compelled me to know more about Relief Society after I had attended that first meeting. I talked with my mother and she told me that Amy Brown Lyman was then the general president. Marcia K. Howells and Donna D. Sorenson were her counselors, and Vera H. Pohlman was the general secretary-treasurer. I gained a sense of the kind of leadership they gave to the women as Mother read one of their statements:

> We stand at the threshold of a new century. We look calmly into the future with faith and confidence that there will be a continuation of growth and success for the organization, a continuation of opportunities and development for its members, and a continuation of the organization's intelligent, helpful service for humanity. We realize, however, that in this rapidly changing world—a world of turmoil and tragedy at present—there is a possibility of temporary interruptions, that new and different conditions and exigencies may call for new and different and even extended service on the part of the organization, and for added duties and responsibilities for officers and members. But we feel assured that the work will continue to go on effectively, and that needs will be met as they come, if we follow the patterns, standards, and traditions of the past and put our trust in our Heavenly Father. Therefore, we face the future with courage and confidence, with faith and hope. (*A Centenary of Relief Society*, p. 9.)

My enthusiasm was boundless. I wanted to read all I could about Relief Society. I picked up Mother's then current copy of the *Relief Society Magazine*. There was a message to the sisters from the First Presidency—Heber J. Grant, J. Reuben Clark, Jr., and David O. McKay:

> For one hundred years you have walked along the paths the Prophets laid out for you. Your service of unselfish devotion, your loyalty to the priesthood, your love for the unfortunate, and your ministrations to the downtrodden, have made prophecies fulfilled of the advice, counsel, and exhortations of the Prophet; for you have nursed those who were sick, cared for those who were called home, comforted those who mourned; you have fed those who were hungry, clothed those who were naked, warmed those who suffered from cold. You have sustained those whose souls

were weary; you have heartened those whose hearts were heavy. ("Message from the First Presidency," *Relief Society Magazine*, March 1942, p. 153.)

I was stirred by those words, but I liked most their next statement: "The prayers of thanks and gratitude voiced by the poor whom you have succored have ascended to the Lord as sweet incense from a holy altar. The Lord has smiled down upon you and blessed you. He has accepted your labors as service to his cause and for his eternal glory."

I read their prayer that the Lord would, in the century to follow, go with the sisters and help them carry to still higher planes the devoted service that they were organized to carry on. They said, "May the Lord bless them even as he has blessed you so abundantly. May the graces of rare womanhood and glorious motherhood which have adorned you radiate from them undimmed." ("Message from the First Presidency," *Relief Society Magazine*, March 1942, p. 153.) I read Eliza R. Snow's poem:

The Female Relief Society of Nauvoo: What Is It?

It is an institution form'd to bless
The poor, the widow, and the fatherless—
To clothe the naked and the hungry feed,
And in the holy paths of virtue lead.

To seek out sorrow, grief, and mute despair,
And light the lamp of hope eternal there—
To try the strength of consolation's art,
By breathing comfort to the mourning heart.

To chase the clouds that shade the aspect, where
Distress presides; and wake up pleasures there—
With open heart extend the friendly hand,
To hail the stranger from a distant land.

To stamp a vetoing impress on each move
That virtue's present dictates disapprove—
To put the tattler's coinage scandal down,
And make corruption feel its with'ring frown.

To give instruction where instruction's voice
Will guard the feet and make the heart rejoice—
To turn the wayward from their recklessness,
And lead them in the ways of happiness.

It is an *order*, fitted and design'd
To meet the wants of body and of mind—
To seek the wretched in their lone abode—
Supply their wants, and raise their hearts to God.

       (*Millennial Star*, October 1842, p. 112.)

That was all it took; my commitment was sure. I wanted to seek for me and mine that godly seed; Relief Society was for me. I knew it—deep inside me. I wanted to be an active, involved Relief Society sister and have my service ascend to the Lord and be a cause for eternal glory. I wanted with all my heart to have the graces of rare womanhood and glorious motherhood radiate from me.

I became a regular attender soon after my first baby, a little girl, was born. After a few years I was called to teach the Social Relations lessons in my ward. Feeling very inadequate, but determined to do my very best, I thought I knew just the place to go for help. My mother-in-law was a stake Social Relations teacher, so I asked her if I might attend her leadership meeting department. She seemed pleased to have me come and always prepared enough extra material for me to take home.

A strong bond of love developed between us as my mother-in-law shared her expertise in ways that helped me feel adequate in my new calling. One of her suggestions was that, before any of us even tried to teach the Social Relations course that year, we pray for the help of our Heavenly Father. The lessons were on the Constitution, and they could be controversial if we were not in tune with the Spirit of the Lord. I did as she suggested.

I knelt down in my kitchen, and as the sun streamed through the window I prayed for a strong testimony of the lessons I was to teach and for direction as I prepared and presented the material. I will never forget the powerful feeling of warmth and light that came to me. The sun's rays were as naught compared to that warm sensation that filled my whole being. There I was, on my knees, following the counsel of my dear mother-in-law and finding myself in tears, knowing that the lessons I was to teach really had the ratification of my Heavenly Father. There was a special joy and strength that came to me that day.

I went to my own stake leadership meetings as well and felt strengthened by hearing the messages again. I don't know how I could have received more help; I was being taught, first, by my mother-in-law; second, by my stake leader; and third, by that joyous experience of prayerful communication with my Heavenly Father.

In time I grew to feel confident and even felt a certain expertise in my calling. I had to smile one day after I had been studying my lesson. My young daughter came home from school and began asking me questions about the Constitution. I answered them. She lifted her little face and said, "Mother, I can't believe you can answer those questions."

"Why not?" I asked.

"Because," she said, "our teacher at school told us that none of our parents would be able to answer any of those questions, and that we would be able to show them that we were smarter than they were. You've just blown his whole theory!"

"Thanks to Relief Society," I said as she walked off bewildered. I was already beginning to feel the power of Relief Society in my life. It was about this time that I learned of the building being planned. Our ward presidency had been told by the Relief Society General Board that each member of the Relief Society would be requested to contribute five dollars toward the erection of a Relief Society Building. I could not believe that they would ask us to give what was then such a large amount of money. I had young children, my husband wasn't making very much money, and we had to count every penny. Wanting my mother to support me in my dismay, I complained to her, "Can you imagine that each of us would be asked to give so much money to build a Relief Society Building?"

Instead of being sympathetic, my mother counseled, "Just give it. You will always be glad you did."

When the Relief Society Building was completed and open to the public, both Mother and I were asked to serve as hostesses from our stake for a few hours each week. When I first walked into that beautiful building I was filled with pride. I was glad I had made my five-dollar contribution, which didn't seem nearly so big by then. I did not have the slightest thought that the day would come when I would remember Mother's words with even greater poignancy as that building became my Relief Society home and office for nearly fourteen years.

A choice Relief Society relationship developed between my mother, my sister, Carolyn, and me when we were all called to serve as Relief Society presidents at the same time. Only another ward Relief Society president could understand fully the depth of responsibility one feels in that calling. Sharing those feelings and desires with persons who were already so dear brought a unity of unusual dimensions. We regularly called each other with ideas concerning executive meetings, board and Relief Society meetings, the visiting teaching program, remarks for ward conferences, and homemaking-day activities.

Best of all, we went to the Relief Society general conferences together. We would each take notes and then share the ideas and inspiration that came to us. Mother had more years of experience and was miles ahead of us, but she was always ready to learn more and was very interested in what we thought and did. Her support and encouragement went a long way toward ensuring our success.

Mother, Carolyn, and I loved the closeness that being in the same Relief Society position at the same time brought us. We often laughed together over some of our experiences and sometimes cried over others. For example, I remember my first ward conference. I misunderstood the time the meeting was to begin. I thought it was to start at nine-thirty in the morning, so my counselors and I went over to the wardhouse the night before to see that everything was ready. We planned that we would meet the next day at 9:15 A.M. That would give us time to get the children off to school and still have our prayer together before our stake visitors arrived. When we got there, however, the stake visitors were waiting by the door for us. The meeting was to have begun at nine o'clock! They were very kind and seemed to understand our mistake. The meeting began at nine-thirty because that was when the rest of the board came. Then, in the middle of the stake Relief Society president's talk, some of the pictures started to fall off of the wall. I could hardly believe both of those things could happen in one meeting. Needless to say, I was embarrassed, but Mother counseled, "There is nothing you can do about it now. Just learn from that experience and see that neither of those things happen again." They didn't.

My first stake calling in Relief Society was frightening. I went into the stake classroom thinking of all the help my mother-in-law had given me and of all the help I had received from my stake leaders. I realized that I would be expected to be that helpful to others. Hortense Young Hammond was sitting there looking into my face. She was to teach the Social Relations class in my own ward. I knew her to be a brilliant woman. I wondered how I could possibly give her any information at all. Then I had the thought that she needed not only to receive information, but to share her knowledge with the class as well. I asked her to tell the class how she had learned so much.

She said: "Learning was a daily ritual in my family as I grew up. My father felt it was just as important that we learn something new each day as it was for us to wash our hands or brush our teeth. Each evening when we sat down at dinner together, he insisted that we bring something new we had learned that day. It couldn't be an old idea warmed over. It had to be something we hadn't known before. The regularity with which he did this, and the stimulation of his probing questions, made us want to learn—first to respond to him, and then, by the time we got so we could handle his testing, he had instilled in us an insatiable desire to learn and to share something even more exciting than the other members of the family had presented. By the time we had continued our quest over the years, we had all become avid students with inquisitive minds. It was a common practice for us to go to the scriptures and give deep consideration to the points of doctrine that were new or difficult, and try to internalize them."

We all learned from her. Soon others began to share. It was more effective than if I had monopolized the meeting myself. I knew I had been enriched.

Another time, I was taught a striking lesson on commitment by Ruth Timpson, who was a Spiritual Living teacher when I was her stake leader. Ruth had multiple sclerosis. Twice she had lost her sight before she was asked to teach the Spiritual Living lessons, and twice it had come back, but never fully. She loved to come to the stake class and learn there because all of us in that department could give her insight into the lesson that she was to teach. She could listen to our discussion and feel that she had more to give than if she had only studied on her own. When I would visit to observe her teach, I would be brought to tears. She had written all of her notes out with a black marking pen so that she would not miss anything of importance. She sat on a stool so that she would not lose her balance while teaching. Her lessons were masterful and always included a testimony of such strength that there would not be an unconverted sister in her class. Again and again, I felt thankful for the choice sisters who were my associates and the rich outpouring of the Spirit I enjoyed while serving as a member of the stake board in Relief Society.

My ward and stake Relief Society service opened my mind and heart in many ways. As I served I learned that the heart of Relief Society was each woman's testimony of the atoning sacrifice of Jesus Christ. This was the great bond that drew us together and caused us to bear one another's burdens.

In little, and sometimes more significant, ways, Relief Society became a familiar part of my children's lives as well. One day I had to conduct a Relief Society meeting and needed to leave my little daughter with someone. My mother-in-law came to my rescue. When I went to pick my child up, my mother-in-law was laughing and said, "I took this dear child with me to our homemaking meeting. When I told her we were going over to my ward to work on some items with the girls she asked, 'Do you mean the girls with the grandma faces?' "

My daughter's childlike candor revealed the grandmother-goodness she attached to the sisters as she looked at their maturing faces. For myself, I knew they were grandma faces I loved—faces of young mothers, and older mothers; faces of women who didn't have any children, but who had added much to my Relief Society experiences. They all belonged; they were all a part of that godly seed found in that divine organization. I loved the many, varied, wonderful faces of all those I knew in the great sisterhood of Relief Society.

3

Bearing Precious Seed

He that goeth forth and weepeth, bearing precious seed, shall doubtless come again with rejoicing, bringing his sheaves with him.
—Psalms 126:6

What I could not learn in the classroom about the Relief Society's work of love, I very soon began to learn from compassionate service provided by visiting teaching, in which women are sent two by two to visit sisters in the ward each month. President Kimball said that when the Lord needs to answer prayers, he sends us to do the task; often it is visiting teachers who receive those assignments.

My companion and I were assigned to visit a couple who had just moved onto the back side of our circle. We were happy to accept that assignment, but when we knocked at the door and stood there for a few minutes before it opened, we felt perhaps we had come at a difficult time. A lovely woman, with black hair pulled back into a bun, opened the door. She was neat and comely, but very businesslike. We introduced ourselves and welcomed her to the neighborhood. Then before we left, we told Sister Anderson that we would come again the next month. She gave very little response.

The next month we did go back again, and that time Sister Anderson had her arm in a sling. She said that she had fallen while putting away some of her household items and had broken her arm. We asked if we might be of service, but she abruptly told us that she was a professional nurse and was certain that she could manage.

The third month came around and when Sister Anderson came to the door, again we were left standing on the porch as she informed us that her husband was confined to bed. He had suffered a stroke. Again she assured us that she was capable of taking care of him and of herself. It seemed to me that there was a bitterness in her that turned people from their door. The months passed with regular front-porch visits and then, on one occasion, I needed to take my baby with me. This time, though reluctantly at first, and almost with anxious concern, Sister Anderson invited us to come in. She said her husband had become very lonely and needed to talk to someone other than her, day after day. She thought he would like to see the baby. She opened the door, and for the first time, we went into that home.

From then on I took the baby with me when we went to see the Andersons. We were delighted to find in this child a common ground that seemed to make our calls more accept-able. Smiles began to appear when we came instead of the stern countenance we first saw.

We became good friends and had pleasant visits, but my companion and I could feel that they did not want the mes-sage. One time, however, it was on love. I thought anyone could talk about love, but I learned it was perhaps the most difficult subject of all for them. Apparently the children of Brother Anderson had been very much opposed to the remar-riage of their father after their mother had passed away. The hurtful things that were said and done had created feelings of bitterness and resentment. We were sorry to learn of the un-happy experiences, but the sharing of them seemed to create a bond of trust between us.

One day my telephone rang, and it was Sister Anderson asking me if I could help her find someone to cut the lawn. I knew several young boys and sent one over immediately. Later, she called to tell me that her husband was sick again. She needed to get to the store and asked if I could help her. I did. When her husband passed away she asked for our counsel about the services and for help she needed with his personal affairs. I can't adequately express the happiness that came to me, knowing that she felt confident enough to call. She started to come out to our meetings and was really loved and accepted, and I know she felt it.

The most thrilling thing for me was to go home one afternoon and find a card in my screen door, with her name signed to it as one of my visiting teachers. It wasn't that way with every experience, but at least in this instance, knowing that we had helped to make Sister Anderson's life more tolerable, more purposeful, and a bit less stressful for her, gave me a feeling of warmth. I found myself facing each day with a little more purpose.

Then another remarkable thing happened in our ward while I was serving as president. My counselors and I went regularly and faithfully to visit an elderly couple. Each month while there, we would inquire about the physical condition of the couple, and the man and woman would always say they were "all right" or "getting along." One time, however, their faces were sad as they said, "We are fine, but our house is so dirty."

We smiled and looked around, but seeing it to be very neat and orderly we said, "It looks lovely to us. You are good housekeepers."

Again they responded, "But our house is so dirty."

It wasn't until the next visit, when they again made the same comment, that we took them seriously. Then we looked beyond the order and saw that the wallpaper was smokey, the curtains did need to be laundered, and the floors could have stood a good waxing.

We talked to our bishop. He asked what we wanted to do about it. We suggested a Relief Society housecleaning day. He added, "Let's include the whole ward. We can have the deacons and their advisers work in the yard, the priests do the basement, the elders clean the wallpaper." It sounded exciting.

The only son of the couple lived out of town, but the bishop arranged for him to come down one Saturday morning and take his parents away for the day. We all began at nine o'clock in the morning. The deacons cleaned, trimmed, cut, edged, raked, and watered the entire grounds. The Relief Society sisters took down the drapes; the priesthood brethren took them to be cleaned. The curtains were washed and put on stretchers. The men cleaned the walls and windows. The women washed woodwork, scrubbed and waxed floors, and polished furniture. It was an all-day job and, although it was difficult to put things back and to remember exactly where they went, by six o'clock in the evening, all was sparkling clean and in place. The doors were locked and everyone went home. The neighbor next door was asked to keep watch and tell us how the couple responded. She said they walked into the front room, looked around, put their arms up in the air and then around each other, and cried. They didn't live long after that, but all of those who participated were grateful to be part of that experience.

It was very interesting, in fact, to see who had been there and had given such willing service. They were, for the most part, those who had problems of their own. One was recovering from a heart attack. Another was the mother of a son with hemophilia. There was one woman with multiple sclerosis. Those who had helped were mainly those who knew real problems in their lives. I learned more about why we have tests and trials than I had known before; they make us aware of the needs of others. If we have only good health, we commonly do not realize that others often function in spite of poor health. I also became convinced that no Relief Society president or set of visiting teachers goes into a home alone; there is a vast resource of ward members behind them, and there is the Spirit of God to lead, to teach, and to prompt.

My ward Relief Society secretary-treasurer told me another remarkable story about visiting teachers. I have shared it with many because I feel it can help other visiting teachers know the importance of the work they do.

Dorothy, David, and their new little baby son had barely lived long enough in a California ward to have visiting teachers assigned. Two sisters were driving down the freeway on a Saturday morning, going to a year-end sale, when suddenly the one who was driving said, "I feel impressed that we should go and visit that sister who just moved into our ward, the new one assigned to our district."

Her companion objected, "No one goes to visit a new woman in the ward this early on a Saturday morning. But if you feel that we should go, let's go to the sale and then stop by there on the way home." The driver of the car didn't say much more, but when they came to the off-ramp, she turned the car onto it and said, "I just feel that we must go now. I hope you don't mind too much."

When she stopped the car in front of the home the companion said, "Are you certain you feel we need to go in now?"

"Yes, I really do," she answered. They got out of the car, walked up the pathway to the door, and rang the bell. Dorothy came to the door with her baby in her arms.

They began, "We are your visiting teachers." That was all they got to say before Dorothy started to cry. "Is something wrong?" they asked.

"Yes," she said, "it's my baby! Every time I put him down he seems to stop breathing, and so I have held him all night long and prayed that someone would come to help me."

"Why didn't you take him to the hospital or call a doctor?" they asked.

"As you know, we're new here. My husband is out of town on business, so I don't have a car to get to the hospital, and I don't know anyone to call to help me."

The visiting teachers were anxious to help and the mother was deeply grateful. As quickly as they could, they drove the mother and baby to the hospital. At the emergency entrance a doctor took the baby, and worked with him for quite some time. When he came back he said, "You are very fortunate to have gotten this child here when you did. He could not have lived but a little while longer." That baby is now a grown man and a strong advocate for the Church. The Lord had a work for him to do, as well as an important work for those visiting teachers. They were a fine example of how responsive visiting teachers can be instruments of the Lord in filling critical assignments in cases of real need.

I remember another inspiring story about the effectiveness of visiting teaching that I heard after I became the general president of the Relief Society. I was asked to speak, early one morning, to the employees at Welfare Square. Before I addressed them, another sister spoke. In her talk she said, "Last night I sat by one of the most beautiful women I have ever seen, and I had to tell her so. I was really surprised by the woman's response."

The beautiful woman said, "If you had seen me a year ago, you would never have said that."

"I think I would have," said the speaker.

"No, you wouldn't have. I was an alcoholic and everything about me was in shambles, especially me," the woman responded.

"What changed your life?" The speaker had asked the woman.

"My visiting teachers," she said. "One day they rang my doorbell and asked if they could come in and give the message they had prepared for me. I said, 'You wouldn't want to come into my house. I'm always drunk, I'm a mess, my home is a mess, my children are a mess, so no one ever wants to come into my house.'"

The woman continued her story: "My visiting teachers said, 'We do. We'd love to come and talk to you and help you if we can.' I let them in, just to show them how impossible my life really was. They said they would do anything I would let them do to help me and that they would come back every day if I wanted them to, and they did. They helped me fix my hair, and myself, so that I gained some self-respect. They helped me learn how to take care of my children and my home. It wasn't easy, but bit by bit they helped me to become who I am today. Now there are many things I want to accomplish with my life. You see me, a year later, as I am tonight."

Those teachers lifted, strengthened, and fortified that sister. This is the work of the visiting teacher, bearing the precious seeds of compassionate service to bless the lives of others.

4

It Must Needs Be a Good Seed

Know that this is a good seed; for behold it sprouteth and beginneth to grow.
—Alma 32:30

When I was the Hillside Stake Spiritual Living teacher in Salt Lake City, I attended my first Relief Society regional meeting. It exceeded my expectations. A member of the general board conducted the department in an outstanding manner. She had us all involved as we shared ideas and thoughts. I felt I learned so much that I could go back to leadership meeting and fill the sisters full of useful information and helps. As I thought about the experience, I said to my stake Relief Society president, "I wish I could meet on a regular basis with other stake Spiritual Living teachers. Do you think that would be possible?"

She said, "I don't know why not. I'm sure you would learn a lot from each other."

I was thrilled at the thought, but when I told my husband I intended to call the teachers in that department from the surrounding stakes, to see if they would like to meet regularly and discuss the lessons before we gave them at our leadership meetings, he said, "I don't believe you are supposed to do that."

I was surprised and asked, "Why not?"

He replied, "I don't know, but I would ask our stake Relief Society president if I were you."

I told him I already had, and she thought it was a splendid idea. I went ahead and asked the sisters if they would like to meet. They said they would, so I asked one to bring sugges-

tions for visual aids, another to bring an introduction and a
conclusion to the lesson, one to tell how she intended to treat
the subject matter, one to bring questions that would involve
the class, and another to look for any trouble spots that might
deserve special attention. It was a very worthwhile session.

We traded assignments each time we met. When it was my
turn to present the subject, the lesson was on the dispensa-
tions. I decided I would prepare a script having the wives of
the prophets tell about their husbands. I thought about researching for further material, but decided against it because I
wanted them to learn the information available in the lesson.
Everyone wanted a copy of the final script I had prepared, because it utilized the lesson material while providing a variation
from the usual Relief Society lesson format. I gave copies out
freely.

A few days passed before my stake Relief Society president
called and said, "Sister Smith, I just hate to tell you this, but
Sister Spafford just called and told me that you have been passing out manuscripts for other stakes to use and that you have
no right to do that. You are called to serve in our own stake
and not in any other stake. She wants the meetings with the
other stake leaders to stop immediately." I was stunned. I had
so greatly benefited myself and had wanted to be helpful to
others, but I had caused a problem instead.

I thanked my stake Relief Society president for the call and
told her I was grateful she had called, rather than having Sister Spafford call me. I was hurt, embarrassed, upset, of-
fended. There were so many ill feelings that swelled within me
I could hardly believe it. Nevertheless, I started calling every
Spiritual Living teacher to whom I had given the script and
told her not to use it, that Sister Spafford had said I had no
right to give it to any other stake. One said, "I've already given
the parts out. I don't want to call them and tell them not to use
it." Another said, "Don't worry. I won't use it." Each reaction
was different, but all of them were disappointed that we
would not be holding any more meetings of our group.

By the next morning I had contacted every sister. I called
my stake Relief Society president and told her she could call

and tell Sister Spafford that each person had been told not to use the material I had prepared. It was so hard for me to get through the next few weeks that I couldn't control the tears. I just couldn't get the experience off my mind.

Not too long after that I received a call from Sister Spafford. I began trembling with those same difficult feelings and feared that I had not done enough to rectify the situation. She said she would like me to come to her office and meet with her. She gave me a date and time. When I arrived at the Relief Society building I didn't know my way around; I went to the wrong office. Someone took me to the right place. Sister Spafford, Sister Sharp, and Sister Madsen all met with me in the executive council room. There, to my surprise, they called me to be a member of the Relief Society General Board.

After I had recovered from my amazement and indicated my willingness to serve on the board, Sister Spafford said, "I want to talk to you about the script you wrote and distributed." A big lump came into my throat. She explained, "If I had read it before I called your stake Relief Society president I would have handled the matter differently because there was nothing wrong with it. The thing that made it difficult was that there was no name on it. Why didn't you put your name on it?" I explained that I had only used the lesson material printed in the *Relief Society Magazine* and I hadn't felt that I had a right to put my name on it. She responded, "I want you to know that because of your obedience when you received that telephone call from your stake Relief Society president, I can call you to now serve on the general board. I had asked for you before, but this time seemed to be the appropriate time for your call to be issued. Thank you for responding in the way you did." Then she added, "I think I'll ask you to serve on the curriculum committee so that you will be able to see how important it is that everyone who teaches has approved material."

As I left her office I felt that a heavy load had been lifted from me. I was relieved to know that my script work had been accepted as a righteous undertaking, that, in truth, "It must needs be a good seed." My heart was finally at peace regarding

that matter. I was ready to commit my service to the work of
the general board. And I had learned important lessons about
curricula and about obedience to those called to preside. Both
were lessons I would need.

Part 2

A Plant
of the Lord

For the vineyard of the
Lord of hosts is the house
of Israel, and the men of
Judah his pleasant plant.
—Isaiah 5:7

5

A Tender Plant

For he shall grow up
before him as a tender
plant.
—Isaiah 53:2

I truly felt like a tender plant as a new member of the Relief Society General Board and knew that I had much growing and learning to accomplish before I could adequately do the Lord's work. I was assigned to be a member of the visiting teaching committee. Our main effort at one particular time was to prepare a presentation for the visiting teaching department of the Relief Society for the general conference. We decided that we would hold workshops designed to help visiting teachers work more effectively with the sisters they visited.

We had heard that a Brother Joseph Bentley from the University of Utah was very skilled in conducting workshops. I was given the assignment of contacting him to see if he would help us carry out our plans. This was a bit difficult since I had very little information to help me find him. I knew his name was Joseph, but that was all. I had no address or middle initial for him. I looked in the telephone book, found two Joseph Bentleys, and I took a chance that I would call the correct one. I dialed the number and asked for Brother Bentley. He answered the telephone. I told him that I was a member of the Relief Society General Board and that we were wondering if he would conduct a visiting teachers workshop in our Relief Society conference. He listened politely and then said, "Yes. I'll do it if you want me to, but I just can't imagine that you would. You know, I am a trucker by profession. I don't know the first thing about conducting a workshop."

He was right; we didn't need Joseph Bentley, the trucker, we needed Joseph Bentley, the teacher. I was more than embarrassed, but couldn't help laughing at his charming response and the way he helped me to make a quick recovery from my faux pas. I called the next Joseph Bentley and made certain he was a teacher before I asked for his participation. He accepted. He told me he would think about the assignment and how to make it effective; then he would get back to our committee. There were planning sessions and preparations that followed, and finally, the day of the conference arrived.

The committee had been there long before the meeting was to start, to make certain everything was ready. Surprisingly, the sisters began coming as much as an hour early. They quietly took their places and sat absolutely still. There was no whispering, shuffling of papers, wandering around—nothing but silent contemplation. The reverence of that time was contagious. The spirit that filled the chapel and the cultural hall could be felt, and it carried over into the meeting itself. Each one who participated was prepared and did well.

When Dr. Bentley's time came he divided the women into groups of four: one woman was the one being taught, two were visiting teachers, and the fourth was an observer. They were given a printed page describing the techniques they were to use in doing their visiting teaching and a copy of the message they were to teach. After each had taken the different roles and discussed their successes and ways they could improve, we moved to another phase. They were then taught how to be sensitive to the needs of the sister they would teach, how to apply the message, and how to utilize other good teaching practices that could help the program of visiting teaching move progressively ahead. It was a spiritual feast for all of us present on that occasion. Everyone went home enriched.

As I reflected on the conference meeting—the expectation of the women who came early and sat reverently, and the excellence of the training given—I thought again of my first faltering phone call and the man who was willing to do what was asked of him but was simply not prepared. I realized that he, too, was an important part of that experience for me, to let me, as a new board member, see that willingness alone was not enough to do the work. It was the learning, training, preparation, and the ability to bring the Spirit that made that meeting extraordinary.

For another general board assignment I was to meet with the Curriculum Committee of the Church. This group had decided to program into the lessons over an eight-year period gospel topics which were important for members of the Church to study. My assignment was the development of a Relief Society curriculum plan that could ensure this.

I had an overwhelming feeling that we should be teaching about Relief Society sisters from around the world. It seemed an appropriate direction for our Cultural Refinement lessons to take. I mentioned the spiritual feeling I had regarding this matter to Sister Louise Madsen, who suggested that I call Sister Spafford and share my feelings with her. I made that call with fear and trembling the next day, although I had felt I must call because the prompting was so strong. Sister Spafford listened to my suggestion and said, "You have been inspired. Please call Sister Marianne C. Sharp and talk with her about it, since she is the counselor responsible for the lessons taught in Relief Society."

Sister Sharp met with our committee and then said, "That idea has been thought of before, but it was felt that the women weren't ready to study about each other. Perhaps the time has now come. Let's work out the details, present it to the Brethren, and see how they feel about it."

Sister Alice C. Smith wrote a sample lesson. We then met with our advisers, Elders Thomas S. Monson, Boyd K. Packer, Marvin J. Ashton, and Bruce R. McConkie. When we had finished showing them what could be done, Elder McConkie said, "Trust you sisters to come to the very heart of what should be taught. We all need that course of study." I had felt that there had been a sweet witness each step of the way, and those words were the final affirmation we needed.

As I might have expected, my next assignment was on the Cultural Refinement committee under the chairmanship of

Alice Ludlow Wilkinson. I was very pleased. We began interviewing people from many lands so that the new curriculum
would accurately portray the sisters and the cultures that in-
fluenced their lives. Many people at Church headquarters and
at local universities gave both support and hard work to our
preparations. The love that developed for our sisters worldwide as the materials were prepared was overwhelming. We
found many differences among the sisters of the Church, but
we also found, perhaps not surprisingly, that there were more
similarities.

When we presented the new material in the Cultural Refinement department of Relief Society general conference,
there was an unbelievable acceptance. Some who had been
afraid to teach Cultural Refinement lessons could be heard to
say, "I can teach those lessons now." Others had traveled the
world; they felt they could easily tell about the sisters in foreign countries, of their music, art, and literature, and they
considered the opportunity a great blessing.

A thrilling part of the new emphasis on the Cultural Refinement lessons was the flow of tenderness, compassion,
pride, and desire—the sisters were truly moved by the lessons.
One woman from Austria said, "I have never really felt that I
belonged before; now I am a celebrity. Everyone wants me to
come and share what I have." Another woman said, "I've always been critical of Mexico. Now I can hardly wait to go
there. I actually look for Mexicans who will talk to me. I love
these people who have given so much to me."

I remember working with Moana B. Bennett to present a
readers' theater that would introduce the Cultural Refinement
lessons. Her cast included women from many different countries. One woman didn't seem to be able to do her part well
enough to deliver the message. I watched Sister Bennett work
long and hard to help her, but the woman could not do what
she was asked to do. Finally I said, "Sister Bennett, I think you
will have to get someone else to take that part. She doesn't do
well enough to be a part of a general Church presentation."

Sister Bennett said, "I can't do that to her. She is so thrilled
to have that part that it would break her heart. I'll work with

her, I'll give her all of the time she needs, but I can't take the part away from her. Her feelings are more important to me than the performance."

I was taught a great lesson by that very special dramatist: people are more important than a few minutes before an audience. I knew, as did Sister Bennett, that eventually the woman would do her part well enough to be proud and happy that she had participated in the conference, and well enough that those people who came to the conference would understand the message. Sister Bennett did work diligently with the woman. And while the woman never reached the high expectations that I had hoped for, she performed acceptably for the conference presentation. It was a big step in helping me learn more about the importance of each child growing before the Lord as a tender plant.

As a member of the Relief Society General Board I went to one of the Latin American missions, traveling with Sister Trilba Lindsay, then general secretary of the Primary. We were there under the direction of Elder Richard G. Scott who was then a Regional Representative. Three things that happened on this trip made a deep impression on me. The first was to feel the power manifested in the leadership of the mission president and to recognize, in a way I hadn't before, the hand of the Lord in the calling of a man to head a mission.

The president had been in his field of labor only about six weeks when we arrived. He told us he had lost nearly ten pounds worrying about the work and about his ability to do it in a way pleasing to the Lord and helpful to the missionaries. I understood his worry, because he was over seventy years old. At first I thought it was too bad that an older man was sent to try to keep up with those young elders and lady missionaries. The country was experiencing some political unrest, and often the missionaries seemed oblivious to the dangers around them. The mission president worried a great deal about them.

While we were there he called the missionaries together in a zone conference, and we were invited to attend. I went, doubtful about what we might see in this elderly man's leadership. I even questioned his physical ability and wondered how his health could stand up under the strenuous conditions of a people living in poverty and under the great work that was required of him.

As the meeting began, I was impressed with the elders who were fulfilling their positions of responsibility. They carried out their duties with dispatch. They gave instructions to the elders of the zone. They used graphic illustrations that would help them relate to the people. Then they called on this good president to talk to them.

He stood and said: "Fellow missionaries, I don't know specifically what your problems are, but I do know that you have them. I want to assure you, each one, that some of the most meaningful words in the scriptures are, 'And it came to pass.' " He continued: "I want you to know that your problems will come to pass. I have had problems and they have come to pass. Let me tell you about some of them. Perhaps you will be able to relate to your own lives my experiences and those words so often used in the scriptures."

He then told them about his three-year-old daughter and how that little girl could wrap him around her little finger. "She was charming, and she loved her daddy very much. If she broke a toy and someone asked if he could help her with it, she would say, 'No, my daddy will fix it when he comes.' She would stand by the window and watch for me to come home, and as she showed me her broken toy she would say, 'Fix it for me, daddy.' And I would fix it.

"One day that little daughter became ill. Her mother took her to the doctor. The doctor said it would not be long until that little girl would no longer be with us, because her illness was one that would take her life. The whole family wept. The time came when her little chair was empty and the loneliness that filled our home was fierce. I almost hated to come home. Then I realized that the terrible hurt would come to pass if I lived worthy of being with her again. I can picture my little girl in that heavenly home with a broken toy and someone there saying, 'Can I help you?' I know that precious child would say, 'No, my daddy will fix it when he comes.' I still long for that child, but the ache of my heart is less as I strive to live worthy to be with her again."

He then told the missionaries about his teenage daughter, and how much he loved her and wanted her to have every blessing that the Lord could give her. He said that as he looked at her he remembered the many times people had asked him how they could keep their children from marrying a nonmember of the Church. He would reply, "It is simple. You just don't let them date anyone who is not a member of the Church, and then they marry in the Church." He had determined that that would be his attitude with his beautiful teenage daughter, and he told her of his plan.

One day this daughter did not come home from work. When a telephone call came, he was told that she had gone off with a young man from the office and that they were married. That young man was not a member of the Church nor of the same cultural background as his daughter. He said that was the most devastating problem that had come into his life. He knew that unless that young man became a member of the Church his daughter could not have the blessings of eternity that he had hoped would be hers. He thought life would be very difficult for her, because the training and home life of the new son-in-law were so different from his daughter's.

He shed many tears and experienced hours of frustration before he came to a decision: he would send the missionaries to teach his son-in-law the gospel. It was a happy thought—until his daughter called and said that her husband had thrown the elders out bodily and told them not to come into his house again. Vividly he described the heartache and the pain he suffered. But, he said, "it came to pass" that some sister missionaries began to talk to that young man. He became interested in what they said. The day came when he joined the Church and wanted to take his family, then consisting of his wife and three children, to the temple to be sealed for time and all eternity.

The president said it was a joyful day as he watched those two people he loved kneel at the altar of God in that holy house with their three children. He realized that "it came to

pass" had again been meaningful in his life, and he thanked
the Lord for allowing him the privilege of knowing the comfort those words could bring.

This president used the experiences of his life to teach those
elders and sisters in such a powerful way that I knew why he
had been chosen to lead that mission. He was exactly the person that could make a difference in the lives of the missionaries
and touch the people in that land.

Next, the mission president went into an individual meeting session with each elder and sister, and then I had the second experience that impressed me deeply. While he interviewed, I talked with the waiting missionaries. I asked them
what they knew about Relief Society. Their answers were
nearly all the same: "I know the sisters make things." That was
all they knew of Relief Society.

I knew that Relief Society was the organization given to
the women of the Church by the Lord to teach them his ways
so they might give unselfish devotion to all of his children and
loyally support the priesthood. I could see that each missionary needed to be aware that Relief Society was an integral part
of the Church and that it was an evidence of our Heavenly Father's concern for his daughters.

When I returned to Salt Lake City I hoped to encourage
the development of a brochure for missionaries to use that
would help them present the message of Relief Society to each
potential female member of the Church; a brochure that could
help not only women but also missionaries to understand the
value and purpose of Relief Society.

That trip was filled with rich experiences. At one Primary
meeting I attended, a sweet reverence prevailed. Suddenly the
door opened and a little boy came in. As he did, a woman
stood up, hurried over to him, put her arms around him, and
kissed him. She then took him by the hand and brought him
over to sit by her. I whispered to a sister sitting near me, asking
if the boy was her son. She said, "No, he is a child in her Primary class." I was so impressed with that welcome that I asked
if they had many problem children in Primary. Her answer

was, "No, of course not. We just love the children. They are no problem to us." I could see that they did love the children. I could also see that the child felt the love that was extended to him.

The third great experience that was such an important part of this trip occurred as I returned home. Elder Scott had at first determined that our trip would cover a three-week period; however, just before we left Salt Lake City he said that it would be cut to two weeks for business reasons. We crowded more into those two weeks than I could have imagined. We returned home filled with a love for the people of the countries we visited.

My father came to see me the night I returned. He had undergone surgery a few months before in which his leg was amputated. He was pleased because he had learned how to use his artificial limb. It was hard for an eighty-year-old man, but very rewarding for him when he could get around and be independent again. The day after we had visited, he went to the doctor to have a flu shot. Almost simultaneously with the shot a terrible pain came into his head. He had planned on going Christmas shopping, but waited instead at the doctor's office for the pain to subside. In a short time he became unconscious and was taken to the hospital.

There in the hospital he struggled to breathe, even to live. He was given a blessing and, as the words were pronounced to bring to pass the will of the Lord, he took his last breath. I recalled those words, "and it came to pass," and I knew that the mission president had spoken not only to the missionaries but also to me. The direction received by Elder Scott to shorten the trip from three weeks to two was not only for him but also for me. Had we stayed another week, I would not have had that last day with my father. I came to realize as never before how keenly aware the Lord is of the needs of all his children and of the means he uses to bless them. I reflected on the Primary meeting I have mentioned. Could the example of the teacher welcoming that child be an indication of the welcome my father would receive? I thought it was.

These three experiences indelibly impressed upon my tender spirit that with the Lord "all things work together" to bring to pass his purpose. It was a treasured insight into the workings of the Spirit and into the depth of understanding I needed to prepare me for the work yet ahead.

6

In the Season Thereof

Yea, all things which come of the earth, in the season thereof, are made for the benefit and the use of man, both to please the eye and to gladden the heart.
—D&C 59:18

The words, "under the power of the priesthood" had a greater meaning for me one Friday afternoon in 1974. I had just returned home from a day spent at the Relief Society Building practicing for the October Relief Society general conference, when the telephone rang. It was Arthur Haycock, secretary to President Spencer W. Kimball. He said, "Hello, Sister Smith."

I said, "Yes."

He continued, "This is Arthur Haycock calling. What are you doing, getting dinner?" I said I was and he said, "Good, save some for me." He then laughed and said, "No, not really. President Kimball would like to speak to you."

In just a moment or two it was President Kimball with, "Hello, Sister Smith, how are you today?" I acknowledged that I was fine before he said, "I would like to talk to you. May I come to your home and see you?" I told him I would be very honored to have him come. He asked, "Is your husband home?"

I said, "No, he is at work."

He asked, "Will he be home when I get there?" I told him I wasn't certain. Then he said, "What I mean is that I would like to have him there when I arrive."

My answer was immediate: "He will be here."

Quickly I called my husband and told him about the conversation. He was in the middle of a business meeting, but told his associates, "I must leave now. I will see you all tomorrow." He left his surprised colleagues wondering what could cause such an abrupt ending to an unfinished meeting.

In the meantime, the ward Young Women's presidency had come to see our daughter. I called Sherilynn aside and explained that President Kimball was coming to our home, and when he came he wanted to talk to her father and me, so maybe she could take them outdoors to finish their conversation. It was arranged. Douglas came home, and almost immediately President Kimball arrived.

President Kimball came into the house, greeted us warmly, and as we sat he said, "I have come to call you, Sister Smith, to be the general president of the Relief Society of the Church and to preside over all of the women of the Relief Society worldwide. Will you accept that calling?"

I was shocked, overwhelmed, and deeply moved. I responded by telling him I would be honored to accept the call and I would work hard to do my very best to fulfill it as he would want me to and as directed by the inspiration of the Lord. He then turned to my husband and asked him if he could support me in that calling.

Douglas said, "President Kimball, I would be very pleased to do so. She has supported me for over thirty years in my Church work and I will be honored to support her in this high and holy calling."

President Kimball next said, "Do you know who you want to be your counselors?" I asked him if I could give it some prayerful thought. He explained that he would be leaving to go to Washington, D.C., soon, and he would like to have the matter resolved before he left. He said he would appreciate a call as soon as possible.

He then asked us to keep it strictly between ourselves until he had an opportunity to talk with Sister Spafford. As he prepared to leave, he put his arms around me and assured me that it was a great honor to serve as the general president of the Relief Society. He told me that he was certain I would do so in a way pleasing to the Lord.

Douglas saw him to his car. I watched them walk together until President Kimball got into the car and closed the car door. Then I slowly closed our front door, leaned on it for support, and wept quietly; I could not control my tears. Being the general president of the Relief Society was not an office I had sought nor would ever have asked for. I knew it was a calling from the prophet of the Lord and I also knew the power of the office and the divine connections it required. I knew whatever good would come from this new assignment would be dependent upon my worthiness and my willingness to be led by the Spirit. I prayed at that moment that I would be able to listen and be guided by each divine prompting as it would come. I knew that he who had called me held the keys of the priesthood on the earth, and therefore "under the power of the priesthood" were not idle words.

As soon as President Kimball's car drove away from our home, our children, the only two that were still at home, hurried in to ask what he had wanted. We told them we were not at liberty to discuss it. They could not believe it—"Do you mean to say the prophet came to our house and you can't even tell us why?" We explained that he had asked us to keep it confidential and that we would tell them as soon as it was appropriate. It seemed as if they asked every few hours if it was all right to tell them yet.

My fasting and praying began immediately to help me determine which, of all the wonderful women I knew, the Lord would have me call as counselors. I considered all of those who were board members. I thought of stake and ward Relief Society presidents I had met as I had traveled the Church during the previous four years that I served on the general board. There were so many capable, dedicated, spiritual women that to select only two seemed an overwhelming responsibility. I knew that many people called to be a president were immediately inspired and knew exactly what to do, but I suffered and I thought of my own inadequacies. Indeed, I experienced an inner struggle that began as soon as President Kimball left our home.

I needed help. I tearfully poured out the dilemma of my heart to my husband, and asked him if he would please give

me a blessing so I could be directed by divine power as I tried
to respond to the call given to me by our beloved prophet. I
was grateful for his petition to the Lord in my behalf; and
again and again I prayed.

Finally I did call President Kimball regarding the two
names that came most frequently to mind. He hesitated just a
moment and said, "Why don't you fast and pray a little
longer, and so will I." I told him that Douglas and I had been
invited to the same meeting that he mentioned he was going to
attend in Washington, D.C., and that perhaps we could discuss the selection further there. He seemed to think that was a
splendid idea. Douglas had some business matters come up,
however, that prevented us from going, so during the days of
President Kimball's absence, I spent most of my time considering the matter of counselors. The decision of one counselor
seemed final, but the other one was never very certain.

When I knew that President Kimball was back in town, I
called his office, but I couldn't get through to him. I felt the
matter was urgent, and the only thing I could think to do was
to pray for help. I did, and almost immediately the telephone
rang. It was President N. Eldon Tanner of the First Presidency. President Kimball had asked him to work with me in
the selection of my counselors and board, and he asked me
when I would like to meet with him. I told him I would come
at his convenience, and that the only time I was involved was
at four o'clock that afternoon. He said that was the only time
he had free. I quickly changed my appointment and was there
in his office waiting at 3:50 P.M.

He welcomed me graciously, by saying, "Bless you! What
can I do to be helpful?" I told him that I felt certain about my
homemaking counselor, but as yet I was pondering over the
one for education. He then asked, "Shall I tell you whom President Kimball has been thinking about?" I was, of course, anxious to know and, after hearing her name, responded immediately that she should be the counselor. President Tanner was
most insistent that I had the right to choose my own counselor,
that President Kimball wanted me to know it was only a suggestion. I explained that I had thought about her because I

had served in capacities where her name had been mentioned, but had never really known her or worked with her. I told him I would, however, like to have her serve as my counselor.

Next President Tanner wanted to know if I had told my family. I explained that President Kimball had requested that we not say anything to them or to anyone else until we had heard from him that Sister Spafford was aware of her pending release. President Tanner said he would take care of that. Then, addressing the matter of the general board, he told me to call anyone I wanted to serve because, he said, the work was important and we needed good women to help carry out the work of the women of the Church. He did counsel me, however, about some women whose home and family responsibilities seemed especially burdensome at that time. I left his office feeling relieved and peaceful for the first time in two weeks.

The next morning, early, a call came from President Tanner. He said, "I just want to make certain you haven't changed your mind on the selection of your counselors." I assured him that I had not and that I felt peaceful about the decision.

The experience of selecting my counselors was an important prelude to the continuing work of this still-new calling. It enabled me to see how the inspiration and direction to fill this awesome assignment might come: sometimes, as in the case of the homemaking counselor, it would be the result of my earlier experiences and knowledge; other times, as with the education counselor, inspiration would be given directly through priesthood leaders. Whatever the process, it is the confirming agreement of inspired priesthood leaders and the personal witness of the Spirit that verifies the rightness of such decisions.

President Tanner also told me that we could tell our children about my calling because Sister Spafford knew about the change. The look on the faces of our children was one of astonishment. They could not believe such a call could come to me. With subdued humor in our countenances, we reminded them that they had the responsibility of secrecy now.

One of the arrangements I had with President Tanner was that I might call and talk with Sister Spafford. I did call her and told her that I would like to visit with her. As I did, I was thinking of how very difficult this change must be for her. She had served for over twenty-nine years as general president, and before that for nine years on the Relief Society General Board. She asked, "What do you want to talk with me about?" I was somewhat taken back until she said, "Is it about your new calling?" I told her it was, and she invited me to come to her home where we would have privacy. So I went over to her house for the first time. She was very gracious. She told me it would now be my responsibility to be an executive member of the Welfare Services Committee and to be on the advisory committee of the Beehive Clothing Mills, with responsibility for the distribution of all of the temple clothing throughout the world. I would serve as a member of the National Council of Women and the International Council of Women, and as a member of the American Mothers, Inc. I would have to manage the Relief Society office, direct the general board, be responsible to direct the Relief Society activities and Relief Society presidents of over 661 stakes, and be responsible for over six hundred thousand women in the Church. The maintenance and operation of Mormon Handicraft would also be my responsibility.

It was a rare and marvelous experience to meet with Sister Spafford, feel of her strength and her buoyant spirit, and to think of the great capacities in which she had acted. I talked with her for over four hours. When I got home my head was fairly swimming. The telephone rang and it was again Sister Spafford. She asked, "Did I overwhelm you?"

I said, "What you really did was confirm what I knew to be true about the heavy responsibilities you have shouldered for so long and so well."

It was at the next Relief Society conference rehearsal that Sister Spafford and her counselors came into the third floor auditorium to make the general announcement to the board. Sister Spafford told them, "There will be some changes in the presidency of the Relief Society at conference. This is a confidential matter until it is announced by the First Presidency. You will all be expected to meet at noon the day of the Relief Society conference, in the auditorium of the visitors center on Temple Square, for further information."

Sister Spafford and her counselors then excused themselves, leaving the members of the general board in total amazement. Some turned to me and asked, "Are you going to be the new general president?" Since I was not at liberty to say, I made some excuse for not answering and hurried away.

The First Presidency met with the general board at the appointed hour and told them of the change in presidency that would take place in the afternoon session, informing them that some of the board members would be continuing while others would be released. It was a very brief meeting, but with a great deal of appreciation expressed to Sister Belle S. Spafford, Sister Marianne C. Sharp, and Sister Louise W. Madsen for their years of devotion and service to the Relief Society.

The Relief Society general conference meeting continued as planned until the last half hour. President Kimball then went to the podium and announced the change, and as he did, it seemed as though the whole audience in unison said, "Oh, no!"

I was heartsick. I knew they would feel that way; I did myself. I had loved the steady hand of leadership we had felt under the direction of Sister Spafford and her able counselors. I began to cry. I became very weak and thought, "I will never be able to walk up to the stand when he calls me to come." My prayer went up to the Lord. In response, the words from the third verse of the hymn "How Firm a Foundation" came to me clearly and brought with them a great surge of gladness to my heart:

> Fear not, I am with thee;
> oh, be not dismayed,
> For I am thy God
> and will still give thee aid.
> I'll strengthen thee, help thee,
> and cause thee to stand,
> Upheld by my righteous . . . omnipotent hand.
>
> *(Hymns, 1988, no. 85)*

I had not committed those words to memory before, even though I had sung them many times, but there they were, indelibly imprinted on my mind and heart. I walked to the stand when called, gave an acceptance response, and felt the presence of the Holy Spirit with me, a presence for which I will always be grateful.

The general conference had concluded before my counselors and I went again to the Relief Society building, this time to assume the full responsibility for the offices to which we had just been sustained. Sitting in conference together considering the work ahead was a situation that was to become all too familiar, but on this first day there was an uncomfortable feeling of not knowing where to begin. Sister Boyer had just the right comment to make that start easier, as she recalled from her vast reservoir of family stories, "My grandfather, George F. Richards, was frequently asked, 'How do you know what to do in your calling as a member of the Quorum of the Twelve Apostles?' He would laugh and say, 'I go sit at my desk and the work comes to me.' "

She had no sooner made the comment than my telephone rang. I was asked to contact my counselors and invite them to bring their husbands and children to meet the next morning, Monday, in the First Presidency board room of the Church Office Building, to be set apart. Our appointment was early, about seven-thirty in the morning, as I remember. We were there promptly and all of us excitedly awaited the entrance of the First Presidency.

A setting apart to a Church calling is a solemn and joyous occasion. The prayers given at that time invoke a genuine feeling of assignment along with responsibility, and the mantle of the office, an almost tangible thing, descends upon the one being set apart.

The First Presidency didn't keep us waiting. They were smiling and happy as they welcomed us and shook hands with everyone in the room. They told us they were very pleased to have us join the headquarters' Church family and that they would immediately proceed with the business for which we had met.

President Spencer W. Kimball asked me to come forward and sit in a particular chair that was waiting. He invited my husband to join with President Tanner and President Romney as he set me apart. They all put their hands on my head while President Kimball set me apart to preside over the Relief Society of The Church of Jesus Christ of Latter-day Saints. He pronounced blessings upon me and counseled me thus in part: "Impress upon the women of this Church their femininity and their great privileges and honors to be the mothers of men, mothers of those who will be in positions to lead the Church, that they may be grateful for that privilege and they will not be affected by the ideals and ideologies of the world."

At that moment I felt something akin to those feelings of peace and comfort I had known the Friday before, when I was in the Tabernacle and the words of the song, "How Firm a Foundation," had come to me. There was a profound impression of the responsibility that was mine to defend the home and the woman's partnership in that sacred family circle. From that insight and that responsibility I wanted never to waver, even though the problems of speaking up for the role of the homemaker, I knew, would become increasingly more difficult. I also felt the joy of all of the events which had taken place and had brought me to the glorious moment of blessing by the prophet of God.

Janath R. Cannon then took her place in that chair. Invoked on her by President N. Eldon Tanner were marvelous blessings of insight into the work she was to do as the first counselor in the Relief Society presidency. Marian R. Boyer was set apart by President Marion G. Romney, her long-time friend, her husband's former business associate, and a co-worker in her ward. It was tender and meaningful to listen to her blessing and to have her father, Elder LeGrand Richards, who was a member of the Quorum of the Twelve Apostles and a long-time advocate of the Relief Society, present on that occasion to support his daughter.

We left that room inspired by our prophets. We knew that we had been empowered to do the work of Relief Society. It was for us "the season thereof." My prayer was simply that we would serve to the benefit of the women of the Church and that our work would build upon the good works of former Relief Society leaders.

Our organization became complete when on October 31, 1974, the newly sustained Relief Society General Board members were gathered for an inspirational meeting by members of the Quorum of the Twelve, and given individual blessings to guide them in their new callings.

Elder Bruce R. McConkie addressed us and explained in some detail the importance of a major change in an organization. He affirmed that Sister Spafford and her counselors had been called of God by revelation. They were those whom the Lord had wanted appointed. They had served with majestic ability and distinction. He expressed appreciation for them and their associates. He stated that there was no question about the inspiration of the past, and that the presidency had been released by the same spirit of revelation. He continued by saying that the Lord had now called three other able women to leadership responsibility in the Relief Society. He said when changes are made by the Holy Spirit, they constitute the mind and will of the Lord.

Elder McConkie said it was most appropriate to have the husbands of board members and certain family members present, because Church service is more than an individual affair; it is a family concern. That is why, when priesthood leaders are called, their wives are also interviewed and involved, so that in the "call" the family unitedly adds its strength to the individual.

The members of the board divided into four groups, and each group went with one of the four members of the Quorum of the Twelve Apostles, our advisers, who set them apart as members of the Relief Society General Board. Each woman was given promises and blessings, as needed, to help her give needed service to the Relief Society organization. Some board members returned with happy, smiling faces to the waiting members of the Relief Society presidency; others were radiant, but with tears being dried. Over the years I saw those same, sweet expressions return to the faces of those board members as they received assignments and reported their successful completions.

I had not been in office long when one of the Brethren called and suggested that Cloy Kent of Iowa City, Iowa, be commissioned to paint the portrait of me that was to hang, along with those of the former general presidents, in the board room of the Relief Society Building. I was pleased with the choice, although there might be some trepidation in putting one's trust in an artist since her representation would be so long-standing. I felt comfortable with Sister Kent. She had painted a portrait of Elder Thomas S. Monson and I liked her work very much. She was also a dear friend of our daughter, Lillian, who lived near her in Iowa.

Before she began with the brush, Cloy Kent gave a great deal of thought to how a finished portrait should look. She said she liked to know the end of the painting from the beginning. She liked to have the spirit, not just the outward appearance of the person, come through in her work. She began the project by taking a number of photographs of me, in which she tried to capture multiple feelings and expressions. She suggested I wear the dress that Becky Sweeten Smith, our daughter-in-law, had made for me to wear when, as the newly called general president, I received guests at a special reception in the Relief Society Building. The fabric was some I had purchased in Australia. Becky had worked hard to make the dress lovely. I was proud of her and of the dress she had created for me. The artist liked its color and the elegance of the fabric, and I was pleased when she selected it for the portrait.

We went to the State Capitol Building where Sister Kent began photographing me. She chose that location because she particularly liked the overhead light that was available from the dome. I felt very self-conscious with so many people looking on while she worked to get just the perfect setting and poses from which she would be able to paint the portrait. She told me that, once she had quality photographs of me, it would then only be necessary to have me come to her Iowa studio for three or four sittings. The rest she could do from the photographs themselves.

Cloy Kent was very interesting to talk with as she worked. She loved the Lord, and from studying his handiwork she wanted to learn more about the art of creating. She wanted to be able to bring forth on canvas a reproduction of human life that would do justice to him and to his creations. She loved the out-of-doors and saw beauty in all of it. It was a pleasure to feel her happiness and sense her desire to understand the Lord's creative power. I looked forward to each visit with her.

Occasionally she would have my daughter and son-in-law over, and would ask them if my spirit were showing through in the painting. She was very receptive to their feelings and suggestions. She said that other people see things differently from the artist and so it was important that she listen and respond.

I thought often then of what we portray to others. Although not on canvas, still nonetheless real is the picture our lives present. How important it is that, in interactions with others, we are sensitive to what they see! Those relationships should help us to listen and learn and do what will help us develop and become the beings we want portrayed. We sometimes speak of brief encounters with people as "brushes." If we are keen in our sensitivity, these experiences can, in fact, be thought of as brush strokes through which we are creating the portrait, or even the mural, of our lives. Having such awareness continually will enable us to enjoy the varied experiences of our lives and use them for our benefit in becoming more like Christ, growing "in favour with God and man" (Luke 2:52).

Part 3

In His Vineyard

A certain man had a fig
tree planted in his
vineyard; and he came
and sought fruit thereon,
and found none. . . .
Three years I come
seeking fruit on this fig
tree, and find none: cut it
down; why cumbereth it
the ground? . . . Let it
alone this year also. . . . If
it bear fruit, well: and if
not, then after that thou
shalt cut it down.
—Luke 13:6−9

7

A Continuation of the Seeds Forever

In all things, as hath been sealed upon their heads, which glory shall be a fulness and a continuation of the seeds forever and ever.
—D&C 132:19

I learned quickly that the general president of Relief Society has literally hundreds of encounters with women—women of the Church and women not of the Church. Although my portrait as general president was started soon after I took office, before it was finished and hanging among those of the other general Relief Society presidents, I had almost circled the globe in meetings with women.

I went to Europe and then to the Far East, meeting with Relief Society women and other groups of which I was a part because of my position. In between trips, I received scores of telephone calls and met with great numbers of women who had traveled to Salt Lake City. Some were from Mexico, Hawaii, Canada, Norway, Sweden, South Africa, and other places near and far. I very quickly found that Relief Society, like the rest of the Church, was beginning to face the multiple challenges of serving an international membership; what we taught in our meetings must answer the needs of women from many lands and with varying cultures. Equally challenging was the diversity of sisters who lived their lives in different circumstances: single, married, and divorced, with children and without children; all were the offspring of our Heavenly Father with needs, wants, and a desire to make their individual contributions in the world.

Talking with groups of Relief Society sisters could never be casual or random. Very soon, it became apparent that I must be part of the continuing discussions going on about the role of women in today's society. I don't suppose that a more vocal and, in many ways, more strident questioning of that role has occurred than during the seventies. The first part of that decade found many women involved in a consciousness-raising campaign to help others become acquainted with, and more concerned about, their situations in life. There was an enormous effort to uncover all the inequities and problems that women faced, and to push for changes. Against this backdrop, a defense of the more traditional role of wife and mother was rarely represented, especially by the media, and when represented, it was seen to be anti-woman or a defense of the stereotype.

It was incredible how often I was made out to be anti-woman; how often the women of the Church were characterized as being exploited by men. Despite the criticism, however, I continued to meet with women individually in my office. They would pour out their hearts to me, and as they did I felt that I was gaining a good understanding of their heartaches and problems. Not only did these individual interviews prove a valuable resource to help me learn of the feelings and needs of women, but I felt the need of calling together a special committee of active, community-minded women who researched the current issues and presented their findings on such subjects as depression, child abuse, volunteerism, employment, and singleness. Together we discussed solutions and directions that could help women know both peace and progress.

I found myself frequently referring to the set of scriptures I had on my desk. Passages that I had read a hundred times and more now began to take on a new and more personal meaning for me. "And God said, Let there be light: and there was light" (Genesis 1:3). As a Relief Society presidency, we felt we needed light. There was an openness and a feeling of light in the Relief Society Building itself. It was spacious and had many windows, but we needed more light. We were con-

stantly praying for the light of eternal vision because we knew
that where there is no such vision, the people perish.

As a presidency we decided we should look back and try to
build upon the firm foundation of the past; Sister Belle S.
Spafford had given strong leadership in her nearly thirty years
as general president of the Relief Society. We wanted to make
certain we preserved those basic policies and plans that the
Lord had directed to be implemented throughout Sister Spafford's administration as well as those given in other times and
eras of Relief Society. We found many past references to certain stewardships, assignments, and tasks that Relief Society
had been asked by the Brethren to carry out. We were constantly inspired by the initiative the women had taken to meet
their special needs. In many instances they have conceived
programs and carefully nurtured them until they became fully
developed departments of the Church.

We were pleased to read again the directions of the
Prophet Joseph Smith in which he outlined the purposes of the
Relief Society in his instructions at early meetings of the sisters.
It seemed to us that when he addressed the sisters the Prophet
was trying to teach the Society ways to manifest benevolence:

> To illustrate the object of the Society that the Society of
> sisters might provoke the Brethren to good works in looking
> to the wants of the poor, searching after objects of charity
> and in administering to their wants—to assist by correct-
> ing the morals and strengthening the virtues of the commu-
> nity, and save the elders the trouble of rebuking: that they
> may give of their time to other duties, etc., in their public
> teaching.
>
> (A *Centenary of Relief Society* [Salt Lake City:
> General Board of Relief Society, 1942], p. 15.)

If we could teach those same things in our day it would be
another step in motivating the sisters, through Relief Society
meetings, to render compassionate service and then to take
that training into their homes. Of course, we knew that learning the homemaking skills and arts was essential for women
in order that they have the necessary time and become ex-

amples of cultured and refined living, able to help others find
relief from poverty, selfishness, sorrow, apathy, ignorance,
immorality, worldliness, mediocrity, fear, personal limita-
tions, and loneliness.

We also realized that while each one of the desirable character traits described by the Prophet could be guidelines for
living, they might require different applications in the many
lands where the Relief Society was organized.

It was our hope that we could organize the program of Relief Society, wherever it was, to be administered with wisdom
and good judgment; that love and understanding would per-
meate all the activities of the Society. We knew that all who
were called to positions of responsibility in the Relief Society
were daughters of God and could receive divine guidance. We
knew too that, being directed by the power of the priesthood,
the women of the Church could develop their own societies
and thus advance the Lord's kingdom throughout the earth.

With these many thoughts engulfing me I felt a particular
need to know what the Lord wanted this new presidency to
do; what directions he would that we should give to the
women and the work at that time. As I studied and prayed,
there came an overwhelming feeling of love and the knowledge that the Lord loves each one of his daughters. Love then
seemed to be the message. I wondered if there wasn't a more
important direction for me to know than that. I returned to
my Heavenly Father again and again, and the assurance came
that each woman is his daughter and that she is entitled to a
continuation of seed forever. He loves his daughters individually and collectively. It was then that I knew all our plans
must be made considering the best means for helping women
to have confidence in the love of their Heavenly Father, to understand the importance of their place in the kingdom of God,
and to know Jesus Christ, "listen to [His] words; walk in the
meekness of [His] Spirit," that they might have peace in Him
(D&C 19:23). Then, it became very clear, they could best do
what needed to be done. They could work together. They
could learn together. They could strengthen and serve one another. A major purpose for Relief Society was to help bring

women to that spiritual understanding and provide opportunities for them to continue developing it forever.

An invitation was extended to me to attend the temple dedication in Washington, D.C. Our priesthood advisers suggested that Sister Spafford and I go there together and make certain that the Relief Society Distribution Center for temple clothing, for which the Relief Society was responsible, was in order. I was pleased to travel with Sister Spafford. As we traveled we talked in great detail about the work of Relief Society. I was surprised at her response when, at one point, I remarked, "I've always admired your great knowledge about Relief Society and its administration, but never so much as I do now that I have become the president. I wish I knew all about it as you do."

She quickly replied, "I just wish I knew everything there is to know about Relief Society. The more I learn, the more I know there is to learn. Each day teaches me something I didn't know before about Relief Society." This astonished me. I thought one could get to the point of knowing all about this work, but her statement made me realize the fact that, as a gift of God to his daughters, Relief Society has unlimited potential.

We arrived in Washington, D.C., on a Saturday. We were thrilled with the location and the beauty of the distribution center. Sister Spafford gave the employees direction on the sacred nature of the center and asked them to maintain that feeling always. She tried to impress upon them that the distribution of temple clothing was a work being done for the Lord. As always, she was powerful. I was then asked to make a few remarks. I did, and was impressed with the reality of the blessing I had received when I was set apart, for although I was new to the work, I could feel the Holy Spirit giving me the power of utterance, and I received the strength and inspiration of my very new calling.

Mary Foulger, wife of Sidney Foulger, one of the builders of the Washington, D.C., temple, took us on a tour of that beautiful edifice. We went from the bottom to the top, and when we arrived in that big assembly room on top, we found

Relief Society sisters busily cleaning in preparation for the dedication. We took time to stop and visit with the women. We met Nona Dyer, sister of my counselor Marian Boyer, who graciously expressed her delight that her sister was in the new general presidency, and said that the women all felt it was an honor and a privilege to be there cleaning the temple. Then she pointed out one sister and said, "Look at that sister. She would not be here today if it had not been for the Relief Society. When she came to Washington, D.C., she had some personal problems and had determined to become inactive in the Church. When we met her, we loved her so much that we felt she just had to be one with us. We are all so happy that she is here in the temple today." It was a sweet commentary on the work of Relief Society.

Then we worked our way around that large room, talking with the sisters and thanking them individually for the work they were doing. Each one responded in a similar way; their faces reflected the happiness they felt to be there together doing a work in the house of the Lord. When we reached the sister that Sister Dyer had mentioned, the sister said, pointing back to Nona, "Look at that sister over there. If she had not been caring and constantly looking out for me and loving me, I would never have been here today. When I came to Washington, D.C., I wanted to become lost. I was very unhappy and decided that I would leave the Church. She would not let me. She organized all of the sisters and had them keep track of me. They loved me and included me in everything they did. How grateful I am to them! I love them and my heart is filled to overflowing with the privilege that is mine of being here now." We put our arms around each other and tears filled our eyes.

Feelings of love were evident on the face of each sister there, reflecting the knowledge each sister had that she was doing a significant part of the work of Relief Society. In those faces I saw at that moment a profound understanding of service and of great love. I remembered again the answer I had received to my supplication, that the most important message of Relief Society is love. When a woman can learn of that love and have it emanate from her, she becomes even more aware of whose daughter she is. Then she can receive all that her Heavenly Father has for her. Although those feelings during that first visit away as a general president were still so new in that awesome responsibility, they have repeatedly come flooding back to me in fond remembrance through the years.

The next day was Sunday. Sister Spafford and I accepted Mary Foulger's invitation to have dinner at her home. She also took us to our Sunday meetings where, to my surprise, when Sister Spafford was asked to say a few words, she declined: "No, thank you. I'm just accompanying Sister Smith on this trip. It is her responsibility to address the group, not mine." Although I was surprised and felt inadequate, I was very impressed with Sister Spafford's concern that appropriate respect be given to the position and the authority that had been transferred. One of the miracles of the Church is the smooth transfer of authority. The mantle of a calling comes to the new officer and shifts ever so quietly from the outgoing officer.

After the meeting was over, Mary quickly excused herself, telling us that her husband would take us for a short ride to see the Washington, D.C., area and that by the time we arrived at their house she would have dinner on the table. We rode through some of the beautiful residential areas near their home, and Sister Spafford commented, "One thing I can't imagine is why these little houses have such big doors. Look at that one. Can you imagine such a little home with such a big door?"

Brother Foulger, with a hint of teasing in his voice, said, "Just one minute. Before you say anything else, let me tell you that is my house."

Sister Spafford laughed and said, "That is just like me, always saying the wrong thing. When I was being entertained one time at the home of a stake Relief Society president, I was so hungry that I decided to take a few extra cookies in my handkerchief. As the hostess said good-bye she handed me a box of cookies. When I went to take them, the ones I had in my handkerchief fell! I was mortified. Another time I was visiting Lady Reading in England. We had dinner. She had a kidney

pie brought in and placed on the table in front of me. She
wanted to honor me by having me cut and serve it. The ladle
they gave me simply would not cut through the crust. I gave it
a big lunge and the kidney pie went sailing off the table onto
the floor." She explained that Lady Reading had good-na-
turedly said, in her thoroughly British manner, "Never mind.
I'll have another kidney pie brought right in." We laughed
with her.

Sister Spafford's delightful sense of humor was another of
her great strengths. She was charming to be with, and witty.
More than her delight in the humorous, however, I sensed in
this great woman a desire to put me at ease as I assumed a new
and monumental role—even if it meant allowing her own mistakes to show. This quality, too, would become a model for me
as I tried to reach out to other sisters. I felt a responsibility to
her and to each woman that the Lord loved; but her shoes
were very hard ones to try to fill. I always felt humbled in the
shadow of her strength.

When I was back in Salt Lake City and at my desk again, I
realized with a start that our Relief Society general conference
was only a month away, and I knew we must get the planning
and organizing for that event under way. We also knew that
we would have regional meeting assignments. Regional meetings were our visits to the sisters in their own geographical
areas, whereas at general conference time the sisters came to
see us. Both were major responsibilities to be fulfilled and time
was quickly passing, so we assessed our needs, reviewed the
strengths of each board member, and prayerfully made assignments.

We realized the inspiration of those assignments when
board members came back from their meetings with experiences such as those of Sister Junko Shimizu. Being a native of
Japan, she had always been assigned to go there for regional
meetings and so she was particularly surprised to be assigned
to attend a meeting in the southern United States. Not only
was she surprised, she was afraid that the people there would
not receive her well because she was not American or Cauca-
sian.

Prayerfully she prepared. Dutifully she went, fortified by her faith. When requested to take part in the opening general assembly, she asked if she might sing rather than speak. In her lovely, clear soprano voice she sang, "I Am a Child of God" in Japanese. The members were moved by the beauty of her presentation and by the inspiration of her message as well.

With that touching introduction she was warmly welcomed by the sisters in her department and was able to give the prepared material, as well as additional helps, very effectively. When the meeting was over, and after thanks and warm embraces from the sisters, she was walking down a corridor to an exit when one of the brethren asked if she would speak with him a moment in his office. He wanted to personally thank her for coming. Then he explained that, although he was now a bishop and for years had been a faithful, active member of the Church, he had struggled with a deep problem. Since his military service in World War II, when he fought against the Japanese, he had not been able to free his heart from the hatred which he had developed for the Japanese people at that time. He had tried, even prayed, to overcome those feelings, but until he heard her sing that song in Japanese, he had retained the terrible feelings. As a result of Sister Shimizu's rendition, his heart had finally been penetrated, and the peace he had so long desired had come to him fully and completely.

Our presidency was so busy that it seemed we had hardly said good morning each day before the day was past and it was time to go home. The next day came quickly and it, too, was rapidly gone. But there was joy in this service, no matter how demanding or how busy. Each day brought with it humor and humility, caring and compassion, inspiration and direction, all drawing us closer in love to the daughters of God with whom we were privileged to serve.

We were going blithely along when, without any warning, it was suggested by some that the name of our organization be changed from "Relief Society" to something more modern and up to date. I began delving into our past history and found that there were some very special connecting links with our past. Not only that, but the idea of "relief" began to have a meaningful, modern application. The more we talked with the members of the general board and with other women who came into the office, or as we talked with women in our travels, the more vivid became our awareness of the individual woman and her need for relief. Women came seeking direction, comfort, and the firm foundation of their organization. They especially wanted the light of the gospel in the strength of the past to help them make their decisions each day. They believed that because of the name of Relief Society, the organization could help them. Relief Society did not have all of the answers but it had been given to them by the Lord. With the light of the gospel, they learned that Relief Society was teaching them the worth of the individual soul, and they felt its reassuring strength. There was an ongoing strength in knowing that God loved and valued his daughters tenderly, wisely, and highly enough to give them a place to go for direction. It was the same organization he gave the women of the past and of the present, and would be the same in the future.

They knew it was not the same kind of sealing upon their heads as that which took place in the temples of God, but it was a preparation for the continuing blessings of eternity.

Each morning began with a prayer meeting. We joined with the staff in a short meeting in which each took a turn reading a scripture, bringing us closer to the word of the Lord, and then each, in turn, would pray. I particularly enjoyed feeling the spirit of those with whom we worked, both those who were paid employees and those who gave endless hours of work on the general board and in other volunteer service. We worked long and hard to understand our callings and to carry them out.

We met as executive officers almost every morning to study the handbook and learn of our joint and individual responsibilities. That time together also allowed us to attend to ancillary problems and project the needs of each day.

The telephone seemed to ring incessantly: a person expressing appreciation for the work we had done, asking for advice or for an interview, a person calling who represented a part of the organization of the Church there at headquarters. There were calls offering congratulations and calls asking for help.

Many persons called from other departments offering to orient us on the interaction that was needed between their office and ours. Appointments were set up, and they came to tell us of their responsibilities and how ours related to theirs. The Tax Department came, the Health Department, the Melchizedek Priesthood Department, the Young Women's organization, the Welfare Services organization—the list went on. Each meeting was meaningful and important to us and enlarged our understanding of the scope of the planning that was before us.

We frequently recalled Marian's Grandfather Richards who had been President of the Quorum of the Twelve; he had said, "You sit at your desk and the work comes to you." What touched me most was the spirit in which it came; surely those in other offices were as busy as we, but they were nonetheless willing to give us the time needed to help us learn our responsibilities. We did not forget their thoughtfulness.

We reorganized the committees of the general board and gave assignments to each member. We tried to equalize the distribution of work, which was extensive considering that representatives of the Relief Society general board met with many community groups such as Travelers' Aid, broadcasting companies, Red Cross, and the League of Women Voters, to name only a few. Many other groups were asking for us to be represented on their boards.

Sister Spafford, as president, had held major positions of responsibility on the National Council of Women and with the American Mothers, Inc. She was indulgent in taking me with her and introducing me to the women who gave those organizations so much of their time, interest, and intelligent action. She was very much at home among those women. She was listened to, respected, and loved.

On one occasion while with Sister Spafford in New York attending a National Council of Women convention I had to smile at her. She stepped out onto the street and hailed a taxi. She did it with the ease of a native New Yorker.

After we had reorganized the committees of the general board, the meetings began with a flourish: welfare meetings, curriculum meetings, Special Affairs Committee meetings, Church education meetings, orientation meetings with new stake Relief Society presidencies, Promised Valley Playhouse meetings, temple clothing meetings and, of course, general board meetings. We often met with committee chairmen first, because we wanted to be brought very quickly to an understanding of their work. We met with managers of Mormon Handicraft and the Relief Society distribution centers. We wanted to know their feelings on the operational procedures and what might be done to continue to improve the service to our customers and contributors. Lessons also needed attention. We felt the responsibility of reading and discussing the lessons with a view toward adapting them to meet the needs of the sisters worldwide. In fact, we gave each facet of Relief Society work a thorough review.

The multiple demands upon our time represented widespread concerns, and the reality of them was instructive. We particularly realized that many of the concerns being brought before us were valid and that the women of the Church whom we served had problems not unlike our own. We were sobered and humbled by our responsibility to respond effectively to the many complex concerns of the sisterhood, in order to help them claim more fully the promises of the Lord.

8

Exercise
Your Faith to
Plant the Seed

Experiment upon my
words, and exercise a
particle of faith . . . let
this desire work in you.
Alma 32:27

In the first few weeks of my term as general president a simple, sweet feeling of energy and significance in the work filled my days at the Relief Society Building. I felt an intrinsic partnership in the work that took place between the men and the women of the Church.

The first of hundreds of talks I would give throughout the Church was given at Ricks College. When I delivered that first address at Ricks I felt again the anchor that comes through faith in the guiding direction of a prophet of God. Before the first three months of my presidency were completed, though, I found that a whole new dimension had come into my work.

A mounting sea of tumultuous issues had been rising during my tenure on the Relief Society General Board. The United States and, in fact, the whole world was entering into a period of unrest, especially insofar as the role of woman was concerned. In November of 1974 I was invited to a meeting with the Church's Special Affairs Committee. The topic under discussion was the Equal Rights Amendment.

This proposed amendment to the United States Constitution had been under discussion for some time. The Relief Society had not taken a stand on it, nor had the priesthood leadership of the Church. I remember saying to Sister Spafford one time that we should do something about the ERA because it was a legislative proposal that would work to the detriment of women. She turned to me and said, "Do what? It is one thing to say you want to do something and quite a different thing to decide what to do." I found that to be a profound statement.

Now I was the general president, and it was my responsibility to decide what should be done. In the meeting with the Special Affairs Committee we discussed the multitude of problems that could be connected with the ERA. We also talked about what taking such a stand could be interpreted to mean. Some would say the men of the Church did not want the women of the Church to achieve, that Mormon men were trying to put women down and have them controlled by men. However, we concluded that a strong stand against the ERA would be the right thing to do, and that was what really mattered.

After further discussion it was decided that as a woman and as the general president of the Relief Society I should make the statement. I was to say whatever I felt would be appropriate. I called together a number of intelligent, knowledgeable women to help me determine what should be said.

It was arranged for me to give the talk at the University of Utah Institute of Religion, as that was a convenient place to address a large audience. The Public Communications Department of the Church contacted the press to allow them to cover what was purported to be a talk against the ERA. I was very nervous. I had never seen so many cameras and microphones—there were at least twenty on the podium.

I was introduced as President Barbara B. Smith, and Douglas was introduced as "President Smith's wife, Douglas H. Smith." It was a strange mistake, but it made the audience laugh, especially considering the subject about which I was to speak.

This talk set me on a course of opposition with many women in America. I would have preferred a less contentious road during my presidency, because so often the work of Relief Society was strained by my taking a public stand against the ERA and the urgencies this created. Nevertheless, I believed then in the position I took, and I believe in it now.

I always felt the need to relate my statements on public questions to gospel principles, for I knew it was that for which Relief Society sisters hungered. Consequently, when I prepared that first public statement on the ERA, I deliberately framed it in the context of the gospel. I wanted to describe what the gift of sacred partnership between men and women should be. I also wanted women to understand that I knew inequities with regard to gender were still present in society and should be corrected. I thought that I clearly enumerated those areas requiring corrections but, in spite of my efforts to state that position, the media coverage tended to define my declaration as against women's rights.

The storm that followed this talk was intense, and organized proponents of the amendment began to say that Relief Society was an unfair antagonist because it was organized both nationally and internationally. It soon became apparent, however, that Relief Society was not organized to accomplish political goals. Our sisters met together united by a bond of testimony, and our traditional service was compassion to meet the needs of the suffering. We also met together to study the principles of salvation.

The work I did was basically designed to persuade against the ERA for some of the reasons I have stated. Nevertheless, the stand did cause some dissension even among the sisters of Relief Society; so as a presidency we worked doubly hard to encourage all sisters to feel that they belonged in all Relief Society meetings. I never wavered in my conviction that the anti-ERA stand was prompted by the Spirit and that, indeed, such a stand was necessary to protect the family from even more devastating forces than were already unleashed in the world.

That talk also caused many to question whether I spoke for the Church or only for myself. The first official response was, "She does not speak for the Church; only the prophet speaks for the Church."

The result was that for many months considerable ambiguity existed in the Church as to whether the stand against the ERA was the official position of the Church. I can only say that I had felt the hand of the Lord in gathering people who counseled me as I prepared that talk.

About a month after the talk, I was at the Beneficial Life Insurance Company dinner with my husband, who was then president of the company. I sat next to President Kimball. I said to him, "Speak to me, President Kimball."

He pursued my request by curiously asking, "Why?"

I said, "As you know, I have given a talk against the Equal Rights Amendment and a lot of discussion and so much criticism have resulted since that if you don't talk to me, people will think you are angry with me for stating such a strong position against that legislation."

So he talked with me the whole evening. We hardly stopped. We just kept thinking of more things about which to talk. That night I knew a sweet feeling of strength and peace as well as support from him.

As the new year dawned I found myself very excited and happy in the full days spent at the Relief Society Building. There was much work to do: planning appropriate programming for the sisters, working with the departments of the Church, trying to respond to the urgent requests coming from so many segments of the Society, and counseling with sisters who came into the building in need of help.

But there was always an underlying awareness of the unrest that was upsetting the thinking of some of our sisters and causing them much pain as they struggled to find harmony in their hearts and minds. My counselors and I spent many hours trying to help women meet their challenges and hold fast to the messages of the gospel.

As a result, we made some changes in the work of Relief Society that we felt would help us better meet the needs of individual sisters. We organized our board with special assignments of developing programs to meet the requirements and wants of the never-married, single parents, divorced, widowed, and other sisters with special needs. We pursued a consistent plan to teach the need for every woman, married or single, to learn to develop a "provident home." We tried to enrich the offering through mini-classes, enhance the lessons on home management, and develop a learning nursery. Thus we hoped to give "relief" to many who had special needs.

The year of 1975 was my first full year in office. I doubt that any previous general Relief Society presidency had ever faced a more constant spotlight than was directed at my counselors and me. Relief Society became the focal point of intense scrutiny. The media tended to pit my associates and me against the proponents of equal rights for women. It was a continuing frustration to be described as against women's rights, when I simply did not feel that the Equal Rights Amendment was a good way to attain those rights.

I was pleased and relieved when, on October 22, 1976, the First Presidency issued their statement regarding the ERA:

> From its beginnings, The Church of Jesus Christ of Latter-day Saints has affirmed the exalted role of women in our society.
>
> In 1842, when women's organizations were little known, the Prophet Joseph Smith established the women's organization of the Church, the Relief Society, as a companion body of the priesthood. The Relief Society continues to function today as a vibrant, worldwide organization aimed at strengthening motherhood and broadening women's learning and involvement in religious, compassionate, cultural, educational, and community pursuits.
>
> In Utah, where our Church is headquartered, women received the right to vote in 1870, fifty years before the Nineteenth Amendment to the Constitution granted the right nationally.
>
> There have been injustices to women before the law and in society generally. These we deplore.
>
> There are additional rights to which women are entitled.
>
> However, we firmly believe that the Equal Rights Amendment is not the answer.
>
> While the motives of its supporters may be praiseworthy, ERA as a blanket attempt to help women could indeed bring them far more restraints and repressions. We fear it will even stifle many God-given feminine instincts.
>
> It would strike at the family, humankind's basic institution. ERA would bring ambiguity and possibly invite extensive litigation.

Passage of ERA, some legal authorities contend, could nullify many accumulated benefits to women in present statutes.

We recognize men and women as equally important before the Lord, but with differences biologically, emotionally, and in other ways.

ERA, we believe, does not recognize these differences. There are better means for giving women, and men, the rights they deserve.

(*Ensign*, December 1976, p. 79.)

It was signed by President Spencer W. Kimball, world leader of the Church, and his two counselors, President N. Eldon Tanner and President Marion G. Romney, who constituted the First Presidency, the chief governing body of The Church of Jesus Christ of Latter-day Saints.

On January 20, Wendell Ashton, director of Church Public Communications, called to say that CBS wanted to interview me in my office. CBS wanted to do a videotape discussion of my stand against the ERA. The reporter would come from New York and the program would be aired on television the next evening, following the interview. Brother Ashton said he would have a member of his staff with me for the interview.

We spent about one hour in the discussion with the reporter. It was most interesting to see how long an interview takes and how little is actually quoted to the viewing public.

January 27 brought a request for an interview with an Australian reporter. I expected the same type of questioning I had experienced with the American reporters. Instead, this one began by asking, "Don't you think American women are terribly spoiled? They have automatic washing machines, dryers, refrigerators, and dishwashers. They spend their time eating chocolates and playing cards with never a thought of how hard their husbands must work to earn the money they spend so freely. And don't their husbands become subservient to them?"

It was a very different interview than I had anticipated. I could not help but respond that perhaps his assertions were true of some American women, but I did not know any like that. The women I knew best were members of The Church of Jesus Christ of Latter-day Saints, and they were good mothers and homemakers, community-minded and hardworking women. They might have many of the modern conveniences to help them do their work more quickly, but they were women of integrity who looked up to their husbands and knew that they must make good use of the money he brought home to provide for the needs of their families.

The reporter and I never seemed to come to a meeting of the minds. After the interview I saw Sister Spafford and told her that I thought I had been very ineffective in that interview and was really worried about it. She said, "If I could only tell you how many times I felt just like that!" It was the kindest thing she could have said to me. There was no criticism, no complaining, no belittling—just understanding. I knew I would always be grateful for those words.

Later on I talked with Wendell Ashton about that interview, and he encouraged me, too. He said it didn't really matter what the interviewer thought, what mattered was that I expressed my own feelings on the issue and that I only needed to be concerned that I was expressing ideas consistent with gospel teachings.

These dialogues prepared me for an interview that Charles Graves, director of Church Public Communications in New York City, arranged with Judy Klemesrud. She spent at least an hour interviewing me and wrote a positive article expressing my viewpoint. It was sent throughout the world. On that visit, George W. Cornell, Associated Press religion specialist, also talked with me. Then it was a San Jose, California, reporter who wanted to talk about my stand against the ERA. Most often the reporters were initially antagonistic, but before we were finished they listened and asked good questions; and most often they gave a favorable, or at least fair, report.

In mid-January I was invited to go to Coeur d'Alene, Idaho, to speak on the rights of women. It was not in a Church setting that I spoke, but in a civic auditorium. It was the first time I had actually felt both real support and real opposition for my position on the Equal Rights Amendment.

By this time I knew it was necessary to make my stand perfectly clear, and I tried to do it by stating, "I am for the rights of women. I could not in good conscience head an organization of a million women if I were not for women's rights." I made it clear that with all my heart I wanted to do my part to ensure continued progress toward equality for everyone in the United States, but that I firmly believed that the proposed constitutional change was neither necessary nor a prudent way to accomplish the goal. (See appendix 1.)

During the entire year of 1975 I was repeatedly called upon to state my position, as the general president of the Relief Society, against the Equal Rights Amendment. It was a faith-promoting experience to stand up to the intense and persistent public scrutiny of such a controversial issue. The issue would remain before the public for the next several years as proponents worked assiduously for passage of the amendment before the legal time frame for passage was exhausted.

Initially I was concerned, and somewhat disheartened, that so much of my effort and time as the general president of the Relief Society was necessarily consumed in maintaining a knowledgeable and rational public stance opposing the proposed amendment. I came to realize, though, especially in retrospect, how vital and effective the participation must be in which one of the oldest and largest women's organizations in the United States was involved. Our voice was heard and, combined with the voices of other thoughtful citizens, the proposed amendment ultimately could not receive enough support for ratification.

That proposed amendment, however, still lies dormant. I am certain the issue will be brought before the American people again. Proponents of the amendment will resurrect it and begin anew their offensive. When that happens, it will be vital that citizens research and review all the accumulated information regarding the issue. By so doing, the populace will be able to take intelligent action and only support legislation which will be in the best interest of men, women, and the family.

A welcomed respite from all the clamor of the women's movement, especially as it involved the ERA, was the prayer vigil sponsored by the American Mothers, Inc., in November of 1975. Recognizing a deterioration in the structure of American family life, this organization requested that every state in the union join together in prayer in behalf of the families of America. If America were to remain strong, the families would need to remain strong and intact.

I was asked to address that interfaith assemblage in the Salt Lake Tabernacle at the conclusion of the vigil. I gave a brief history of the origin of the famed Tabernacle organ, explaining that while its power source is now electricity, before 1895 the power for the organ was supplied by hand. In fact, it took four pairs of hands to pump the large bellows that gave the organ the needed air to produce its magnificent sounds.

On one occasion in those early days, Professor Joseph John Daynes was giving a recital on the organ. He pulled out the stops to begin his performance and gave the signal to the four men to begin pumping the bellows. He put his hands on the keys, but to his surprise there was no sound. He left his seat, went around to the back of the organ, and there found the four men comfortably seated and talking amiably to each other. When he questioned them, their spokesman said, "Professor Daynes, whenever you give a recital here you always get all the credit, and we wish to say that without our help there can be no recital." Professor Daynes promised to rectify the error. He went back to his seat at the organ and it was announced that Professor Daynes would begin his recital with the help of his four assistants, who were named one by one.

We find ourselves in a somewhat similar situation. We continually face major problems as individuals, in cities, states, nations, and the world. No one man or woman—in fact, no group of men or women—will be able to solve such problems alone. But behind the mighty "organ" of our human experiences lies a power source seeking use. It is the power of him who created us all. He has repeatedly told us to ask him for wisdom and knowledge, and has promised that he would be responsive to our petitions and to our needs. In the troubled days of our experience now and in the future, we must seek and utilize that eternal source of power and light which will provide us with the inspiration and direction we need to meet our challenges.

I certainly knew early on in my Church assignment that I must exercise a great deal of faith and rely on the only dependable power source as I spoke for Relief Society in addressing the difficult issues of the day.

9

Much Seed Out into the Field

Thou shalt carry much
seed out into the field.
—Deuteronomy 28:38

I thought often about my call to serve the women of the Church, of the promises given me when I was set apart under the hands of the prophet, and of the rich outpouring of the Spirit I knew on that day. I so much needed to feel that sustaining influence of my Heavenly Father following the talks I gave on the Equal Rights Amendment, because I struggled with the divisive spirit that seemed to descend upon many men and women in and out of the Church.

Even so, during 1975 I experienced great personal growth. Almost every day it became more clear to me that the issues of our times could not be ignored, even within the relatively calm and enjoyable confines of Relief Society. The unity of faith shared by the women of the Church was being ruffled by the difficult discussions about women taking place, and by the media's attack upon the women who were in the home rather than participating in the work world often glamorized by the media.

One of the fundamental and urgent questions being explored was that of the right of women to choose the direction of their lives. Energy and time were also devoted to raising women's awareness of their situations in life, with an emphasis on what were perceived as inequitable situations.

In February, Marian, Janath, and I had a pleasant surprise as we were presented the Elect Lady Award by the Lambda Delta Sigma sorority. This recognition is given annually by the sorority to an outstanding woman of their choice. The fact that they awarded three at once gave added importance to the ceremonies. We were truly pleased to receive the distinction, not only for the personal acknowledgments but also because of the recognition it brought to Relief Society. Barbara Winder gave me mine, Winnifred Jardine presented Janath's award, and Nedra Warner gave Marian hers. Each had talked with our families and had prepared personal and meaningful tributes. This took place at a lovely luncheon held at the Lion House with the national officers of Lambda Delta Sigma and the local chapter officers.

Just a week later we were invited to the Church Office Building for a luncheon honoring the wife of the Korean ambassador. She was a dignified and charming woman. In Korea women are not called upon to speak, but Elder Hinckley, although knowing this about the Korean people, called upon her to say a few words to us. She expressed her surprise that she would be asked and then, very quietly and carefully, she began to express her appreciation for the kindness she had been shown while she was in the United States. Her love for her own country was obvious, but her understanding and appreciation of other lands had been enlarged as she had traveled with her husband. We were all captivated by her charm in responding to all that was done for her and her husband. I left that meeting with an increased awareness that every nation has greatness to offer, as does every child of God.

As that day drew to a close, I suddenly realized that the next day I had a lecture to give at Brigham Young University. It was to be part of the "last lecture" series on campus. The talk was to be given in the Joseph Smith Lecture Hall and was to express what I would say if it were my very last lecture on earth. I had been thinking from time to time of what I might include, but found the topic difficult and had come to some only partly conclusive thoughts on the subject. Then came the trip from Salt Lake City to Provo. There was a terrible snow storm. The roads were slippery. It was late in the afternoon and the traffic was heavy. The trip was a frightening experience. I began to feel that perhaps it was all part of the plan—if I became frightened enough, I would speak with realism, thinking any moment might be my last.

The auditorium was not full for my lecture, but the students were attentive. I appreciated the experience because it helped me realize how very much I had to learn. In some ways it seemed more like a first lecture than a last. When I was called as Relief Society general president, no one had asked me whether I was prepared to deliver major public addresses, but I could see that this was to be a significant part of the work. I thought, as I was standing there before that group of intelligent young people who wanted to be taught, I had no right to take their time unless I could give them a message of worth; yet my days had been so full that it had been difficult to prepare properly. I wondered how I would manage to fit everything in.

Even our family life reflected the busyness of my new calling. Sunday dinners had been an important part of our family life and I wanted them to continue for as long as possible. Each of our children, as well as my husband, had Church responsibilities, so it was difficult to arrange our schedules for a gathering. Sometimes some of them just could not be with us. Still, even with our time constraints I continued to offer invitations and they would come if they could. This continued until Sherilynn, our youngest daughter, was married. Then, quite suddenly, preparing Sunday dinner became harder to do. I found out very quickly how dependent parents can get on their children. Too many parents think only of the ways in which their children are dependent on them; but when I think of how our young family members ran errands, did household chores, and helped complete the tasks that needed to be done, I can appreciate all the ways we really need them.

Finding ways to bring the family together, although increasingly difficult, meant as much to them as it did to my husband and me. Our son, Barton, expressed this one day when he said, "Mother, I have just heard the most terrible thing."

"What is it?" I anxiously inquired.

"My friend and his family no longer go to his parents for Sunday dinner," he said.

I had to smile, because I had expected a tragedy. Then, realizing that Barton was only half joking, I perceived he had helped me recognize that when a family stops having that sweet, close association together, it is a tragedy if some other activity does not fill in. It leaves a void in the communication link, in the talking time that keeps a family close. We continued trying to create family occasions. They were always precious moments, treasured islands in the sea of work that surrounded all of us.

Each workday brought some new experience. One Monday in February began with a recording session for the Relief Society general conference. It was amazing how I could shake in that soundproof room, all alone with only a microphone. My mouth became so dry it was difficult even to read simple words from a page without making mistakes. I quickly learned that making a tape recording was a little like the process of repenting. If I made a mistake, only I could go back and correct it. If I made the correction, the technician could cut out the mistake and it was as if it had never been made. If I didn't correct it, there was nothing he could do. My mistake would stand recorded forever.

After the recording session, I hurried to catch a flight. A blizzard had suddenly arrived, making it difficult even to get to the airport, and once there I found that the plane had been delayed. I called the Relief Society president hosting the meeting I was to attend and told her I would be late but would come as soon as weather conditions permitted. The sisters sat in their meetinghouse for three hours until I finally came. I was impressed at their dedication and, after those three hours, their willingness to listen for as long as I wanted to talk to them. "Thou shalt carry much seed out into the field" became a directive to me, and is a responsibility that each woman in the Church must assume as well, whether we participate in activities or share ways that the gospel of Jesus Christ has strengthened us and blessed our lives.

Tilling
the Ground

And we began to till the
ground . . . with all
manner of seeds.
—Mosiah 9:9

Representing the women of the Church in a general welfare session allowed me to enthusiastically reaffirm the
wisdom of the plan presented to develop specific welfare programs that would bless the individual family. I pledged both
my support and my every effort to encourage the women of
the Church to assist in carrying out the great welfare program,
and offered the resources of Relief Society in both its planning
and implementing stages.

The need for that kind of cooperative action between
priesthood and Relief Society was made evident when, on one
cold January day, two visiting teachers called at the home of a
family that had recently moved into their ward. There was no
immediate response to a knock, but a feeling impressed them
to try again; they knocked a second and then a third time.

The door finally opened a few inches, revealing a woman
and a child bundled in coats and pajamas. The visiting teachers were reluctantly invited into an ice-cold house where, in
answer to questions asked in understanding and love, the
woman tearfully revealed the family's situation.

The student husband was desperately ill and in the intensive care unit of a local hospital. The doctor and hospital bills
were taking all the money the couple had saved for years to
allow the young father to obtain additional schooling. When

their supply of fuel was exhausted, the young wife and the
child stayed in bed to keep warm. The mother was trying to
make one quart of milk and a half-loaf of bread last for the re-
mainder of the month.

The visiting teachers offered help, but the sister replied,
"My husband is proud; he wouldn't want us to accept
charity." The visiting teachers wisely explained that the Lord's
program of welfare is not one that robs the receiver of his self-
respect or independence, but rather contributes to it. By
gentle, loving persuasion, the visiting teachers convinced the
young wife to let them call the Relief Society president.

Within a short time both the Relief Society president and
the bishop arrived at the home. Soon fuel was delivered, the
furnace was started, good food was immediately provided,
and additional supplies ordered. The bishop visited the husband in the hospital and gave him encouragement by assuring
him that his family was well cared for. An administration followed in which the young man was reassured concerning his
own condition. From that point, he began to improve.

When I was asked to serve on the Church Board of Education, I again witnessed the joint efforts of the priesthood and
Relief Society. Sister Spafford continued to serve on the board.
She and I were the only women among an august group of
General Authorities. It was humbling. I appreciated being a
part of it. There is no sweeter experience than listening to the
prayers of the prophets and Apostles of the Lord; I particularly
felt that way as they offered the invocations in those meeting.
Because they prayed so personally to the Lord I always felt a
little anxiety when it was my turn to supplicate the Lord in
their behalf, even though I know presenting ourselves to our
Father in Heaven is always a privilege. When I was called
upon to pray I was very grateful that as a child I had been
taught to pray to and to love the Lord.

At one meeting of the Church Board of Education, Elder
Boyd K. Packer responded to my proposal that Brigham Young
University teach students not only the importance of gaining
knowledge but also how to apply that knowledge in the home
setting. He suggested that the family science college change its

name to the College of Home and Family Science. The added emphasis in the departmental name should also be reflected in classroom instruction, by applying general knowledge to areas of home living. The motion was passed. The name of the college department was changed and Elder Packer helped maintain that designation from that time forward, supporting my attitude about that important facet of learning.

Serving on the Church Board of Education was a new responsibility that was especially meaningful because I had always known the importance of education, an appreciation possibly inherited from my ancestors as far back as Reverend John Rogers, who, on February 4, 1555, was burned at the stake for learning and teaching about God. From at least that early history on, my family had always sought knowledge.

I thought of how it would have pleased my physician grandmother if she could have known that her granddaughter was serving on this particular board. She had been in the first graduating class when Brigham Young University was still an academy, and had completed her education with honors under the superior tutelage of the renowned Karl G. Maeser.

Former general presidents Belle S. Spafford and Florence S. Jacobsen, along with general Young Women president Ruth H. Funk and I, were all in New York for the National Council of Women meetings in May of 1975. It was helpful to have the three of them introduce me to the other council members. They also participated in the discussion of the ongoing items regarding financing the council and the proper use of money that had been willed to the national and international councils.

Some of the women's ideas under discussion there were quite different from those ideas I worked with in Relief Society. They were as different as "sheum and neas" used when planting with grains and all manner of fruit was done (see Mosiah 9:9). Different to me, but listening to them comprised one of the expectations of the calling. The businesswomen who made up a large part of this group were determined to promote issues of the day that seemed important to them: actively supporting the Equal Rights Amendment and abortion ranked high among their priorities. Sister Spafford reminded them of the founding days, when the organization was established for the purpose of providing information on issues of particular concern to women; then each group took back to their councils the current thinking and ideas to increase the awareness of women in their locales. This appeared an unacceptable stance for some of those present; they wanted to become an action group.

Florence Jacobsen presented a possible format for the Home and Family Conference the council would sponsor that October. Her proposal, as well as the handmade articles she donated to be raffled off, was appreciated. The items were a lovely quilt and a needlepoint bag. Both were beautiful. Because I had helped make more than one quilt in days past, I realized the value of her gifts. I wondered if these women could really appreciate the offering that was made.

A deep feeling of gratitude welled up within me. I was more appreciative than ever before to be under the direction of the priesthood with a divine plan to unite women. I thought about the great accomplishments that could belong to those women of remarkable talent were they directed by God, instead of deriving their initiative from the competitive working world where they struggled for power and acceptance. I could hardly wait to get back to the Relief Society General Board members whose loving, cooperative use of time, talents, and energies were directed toward building the kingdom of God.

I looked out of the window and saw just across the street the United Nations Building. I began to realize that this was but a minuscule experience and that the time must surely come when we would be of one heart, one mind, and one thought as the work of converting the world came to fruition.

After attending those National Council of Women meetings, it was increasingly apparent to me that we needed to consider problems facing women in the light of gospel principles. All women, if they will, can receive wise counsel from the scriptures and through the words of modern-day prophets of the Lord. Relief Society as well, from its beginning, has taught women:

1. To assist in correcting the morals and strengthening the virtues of community life.

2. To raise human life to its highest level.

3. To elevate and enlarge the scope of women's activities and conditions. (Relief Society Minutes, March 17, 1842.)

Occasionally my schedule would permit me to accompany my husband on his Regional Representative assignments. One assignment took him to the Park Stake conference in Salt Lake City. I was invited to sit on the stand with Douglas. I was surprised, as I looked over the audience, to see not only young people, but many older people, multinational people, and handicapped people. But the deaf group caught my eye and interest.

I had never watched anyone sign for a group of the deaf before. The interpreter was masterful and had a proficient assistant who rotated with her for every alternate speaker. I could see that it was a very challenging and demanding skill to listen and, very quickly, sign the message while still being aware of what the speaker was saying. The deaf, interested and responsive, were engrossed in the meeting. It struck me that, although many of life's experiences such as this one come about in ordinary ways—like a visit to a stake conference with my husband—they can carry with them a significance that portrays the importance of growth for each of us as children of our Heavenly Father.

It was as important for the deaf members of that stake to have the benefit of the teachings in that conference as for those who were not hearing impaired. It was necessary for some members of that stake to prepare in extraordinary ways to make this necessity possible. I thought of those who depended upon me and upon each of us because of the callings we have, and I realized that only through our extraordinary preparation and growth could we be equal to the call and be the servants the Lord needs us to be.

In June, Douglas and I were off to London for regional meetings. I can't describe how much I enjoyed being in London. I thought again about my ancestors who had come from England, and felt a kinship with them in just being there. I wanted to bask in the sights, sounds, and symbols of this city that was so much a part of my heritage. It was also so pleasant to have people I knew and admired there to meet us; Elder Robert L. Simpson, and President George I. Cannon, then serving as a mission president, and their wives made our days there happy, memorable ones.

I went to England longing to learn of the diversity and commonality of the Church in the lives of the women there. I found them as I asked the sisters to share their conversion stories with me. One Relief Society president told me that it was because of her son that she had joined the Church. I asked for the details and was very touched by the story.

She had been baking a cake when the doorbell rang. She went to the door and found two young men who wanted to tell her about the gospel. Knowing she had a cake baking in the oven, she thought if she could stall them long enough, the oven-timer bell would ring and the missionaries would know that she must go. That happened and she all but closed the door on them on her way to the kitchen. When she returned she was triumphant because the missionaries were no longer in sight. But as she shut the door and turned around, her little son called, "Mum, they're in here. I invited them to come into my room."

She then felt obligated to listen. She loved what she heard. She had them come back and share their message with her husband. They joined the Church and, in due time, went to the temple, sealing their little son to them. The mother was pregnant at the time, and when the baby was born her older son asked, "When are we going to take little brother to the temple and have him sealed to us?"

The mother's proud response was, "We don't have to take him because he was born in the covenant."

Her son began to cry. "That must mean he was more faithful in the world before this than I was, doesn't it?"

"Oh, no, my little son," she told him. "You must have been very faithful because, if it hadn't been for you, none of us would have had the gospel of Jesus Christ." She put her arms around him and loved him tenderly.

The conversion stories were as different as the women themselves, but each partook of that same miraculous power which is manifest when the Lord gives someone a new heart. Each of their stories enriched my life.

As I listened to similar experiences, I became aware of what very special spirits the Lord had gathered together to do his work in England. My heart went out to each one who was able to overcome the misunderstandings of friends, family, employers, and fellow workers, and was able to leave the church of his ancestors to remain a valiant member in The Church of Jesus Christ of Latter-day Saints.

As I traveled and met with Relief Society presidents in England, I found, as I had hoped I would, that there were ways I could be of help to them. One president told me of her difficult situation. She said, "I can't get anyone to give me funding on which to operate the Relief Society. We are frequently asked to hold bazaars, which we do, but we are never given any money for our organization in return. How do we operate Relief Society without any money?" she asked.

I was pleased to tell her that we could discuss her problem with the proper priesthood authorities. She gave a sigh of relief, thanked me, and told those with me that she knew the Lord had sent us to help her; she had tried every means she had known to arrange financing.

Although talking with the Relief Society presidents was gratifying, I began to realize that to truly gain perspective on the needs of the sisters there I would have to go into their homes. I needed to see where and how they lived, what their successes and problems were, before I could initiate changes in the Relief Society curriculum that would be beneficial to them. I visited several homes during my stay in England and marveled at the sweet Spirit of the Lord that was manifest there.

It was at the mission home in Birmingham, where some of the missionaries were living, that I gained some insight regarding missionaries. We were invited to stay over at the mission home, and to be up at five-thirty in the morning for a study class conducted by President Reed L. Reeve. I marveled at those young elders, up and dressed so early, and thought of most teenagers and how different their life-styles were compared to those of the young missionaries. As I talked with President Reeve about my observation, he said that it didn't take the missionaries very long to adjust to the routine of the mission field. His biggest concern was that it also wouldn't take them very long, after they got back home, to change back to their old ways of living.

One memorable experience on that trip to England was an interview with a representative from the *Manchester Guardian*. The reporter and his photographer came to my room. Douglas was there, but he let the interview be mine. In previous encounters with the press, I had the opportunity to talk about Relief Society. That was relatively easy, but this reporter was only concerned with the controversial issues of the Church dating from earlier times. He wanted to know about polygamy, which hadn't been practiced for nearly one hundred years. Next, he focused on why black male members of the Church couldn't, at that time, hold the priesthood. Of course, the conversation turned to why female members of the Church were repressed and could not progress side by side with the men. I answered his questions, but my responses did not seem to satisfy him. After about an hour of being grilled, I became concerned that I might ruin the Church's reputation, because my answers were less than facile. Church Public Communications had arranged the interview, and I had really wanted to do well and express my feelings and testimony in such a way that I could help promulgate the gospel. When the reporter left, however, I felt like crying.

Douglas could sense my frustration and suggested a tour of London. We took streetcars and taxicabs and walked until it was late. We went to Greenwich, the prime meridian of the earth used to measure time zones for the world, but time hung heavy for me. Not Greenwich, nor any other site of London, could raise my spirits that day. I can see now that I should have had more faith in the power of the calling I had been given, but at the time I was filled with great concern.

It was years later, when I was in New Brunswick, Nova Scotia, that I met a man who said, "Sister Smith, I am so glad to meet you."

I responded, "Thank you. I am happy to meet you, too."

He responded, "I mean I am really pleased to meet you because, thanks to you, I have joined the Church."

I protested, saying that I had never been to Nova Scotia before. "But you have been to Manchester, England," he replied. "When there, you were interviewed by the *Manchester Guardian*. I was studying for the ministry there at the time. I read the article and began to investigate the Church, and later I was baptized."

It was later still when I was told one of my husband's relatives in England had been sent a copy of that article; it had also helped her to become more accepting of the Church and its influence in the lives of her family members in America. It was consoling to me to eventually learn that the London press interview had reaped some harvest that served for good, and was not the dismal failure I had supposed it to be.

Seed of
the Blessed

For they are the seed of
the blessed of the Lord.
—Isaiah 65:23

M y thoughts could not have portended all that would follow on the day President Spencer W. Kimball called me into his office and asked if I was familiar with the monument to Relief Society in Nauvoo, Illinois. I told him that Sister Spafford had talked with me about how it had deteriorated to the point that it needed to be replaced; she also told me that she had hoped that a big monument might be erected to appropriately honor the Relief Society as the only organization of the Church that actually had its beginning there in Nauvoo. President Kimball wondered if, as a new general presidency of Relief Society, we would be interested in undertaking a project to promote such a monument. I told him I certainly was, but that I would like to talk about it with my counselors. As our meeting finished, he asked me to get back to him after we had considered the matter.

I was excited to tell Sister Cannon and Sister Boyer about the proposal. They were equally enthusiastic and immediately we began contemplating: What would the monument look like? Where would it be placed? Who would finance it? What could its purpose be in addition to serving as a marker of the place where Relief Society was initially organized? Our discussion continued for quite some time. We decided that before going back to President Kimball, we would ask Florence Hansen, a local woman sculptor, if she could give us any ideas for a monument.

I called Florence and asked her if she could draw up anything that would be appropriate for us to present, as a suggestion for a monument to women, to President Kimball. She asked for time to think. After waiting nearly a month and not hearing from her, I called again. She answered that she simply had not been able to come up with anything that she could put on paper. I was disappointed as we concluded our conversation, but in a short time she called back to say that perhaps if she could work with clay . . . That was fine with me.

The next week she brought in a beautiful figure of a woman and child, the child holding a violin. The woman was in pioneer dress and had a tablet on her knee; her arm was around the child. It was lovely. We immediately made an appointment with President Kimball. In our subsequent meeting we told President Kimball that we really would like to have a monument in Nauvoo and showed him the model Florence had made. He asked if the model provided the representation we wanted. We explained that while we felt a woman with children should be an important part of the message, children did not represent all of the work of the women of the Church. We would like other sculptors to submit ideas for the monument. We also suggested the project be financed by the contributions of the women of the Church, believing that they would then become an integral part of the project. We thought it would be appropriate to announce the project at the annual Relief Society general conference.

The project was approved and the announcement well received; a number of sculptors asked if they could participate. Dennis Smith, one of those sculptors, suggested that each sculptor's work be kept strictly confidential until all work was in, thus avoiding duplication of another sculptor's work. After that, we did not leave models on display until after the commission had been granted.

We invited Bishop John H. Vandenberg, Elder Mark E. Petersen, and Elder Thomas S. Monson to give us their opinions on the most appropriate monument to place in Nauvoo.

We also asked the members of the general board to select the most meaningful sculptures to them. Dennis Smith's renditions were unanimously selected because of the broad vision they gave to the work of women. Dennis Smith suggested a garden of monuments, with multiple statues. Since we loved the piece submitted by Florence Hansen, of the pioneer woman, Elder Petersen suggested that we give the commission to Dennis Smith to do the eleven pieces, and commission Florence Hansen to do her pioneer woman and child.

It was a happy moment when the Brethren suggested that we add one more sculpture, a monument of Joseph Smith and his wife Emma. They felt it would be an appropriate way to represent the founding of Relief Society and that it should be in a prominent place in the garden, perhaps at the entrance, to show the companionship roles of husband and wife.

Dennis Smith said that he could not take on more work than he was already commissioned to do, and it was decided that Florence Hansen be given that additional monument to sculpt. Florence was thrilled. She said that it took her breath away to think that she would have the opportunity to design a work that would portray the first Prophet of the Lord of this dispensation and Emma, the first president of the Relief Society, and that she would do it as accurately as possible. She wondered how to portray them. I suggested that it might be with the Prophet giving his contribution of a five-dollar gold piece to Emma at the first Relief Society meeting. She welcomed the suggestion and used it in creating that piece of statuary.

Having commissioned the sculptures, we turned our attention to financing the project. I was told that if we did not get at least 50 percent of the money we needed during the first six months of our drive, we would never raise the entire amount.

That heavy responsibility was made lighter the day my sister Carolyn called and said she wanted to bring the contribution of her stake for the developing Nauvoo monument into my office. As the stake Relief Society president, she had worked with the ward Relief Society units and reminded them that both Sister Belle S. Spafford, the former general president of Relief Society, and I had been members of their stake. Therefore it would seem an appropriate tribute if the sisters of the Wells Stake were to be the very first in all the Church to contribute their money in support of the Garden of Monuments to be placed in Nauvoo, Illinois. The women were enthusiastic in their response and Carolyn was calling to make an appointment to present their contribution. I was deeply touched and delighted. She has always been supportive of me.

I am sure not every sister would be willing to do whatever she was asked to do by a younger sister. Laman and Lamuel were not able to give that kind of loving support to their younger brother. I was so pleased with the service of my sister. Everything that came as a directive from Relief Society she accepted as a challenge and an opportunity. I suggested that I call and see if Sister Spafford would come into the office when Carolyn made that presentation, telling her it was a memorable moment and we could also have our pictures taken together. Sister Spafford was delighted to be there and praised the Wells Stake for its great influence in her life. She expressed her gratitude for Carolyn, and all leaders like her, who conscientiously support the purposes and programs of Relief Society.

We tried very hard to encourage each woman in the various Relief Society units to collect contributions to the monument and send in the money, but we did not have 50 percent of the necessary funding by the end of the first six months. Needless to say, we were concerned, but, as if in answer to our prayers, at about that time President Kimball called me and asked, "When I go on my tour of the Latin American countries and to the Far East, would you like me to encourage the women to send in their contributions for the Garden of Monuments?" I was more than delighted. We prepared some information and pictures of the monuments for him. When our prophet made the request, the sisters could not wait to participate. We felt that we were witnessing a miracle as the money came in, and we soon had all we needed for the project.

I recalled the trip Edythe K. Watson, board member, and I took to spend some time, at the invitation of President LeRoy

Kimball, Nauvoo mission president and brother of Edythe, to select a site for the monument project. He welcomed us to his lovely home overlooking the beautiful Nauvoo Visitors' Center and the sweep of land that continued from it right down to the Mississippi River. We talked for a long time, considering possibilities for the site of a monument to the Relief Society in Nauvoo. He said, "Tomorrow we will drive over this whole area and let you find the perfect place where the monument should be placed. Don't hurry into this decision. Take your time and let the Lord inspire you and help you to make this monument one that the whole world will want to see."

President LeRoy Kimball invited the missionaries who were serving in Nauvoo to come and be guests at his home for dinner with us that evening. They sang, talked, and shared experiences that they had had since being in Nauvoo. It was obvious that they were imbued with the spirit of "Nauvoo the Beautiful" and that they were very effectively teaching and preaching the gospel as they hosted guests in the early Church homes that had been restored.

We then retired, and all night long I was very cold. The next morning, Dr. Kimball expressed his regrets that the heat had gone off during the night. I teased him, saying that he must have wanted us to have the feeling of Old Nauvoo when it was bitterly cold and the people were living in army barracks on the Montrose and Commerce side.

That day Sister Watson and I were accompanied by the president as he drove us to each of the restored homes in Nauvoo; all the while we looked for just the right place for the Relief Society monument. As we left the blacksmith shop, I happened to turn and look up—the roof of the shop was on fire! People quickly ran for the hose, but it was frozen. Buckets of water were carried up to the roof, finally quenching the destroying flames as well as the fire used to forge the horseshoes and nails. I thought, "First the cold, then the fire." The reality of these experiences will forever remain with me.

Each time we passed the Nauvoo Visitors' Center I mentioned to President LeRoy Kimball that the area behind the center, beyond its beautiful windows, looked like the perfect site to place the statues we were having created. He would say, "Well, that is a possibility. Now let's look further." He spoke of the practicality of taking some of the ground the Church owned and developing a park for the monuments. Then he took us to see a natural amphitheater. All day long we looked for the place.

Night came and Sister Watson and I went to the meeting-house, where a group of Relief Society members had been assembled. We gave addresses about Relief Society, expressing our delight at being in the very city where the Relief Society had been originally organized just 133 years before. Afterward it was thrilling to have people come up to speak with us. There were some who had just joined the Church, long-time members, people prominent in politics, and people who wanted to help build up the Church again in the Midwest.

Edythe and I had the privilege of speaking to the sisters as part of the Nauvoo Branch anniversary of Relief Society. It was an especially good opportunity to share with them some of the experiences that Sister Watson and I had been having in Nauvoo.

We still had some difficulty in determining a site for the garden until a letter was drafted to our advisers and to the First Presidency with our suggestions, asking them for a decision. It was determined that the garden should be located in back of the Nauvoo Visitors' Center. It would not be too near the river and could be protected; extensive and expensive preparations would not be necessary; and the park would be in the very heart of Nauvoo, where it would receive adequate attention from the directors of the center and from the caretakers who continually worked to develop the Church interests in Nauvoo.

It was a thrill to take the General Authorities to see the first statue when it was completed and ready for inspection and approval. None of us knew exactly where Dennis Smith's home and studio were, so Elder Monson said he would simply go to one of the houses and ask which home belonged to Dennis Smith. I tried to dissuade him because I thought it would be frightening to whoever opened the door to see an Apostle of the Lord standing there. Before anything else was said, Elder Monson was out of the car knocking at the door. A child opened the door, but soon many faces were in the windows. I have often wondered about the conversation that took place after that very special visitor left.

We could easily recognize the blessings of those experiences resulting from the Garden of Monuments but wondered what other seeds had been sown.

Thou Shalt Prune Thy Vineyard

America's 1976 Bicentennial Year afforded the Relief Society organization opportunities to help the United States members renew their pride in, and strengthen their commitment to, our national heritage. We wanted every American Relief Society member to better appreciate that our nation was discovered and preserved by divine providence and was a country of destiny.

The Relief Society General Board sponsored several patriotic presentations. These included the dramatization "Melt Down My Pewter," given in the Relief Society general conference to portray how mothers had kept the dream of liberty alive through lullabies sung to their children; eight vignettes spotlighting revolutionary war heroines; a readers' theater; and suggestions for choir presentations. We encouraged the writing of family histories, personal writing projects, and community service, in celebration of the Bicentennial.

Meanwhile, in Mexico City, a meeting of women was convened by the United Nations that would have profound effect on the identity and concerns of women. From that meeting an agenda was drawn up for conventions the following year, a year designated as "International Women's Year." Each nation of the world was challenged to determine and respond to issues of concern and substance for women.

As the Relief Society General Board, we discussed the problems of women, as well as the posture and responsibilities of the women in the Church for this day. We decided to ask all Relief Society units to pray that we might be more effective in bringing sisters to the meetings, for we knew active participation in Relief Society could help them to face the problems of the times squarely and to respond in appropriate ways. We also encouraged sisters everywhere to take advantage of their opportunities to put the gospel principles into action. They did, and my appreciation of the women of the Church consistently increased. It was evident that during this period, Relief Society must not only strive to renew national pride in the Bicentennial celebrations, but try to calm the strident voices of the women's rights movement, help women become their best selves, and participate in meaningful activities.

Many television programs portrayed women who stayed home as inferior and discontented with their place in society. Because of this portrayal, I was especially delighted with the opportunity to serve on the Promised Valley Playhouse board. It was my hope that I could help bring to the membership of the Church programs that would let them see women and their responsibilities in their true light. I appreciated the influence of good productions. I had seen the change that took place in the lives of participants in the plays my mother had directed, and I had felt a difference in my own life when I was given parts in our ward dramatic presentations. I felt certain that the Playhouse could give good direction regarding women to the membership of the Church, and I wanted to help implement such a direction.

Almost simultaneously our son was called to be the bishop of the ward in which we lived. Seldom do parents have the opportunity to realize as directly as we did at that time the hope that a son will follow the way of his father. My husband had years earlier served this ward as its bishop, and it was truly rewarding to see our son now have that same privilege. We knew the importance of supporting him as he had supported us. We also knew of the joyful feeling of love he had for the people of the ward. It was his desire to serve them well. He was renting at the time, and the house seemed to decrease as his family increased. Douglas and I talked about the possibility of moving from our home, almost too large for us since most of our children had married and had homes of their own. We talked about selling him our home; then he could still be in the ward and fulfill his responsibilities. That seemed to be the best plan, and he and his wife were delighted. Our only regret was no longer having him as our bishop. We also had a difficult time leaving our many friends in that ward and stake.

When Douglas, Sherilynn, Lowell, and I attended our first sacrament meeting in our new ward in the Ensign Stake, we were warmly welcomed. We met people we knew and, of course, many we did not know. One lovely mature sister bore her testimony that day. She said that she was to be released as the Spiritual Living lesson teacher and that she knew she was being put on the shelf. As I listened to her I knew that, after her many years of rich and rewarding lessons in the ward, this sister should realize, as all older people should, that instead of being put on a shelf, she had been prepared to be self-motivated; that instead of expecting a position in the Church to help them do what needs to be done, older members could render as much compassionate service as they could recognize a need for; that they could study and share what they learned with others in the family, in the neighborhood, in church circles, and even in the community. It was a time this sister could use to be involved in missionary endeavors. There was far too much still to be done to advance the kingdom; there was no time for her or anyone to be put on a shelf. As the scriptures note, after many years of pruning the vineyard, or helping the trees to mature properly, she was ready now to enjoy the harvest, to taste the fruit of her labors.

In October of 1976 I was asked to talk to the Church women employees in a seminar being held for them. I had been to see the movie "Just a Matter of Time," in which a countess tried to teach a chambermaid that the most important thing she could do was to have a beautifully framed mirror. Then, every time the chambermaid looked into the mirror she would be able to see herself in beauty. If each employee could see herself as a successful, beautiful woman, she could strive to attain that goal, for Helena Rubenstein, the great make-up artist, said, "There are no ugly women: only lazy women" (Barbara Rowes, *The Book of Quotes* [New York: E. P. Dutton, 1979] p. 109). I wanted to help each woman employee feel equal to everyone else, and to treat themselves and others with dignity and respect.

Brigham Young counseled wisely:

> Let the sisters take care of themselves, and make themselves beautiful, and if any of you are so superstitious to . . . say that this is pride, I can say that you are not informed as to the pride which is sinful before the Lord; you also do not understand the excellency of heaven and the beauty which swells in the society of the gods. Were you to see an angel, you would see a beautiful and lovely creature. Make yourselves like angels in goodness and beauty. (*Journal of Discourses* 12:201.)

When I returned to my office after participating in the seminar I had my first real contact regarding the International Women's Year. I was aware of it because the special committee I had called together to advise me on women's issues and concerns mentioned that IWY meetings for the state were scheduled to be held in Salt Lake City soon. Each state would hold IWY meetings and then representatives would be selected to go to Texas for a national meeting.

Jan Tyler, the Utah State Chair for the IWY meeting, made an appointment with me. We discussed the issues of concern to Utah women and how to make them part of the national agenda that would be formulated for the IWY meeting in Texas. The discussion of the Texas meeting would be based on the state meetings held across the United States. She suggested that I invite the women of Relief Society to attend. I told her that if I did, and if they came, the conference would not have sufficient room to hold them. She said that she really did feel they should be included and that she would appreciate my support for the IWY meeting.

After Jan Tyler left, I talked with my counselors about the meeting, and we decided that it would be folly for the state of

Utah to be represented only by nonmembers or by inactive members of the Church, and that the issues to be discussed needed to be addressed by all Mormon women. We talked to our advisers and proposed that we invite the Latter-day Saint women.

It was our suggestion that we send a letter out to every stake Relief Society unit in Utah and encourage ten women to represent that area at the conference. Our advisers asked how we could prepare the women enough to address the issues. We thought about that and suggested that all communication be made directly through the newspaper. That way we could increase awareness of what we were saying on the issues, not only among Mormon women, but also among all people in the state. Both of those suggestions received their approval. We prepared the letter, signed it, and sent it out, and the articles were written and published in the newspapers.

The response was overwhelming. Many conservative groups came in and asked if they could instruct our Relief Society sisters on how to deal with women who would come to the conference with hidden agendas. Those women could be very powerful in putting through actions by working with parliamentary procedures that would be unfamiliar to many Mormon women who had worked neither with the issues nor with the methods that would be used in the meetings.

Over and over again we told these groups we would not call the Relief Society sisters together. We would only give them information through the newspapers. We said that we would not even tell them what they could or could not do. But there were those who contacted friends and held meetings to tell the women of the dangers that they would face and how they might be railroaded into accepting proposals that would not really represent their beliefs. By the time these groups had contacted those who would represent the Mormon women, fears and anxieties arose and walls of defense were built. A vacuum was created because the Church and the Relief Society wanted to remain impartial. The women themselves came ready to block anything that was said, for they did not want to be falsely persuaded to accept attitudes or actions that could be damaging to them or to the Church. Some had been told that they would be safe if they voted no on everything. The Latter-day Saint women came by the thousands. They attended the workshops and defensively participated. I was told that sometimes they would not even listen to those who were presenters.

Helvie Sipila, from the United Nations, was sent to represent the national IWY officers. She spoke out strongly and clearly and the women listened and applauded her words, but when it came to those who presented information in support of the Equal Rights Amendment, a majority of the women were loud in their objections. Night came and it was time to adjourn, but the women would not go home. They had been told that motions might be passed after they left. Finally the leaders came to me and asked me to tell them it was time to go home. When I stood before them they were polite and responsive, but they still expressed their fears. Dixie Nelson, former state PTA president, stood with me and explained that once a meeting was adjourned, it could not take further action until it was called to order again the next day.

Some women turned to me and asked if what she was saying was true. I affirmed her statements and they said they would leave and go home, but they needed to be assured that no vote would be taken until the next morning when they would come back to the meeting again.

The forbearance shown by most of the IWY committee members in completing a conference which very soon left their control was a great lesson in respect for differences. However, the conference received a great deal of adverse publicity. Most of the sensationalism reported occurred as a result of extremist views voiced in the open forum. The work of the conference went on among the official delegates, although the debate and the actions taken in those meetings were inadequately reported in the press. Even so, many women leaders who attended from around the country did feel that real and substantial good came from the deliberations.

Much of the confusion and bitterness might have been avoided had information from Relief Society leadership been more direct and visible, but the decision made from long experience of Church leadership has been to let people act upon their convictions. And, in retrospect, the long-range problems of direct intervention would have been far more destructive that the short-range difficulties we experienced.

In a meeting with Relief Society stake presidents following the IWY meeting, it was strongly expressed that Mormon women wanted more information, help with skills in parliamentary procedures, and a clear understanding of expectations so that they might participate more effectively in future community and state meetings. We decided to provide instruction in the curriculum and to encourage Relief Society members and leaders to constantly strive to be more knowledgeable about, and responsive to, the issues involved in each community, not just those pertaining to International Women's Year. Women were encouraged to learn how to conduct themselves in public forums, how to have influence as individual citizens, and how to use parliamentary procedures in public meetings. Members were urged to become involved as citizens in sessions of the International Women's Year in every state where IWY meetings were being held. We encouraged Latter-day Saint women to join with wholesome community organizations to fight pornography, homosexuality, the ERA, and abortion.

All of those things seemed difficult enough, but when I met with some of the Brethren and discussed their visits to various military posts they told me they had found that many of the women, members of the Church who had enlisted in the military right out of high school, were participating with their peers in immoral acts. So there was another difficult problem to address.

I prepared a talk to try to help Church members take a serious look at having our young women enlist in the military. I was invited to speak at Brigham Young University and, knowing that the topic would be controversial, I spoke beforehand with President Dallin H. Oaks, then president of Brigham Young University, and told him of my topic. I wanted to know how he would feel about my delivering that kind of an address at the university. He said he felt fine about it, but that before I delivered it he would like to read the text of the speech and inform the military leaders on campus, so that it would not surprise them.

In due course the day for the address arrived. (See appendix 2.) I was concerned about the reaction that would come from it and asked President Oaks about how the military officers had responded. He said, "I have been out of town and just returned late last evening. I haven't had a chance to read it, nor did I get it to them. Don't be anxious. We'll handle it."

I looked down from the stand and saw that the whole front row of seats was occupied by the military personnel who worked there at the university. I was panic-stricken. I didn't want to hurt them or the military effort, but I did want our young women to take heed of the counsel I had for them. Young women in our day are encouraged to reach and fulfill their potential in many ways. It is vitally important that they do some very careful pruning—cutting away what is not wanted in their lives—in deciding how they will spend the years ahead of them. Used wisely, such years of preparation will make it possible for them to gather the good fruit of life and to fill their minds and hearts with the eternal perspectives of the gospel. Neither the Church nor our nation can afford to waste any of its precious human resources. Both must use our youth in ways that will be in keeping with true values and divine principles. I was surprised that such comments could cause so much controversy as they did.

Pruning the Lord's vineyard and gathering the fruit was much more difficult than I had imagined.

13

Consider
the Seed
that Follows

And thou shalt be a
blessing unto thy seed
after thee.
—Abraham 2:9

An almost casual comment of President Kimball's served as important counsel to me. One day when he came to the Relief Society Building to see the displays of the newly created resource center, someone asked what we used to have in the building. President Kimball answered simply, "Chairs."

The Relief Society Building had served many useful purposes in its lifetime, being the headquarters for numerous undertakings: The publication, printing, and distribution of the *Relief Society Magazine*; headquarters for the temple clothing operation, which in earlier years included the construction, as well as the distribution, of sacred clothing; and center for the Relief Society Social Services, including adoptions, care of unwed mothers, mother counseling, and the placement of Indian children in member homes for the school year. As Church growth accelerated, many of these functions became part of larger, more specialized Church operations. Relief Society had nurtured these departments until the growing Church's needs required expansion. Also as a result of the rapidly increasing size and diversity of Church membership, the annual Relief Society conference was discontinued. These changes left Relief Society with a beautiful and spacious building with, as President Kimball indicated, many chairs. I felt a definite responsibility to make certain that this lovely edifice constructed with the contributions and, in some instances, sacrifices of the Relief Society women served an increasingly excellent purpose in their lives.

The occasion of the prophet's visit, on the day of the "chairs" comment, was to view the resource center. Given the need growing out of the discontinued Relief Society conferences, we as a presidency were led to direct the creation of a center to provide leadership assistance for Relief Society women. It was most appropriate to provide these resources within the walls of the building that their donated funds had made possible. As President Kimball toured, I told him that hundreds of women had already received inspiration, instruction, and renewed desire to improve their homes and their response to Relief Society callings as a result of their experiences in the center. Until the area conferences for women were a reality, the resource displays were providing direction in the interim.

Having heard President Kimball's candid answer to the question I was glad that he seemed pleased with the change in the building, but even more anxious that we should never again have a structure known for its chairs. I determined that this home of Relief Society would represent every good and lovely quality of a home, and that it would be a place from which leaders throughout the world could take back to their wards and to their homes ideas for development and progress. There had to be something special there for women that would elevate them and help them to realize the great importance of the work they do in creating and safeguarding their homes.

Displays were continually upgraded and refined, both in form and content. Even the materials used in preparing the displays were monitored to make certain their quality was consistent with the important messages they expressed. We desired the Relief Society Building to be a place where women could come to be renewed in faith and inspired in their callings, where they could experience the power of beauty in a home and attend workshops and demonstrations that would teach them how to give skillfully and broadly to others.

As we planned and worked, we learned the importance of the process that was a part of each teaching display. In the beginning of our preparations, we called upon the exhibits division of the Church for their professional input and found their suggestions extremely valuable. We learned that long before we determined how the display would look and what activity might center around it, we needed to ask and find answers to some very basic questions: What difference did we hope this display would make in the life of a sister, in that of her family, or in her Relief Society calling? What did we hope a woman would do, or think, or perform in her calling because she had experienced the presentation? After considering such ends prayerfully we were then prepared to determine what we might do to accomplish them. Only after we were certain the exhibit could accomplish what it was intended to do could we begin to think of appearance, design, materials, and color. At one point our mentor from the exhibits division explained that, in this rather extended process, we were learning something about an eternal principle—the need to have first a "spiritual creation" before a thing can be naturally established.

The center was soon recognized as offering presentations and ideas valuable in enhancing and strengthening every facet of the work of Relief Society. Emphasis was given to show women how to use their talents and develop skills that would enable each one to express herself individually.

First, under the leadership of Sister Shirley W. Thomas, the displays were created to give women ideas that could easily translate into use. Typical was a room in which a year's supply of food and necessities shared the living space of a family. Wheat barrels became the base for a table. (Covered by a cloth, they were completely disguised.) Bolsters on the sofa contained extra blankets. Salt was tucked into the hollow space of a table's base. Canned goods were stowed in bookcase supports. The room was appealing with its charming decor; modest in size, it was nevertheless convincing in its message that a determined family can find space to store a year's supply. Hundreds of people caught the vision and this same display was seen recreated exactly, or with local modifications, in scores of welfare or homemaking fairs throughout the Church, giving convincing evidence that it had been an effective resource.

Equally practical and popular were rooms devoted to gardening (with actual beds of growing plants), money management, and sewing—from money-saving make-over ideas to heirloom-quality quilts and fine stitchery. Cooking displays, too, had variety, ranging from basic breads to Christmas candies. Home beautification was an important area shown, always stressing principles that could have application in any home. On special occasions, displays were made even more meaningful with accompanying demonstrations. Leadership training workshops were held at general conference times and orientations were offered for new Relief Society presidencies. These workshops filled a great need for many women who were called to positions in Relief Society without former experience or training.

An outreach feature of the resource center was the code-a-phone, a twenty-four-hour service. Anyone who desired could call, day or night, and receive a Relief Society message. The recording was changed monthly so excessive calling was not required, but each three-minute presentation focused on information valuable to the sisters of the Church. The presentations concerned welfare, the safety of women and children, teaching tips, and inspirational holiday messages. All were designed to give help and create a sense of belonging in addressing the needs of the sisters of Relief Society.

Perhaps the most exciting period in the resource center was general conference time with its special workshops, live demonstrations, and the scores of out-of-town visitors. The center extended its hours during these days to make it possible for more people to enjoy its offerings. One of the finest experiences was at the semi-annual orientation for new bishops and priesthood leaders from around the world. They and their interpreters were taken through each department and through all the displays where they could gain a sense of the scope and importance of the work of women.

In the fall of 1975 President Kimball directed that the general auxiliary conferences be discontinued in favor of area conferences. This announcement was given at a time of great questioning occurring among women, with the ERA on center stage, and change is often unsettling. But it was not difficult to see the benefit of a new plan that allowed more members in distant areas to attend and participate in such conferences. I looked forward to this Churchwide innovation, which had first been experimentally implemented in Asia. It was then instituted in parts of the United States, Canada, and Australia prior to the fall general conference.

The departmental sessions of that last Relief Society conference gave sisters valuable help in lesson presentations and instructions in teaching principles. Nursery leaders were treated to an array of suggestions for creative play. The homemaking demonstrations featured quilting and patchwork, Christmas decorations, basketry, canning, and organic gardening. Bicentennial projects and beautification skits added dramatic spice. Attention was given also to youth, Young Adult, and Special Interest sessions of Relief Society.

We had felt a heavy responsibility to make the last general Relief Society conference a memorable one, in the long tradition of great Relief Society conferences, and also to have it provide the kind of training and emphasis on principle that would give stake leaders the confidence they needed to provide strong leadership in their local areas. We worked very hard, and as President Kimball gave his blessing in the concluding session we felt a sense of peace and believed that our desires had been realized: "I hope that all of your lives will be brightened and blessed by having come to this conference. May God bless you, bless you in your homes and in your families, and especially with your husbands, that they may recognize in you a great power so that they might better fulfill their responsibilities in life. This is the work of the Lord. God Almighty is responsible for it." ("Report of the Relief Society General Conference," *Ensign*, November 1975, p. 140.)

The annual fall Relief Society conference that year, then, was the first and only one of its kind over which I presided.

Three particularly significant undertakings came out of that final conference:

First, we announced the Nauvoo monument project and inaugurated our fund-raising effort. Second, we introduced a production called "Melt Down My Pewter," written and directed by Moana B. Bennett, to be used during the 1976 United States Bicentennial Year. And third, we presented a platform for Latter-day Saint women that gave gospel perspective to issues of the day and helped define some of the problems needing to be addressed to make society in general more equitable for women.

As I spoke to the women at that last Relief Society conference, the words penned by the poet Henry Wadsworth Longfellow, who was writing in America during the period when the Relief Society was organized, seemed appropriate:

> Lives of great men all remind us
> We can make our lives sublime,
> And, departing, leave behind us
> Footprints on the sands of time.
>
> . . . .
>
> Let us then be up and doing,
> With a heart for any fate:
> Still achieving, still pursuing,
> Learn to labour and to wait.

Footprints of all those who had gone before us in this great Relief Society work had left a clear path guiding our way. Grateful for their vision, their faith, and their good works, we also needed to be "up and doing," but we needed to be wise as we did so, looking for beauty and operating upon eternal premises.

I had traveled about the world from Europe to the Orient, and I had come back aware that no matter where we live, God has created a world of great beauty. Now and then, if we stand still and contemplate his wondrous works, we will begin to see life in its eternal perspective.

The composer, Haydn, after walking in the fields near his home one day, went back to his piano and began his mighty oratorio, *The Creation*. As he finished the last notes, he declared, "There it is; it is my response to the wondrous creations of God." We live in a beautiful, exciting world, and like Haydn, we can respond to it by doing, achieving, pursuing, and creating in our own lives.

We all remember the story of Aladdin and his wondrous lamp. Although the lamp was old and tarnished, it had the magical power to make Aladdin's every wish come true. One day someone realized the power within the lamp and conceived of a way to obtain it. He dressed as a peddler, then walked by Aladdin's home, calling out in a loud voice, "New lamps for old, new lamps for old!" Tempted by the appealing offer, Aladdin's wife seized the opportunity and chose to trade the old lamp for a new lamp of momentary brilliance.

During my presidency hundreds of pieces of mail had come to my desk from all parts of the world. Some were statements of platforms about new goals for women; some were cries for help from individual sisters who did not clearly understand what the Lord expected of them; a few were angry statements from sisters who had been hurt or treated unfairly; some held questions about the role of women in current society. Built into each of them was a common thread: Latter-day Saint women were seeking to work out the complexities of their lives within the Church and within the context of the gospel. How unfortunate if any of those women, like Aladdin's wife, were deceived and chose to trade the trendy answers of the world's offering for the patient, long-suffering search for real solutions —to trade eternal blessings for momentary satisfactions!

In the thirty-third section of the Doctrine and Covenants we read: "Wherefore, be faithful, praying always, having your lamps trimmed and burning, and oil with you, that you may be ready at the coming of the Bridegroom." (D&C 33:17.)

In these critical days when new lamps are continually being offered for old, take the responsibility for your own actions with intelligence; unlock the treasures of heaven and the powers of God to bless you and your family. Be an instrument in his hands to help solve those age-old problems with which humanity struggles. Wisely choose him and proclaim:

The Lord is my light; then why should I fear?
By day and by night his presence is near.
He is my salvation from sorrow and sin;
This blessed assurance the Spirit doth bring.
The Lord is my light; he is my joy and my song.
By day and by night he leads, he leads me along.

("The Lord Is My Light," *Hymns*, p. 89.)

Toward the end of my term in office, Queen Siracut of Thailand and the queen of Samoa had, on separate occasions, come to visit at Church headquarters and also with us as a Relief Society presidency. The queen of Samoa met with Sister Marian Boyer and they had an enjoyable time talking together. During a luncheon in honor of the queen of Thailand, I spoke with her about programs of the Church that could assist the hill people of her country. We talked about the welfare program and about principles of nutrition and sanitation. The components of literacy and self-reliance were discussed as important factors if Thailand were to be a progressive society. The queen was most gracious and extended an open invitation to me to visit her in Thailand.

Certainly Sister Boyer and I both felt honored on those memorable occasions—royalty paying their respects to us as leaders of our people. It was at least a partial fulfillment of a prophecy uttered by Joseph Smith in 1842, that "Queens of the earth will come . . . and pay their respects to the leaders of this people." (Joseph Smith, *Teachings of the Prophet Joseph Smith*, sel. Joseph Fielding Smith, [Salt Lake City: Deseret Book Company, 1974], p. 227.) I will never forget that visit from the queen of Thailand, but as I reflected on that experience I was aware that I had been in the presence of queens on myriad occasions.

Over the years, and more so during my presidency because of my travels throughout the world, I met with refined, attractive women of queenly stature with high public profiles, fine caliber women like Mrs. Nancy Reagan and Mrs. Rosalynn Carter, wives of two of our country's presidents. Many of the highly visible women of the Church carry the virtue and demeanor of queens. I have met countless other women of the Church without high profile and royal governmental status whose divine heritage and promise bespeak an enduring royalty surpassing any earthly grandeur. I have felt honored to be in the presence of all such women.

14

Whatsoever Ye Sow, That Shall Ye Also Reap

Be not deceived; God is
not mocked: for
whatsoever a man soweth,
that shall he also reap.
—Galatians 6:7

On January 7, 1977, another grandchild was added to our ever-increasing family. I was filled with gratitude for the safe arrival of this seven-pound baby girl, whose parents called her the most beautiful baby ever, although she looked suspiciously like their other children. They decided to name her Barbara, after me. I was delighted. I hoped her name would be a blessing and a joy forever. I became all the more aware of the importance of sowing worthy seeds so that not only my namesake, but also all people, might reap blessings from our efforts in righteousness.

Our presidency was involved that year in seeking ways to help improve the lives of our sisters Churchwide. Individual and joint responsibilities were stressed, and in the first months of 1977 several changes and events took place: four Relief Society lessons on genealogy were coordinated with Melchizedek Priesthood lessons; Lambda Delta Sigma, the national sorority for Latter-day Saint college women, was brought under the umbrella of Relief Society, with the national officers coordinating their work with that of Relief Society; and Relief Society was given a citation by the American Cancer Society for its contribution to cancer detection through public education and cancer screening.

Because women's needs and rights were becoming more and more the focus of news items, articles, and debates, and because the work of women had become more varied and their role in the home and family under scrutiny, we felt that a fact-finding, information-gathering process was needed. The idea was suggested that we form a Women's Research Institute and house it in the Relief Society Building. Studies and research could be carried out that would make vital information available and help the Relief Society become a source of strength for all of its members. When we discussed it with the Brethren, it was determined that the effects could be more far-reaching if the resource center were housed at Brigham Young University and made available to students, leaders, and Relief Society members in general. BYU president Dallin Oaks, Marilyn Arnold, Jeffrey Holland, Richard Chidester, Ruth Funk, Janath Cannon, and I participated in the organizing of what is now the Women's Research Institute. We did it with every hope that, as research and statistics regarding women were gathered and considered according to gospel perspectives, the women of the Church would be able not only to counter but also to stand strong against inaccurate, worldly assessments that desecrate women's feminine responsibility as defined by the Lord.

The information housed in the research center was most helpful when Elder Ezra Taft Benson, President of the Quorum of the Twelve, encouraged me to go to Graham, Washington, and participate in an anti-abortion meeting. He felt it was important that I attend and talk against abortion. (See appendix 3.)

When I arrived in Graham, I had my first encounter with citizens actually picketing against me, claiming their "right" to abortion. I was amazed that I would draw their attention and I was brokenhearted to see and hear such very young people marching and chanting in the rally. I had always wanted to be known as a peacemaker and a negotiator, a person of conciliation rather than divisiveness, yet my conviction that destroying newly begotten human life, except to save the mother, brought with it moral and eternal consequences and allowed me no other course than the one on which I was set. It would never prove an easy path, but, as I was standing with the prophets, I never doubted that it was the right one.

On a former visit to the state of Washington I had been greeted with "Welcome to the apple bowl of the world!" Those who met me were proud of that beautiful state. They were pleased to live in a place noted for its production of superior apples and were eager to tell me all about the apple industry. I had received a big box of delicious Washington apples each Christmas for the previous six years, and so I listened with genuine interest to every claim they made.

On that particular visit, as we rode toward my destination for the speech, I enjoyed the discussion about the apple industry, and I learned a lot. I came to know that quality apples don't just happen; producing them is an exact science. A great amount of money, time, and effort is expended in scientific research. Scientists teach the orchard owners how to make good use of the state's natural resources.

I was told of the important work orchard owners do during the winter months when the trees are pruned by hand to eliminate branches that will not produce good fruit, branches that keep out the sunlight, or branches that cause the fruits to rub against each other. I learned about the sprays used against mildew, cutworms, leaf rollers, aphids, and other insects. I saw the elaborate watering systems that had been installed. I was fascinated when I was told that the orchard owners knew exactly when the trees would blossom. They just add gradation of temperature in fifty-degree increments until one thousand degrees are counted and the trees burst into full bloom. I could hardly imagine importing thousands of beehives to ensure pollination, or knowing that there is a "king" blossom that can most easily withstand the forces of nature. The blossoms are protected, and it is planned that thirty to forty leaves will nourish each apple. I was told of the supports used to keep the branches from breaking under the weight of the fruit. I learned that professional pickers are hired to carefully, yet swiftly, pick the fruit so that it will be of top quality when it is delivered to the apple shed.

Apples are a multimillion-dollar business that brings rich rewards to the orchard owners, pride and revenue to the state of Washington, and health to those who eat and enjoy that superior fruit. I couldn't help but contrast the apple industry with the multimillion-dollar business I had come to Washington to speak against, one that had developed in the United States since the Supreme Court decision of January 22, 1973, and one that cannot bring the rich rewards of beauty, of satisfaction, of health, and of life—but only a harvest of a different sort. That decision states: "An unborn child is the property of the mother and she may dispose of it for any reason during the first six months of pregnancy, and at any other time, if in the opinion of a single licensed physician it is necessary to preserve her life or health."

In the name of human rights a multimillion-dollar business had grown up in America which facilitated abortion to prevent the birth of the unwanted child; abortion to supposedly give men and women the right to participate in illicit relations free of responsibility to a child conceived; and abortion to control the population and presumably preserve the quality of life already existing in the world.

Abortion continues to receive the support of those who propound such insidious reasoning. All God-fearing people must oppose that legalization and instill in the rising generation an understanding of the importance of being obedient to the word of the Lord and of protecting each human life.

15

Wholly a Righteous Seed

Yet I had planted thee a
noble vine, wholly a right
seed.
—Jeremiah 2:21

Nineteen seventy-eight was destined to be a wonderful year because we would dedicate the Garden of Monuments in Nauvoo, the birthplace of the Relief Society organization. I had no idea how special that event would be until Charles Graves, New York public communications representative for the Church, had listened to our plans and added, "You should invite Rosalynn Carter, wife of the president of the United States, and many other notable women from around the country to attend an event of this significance." I protested that I didn't even know how to go about arranging an appointment with the First Lady. He suggested that it could best be done through an influential woman, possibly the wife of a fine Democrat. It only took a few minutes to come to the conclusion that he was right. We contacted Bethine Church, the wife of Senator Frank Church of Idaho, who successfully made the necessary arrangements for me to meet with Mrs. Carter.

I bought a new suit, blouse, and shoes for the occasion. I described them to Mrs. Church, so that she would recognize me when we met. Upon meeting, we were immediately comfortable with one another. She had met so many people over the years that she was naturally charming, friendly, and knowledgeable. She had planned that we eat lunch together at the Capitol in the senators' dining room, where we could visit.

I asked Bethine if she would go with me to see Mrs. Carter. She declined, saying she hadn't been specifically invited and so had not cleared herself with the White House security for the visit.

She did take me to the gate of the White House and pointed out the direction for me to go. The helpful suggestions she gave also made my time with Rosalynn Carter a little more relaxing, if that is possible with such a prestigious person.

My appointment with Mrs. Carter was scheduled for a half hour. Actually it lasted a little longer, but it seemed much too short by the time I extended the invitation for her to attend the dedication services for the Garden of Monuments. We talked about the dedication and I showed her pictures of the completed monuments.

To my request she replied, "I would come without any hesitation if it were not for one thing."

I asked, "What is that, our differences over the Equal Rights Amendment?"

"Yes," she said. "I cannot understand why you or your church are against equal rights for women."

I explained, "We are not against equal rights for women. We are against the Equal Rights Amendment as the way to achieve them."

Then she said, "I'll have to talk with my advisers and see what they have to say."

I questioned, "If they tell you not to come, would you please at least send a representative?"

"I feel certain I can do that," she kindly responded.

She was lovely, and that charming southern hospitality captivated me. What an exciting way to begin a year! My purpose was righteous; my experience was never to be forgotten.

It seemed that almost no time had elapsed from my visit with Mrs. Carter until I was stepping out of the car and looking to see if the Nauvoo Garden of Monuments was all in place graced by beautiful flowers. It was, and I thought of the notable people that were due to arrive. June 27, 1978, the day of the dedication, was upon us. We had planned the dedicatory celebration for a long time, hoping to make it a fitting tribute to the noble work of the past, present, and future women of the Church. The dedication would honor the blessed nature of the Relief Society with its prophetic beginning, the magnificent contributions made by Relief Society women, and all others who helped to build the monument.

I remembered a man so happy for his new baby daughter that he wanted to pay tribute by making a contribution in her name. I thought of all of the women who had remembered their mothers, as I did, by making a similar donation, and the woman who had sold her rings, wanting to pay her share on the monument. Then there were those who, because of the death of a dearly loved woman in their lives, memorialized them through contributions to the monument.

Many women had expressed a desire to come to Nauvoo to share in this special event, which thrilled us because we very much wanted them to feel that this was their monument; we wanted it to represent their hopes and commitment to the righteous ways of the Lord, but only as the women began to arrive did we sense the magnitude of expression that was coming from the women. First one, then six, then ten and more came, and guests from many women's organizations from across the nation came. We watched the chartered buses loaded with Relief Society sisters arrive. Women had come by car and plane from all over the United States and Canada, and from as far away as the South Pacific. The dedication of the monument to women brought more than twenty thousand Church members to the little town of Nauvoo during the days of June 27 to July 1, 1978. We knew that these thousands who had come, in many instances at great sacrifice, and who represented other thousands not able to make the trip, brought with them a spirit that would help sanctify this unique dedicatory project.

A banquet in the visitors' center on June 27 began the festivities that took place to dedicate the Garden of Monuments. Bethine Clark Church was there to represent Rosalynn Carter. We were pleased that Mrs. Church was there. She had been most helpful in arranging my visit with Rosalynn Carter and in speaking up for the women of the Church. The dinner was served with perfection in spite of the fact that the food was kept warm after being cooked in the kitchen of a congenial

Catholic school nearby, brought to the basement of the visitors' center, and then finally served to all the distinguished guests who were present for that singular occasion.

Illana D. Rovner, assistant deputy to Illinois Governor James R. Thompson, attended the prededicatory dinner and charmed everyone when she said, "After having had the pleasure of seeing Nauvoo, the statues, and the magnificent drama last night, I think I ought to bring the governor's apologies for what Illinois did 130 years ago. Please come back! We need you." She also read a proclamation by Governor Thompson that designated June 28, 1978, as Nauvoo Monument to Women Day in Illinois.

Eight thousand Relief Society leaders came for the ceremony, which lasted for three days. President Kimball stayed all three days. A magnificent pageant written by Moana B. Bennett, *Because of Elizabeth*, was presented. It was scheduled to run for five nights; the two extra performances were for the local people. It was only performed three nights, however, because of heavy rainstorms. It was a play based on the true story of a pioneer woman and the legacy she left to all of those who followed her.

The dedicated cast and crew traveled thousands of miles over a three-month period to prepare the commemorative production. The dinner and the pageant were prelude to the actual dedication of the Garden of Monuments. The dedicatory service itself was deluged by showers, but President Kimball calmly counseled, "After the rain comes the sunshine." Then commenting upon the statuary garden, he said, "As we walk through the garden, we are reminded of the great, powerful influence of women upon the world." In the dedicatory prayer, President Kimball expressed gratitude that the early Church members, exiles from Kirtland, Adam-ondi-Ahman, and other places, finally found their way to the marshland on which they developed this beautiful site for homes and home-loving people. He referred to Nauvoo in those days as "an uninviting region, but a place of possibilities, where solid ground could be found, where rude huts could be built, and a magnificent temple could be erected to thy name and glory." Expressing gratitude that much of Nauvoo's beauty and glory had been restored, he said, "We are grateful that the Relief Society organization, with its millions of wives and mothers of patriots and pilgrims, has found the place to beautify and to memorialize the great work begun by the Prophet Joseph Smith when he gave the keys to his wife, Emma."

"The Spirit of God" was the majestic anthem we sang. It was most appropriate for singing in Nauvoo the Beautiful, for Nauvoo's founders were a people led by the Spirit of God. Nauvoo is a monument to those people, a testament to their virtuous living and to their faith and courage.

I encouraged everyone to look carefully at Nauvoo so they could go away pondering what happened here more than a hundred and forty years ago. It is a city of endless impressions, a site chosen as a haven that later became the scene of bitter battles.

Nauvoo grew from a population of three hundred to more than twelve thousand in about six years. It was a city of promise and vision, a city of industry, and finally, a city of silence and emptiness.

During the time the visitors were in Nauvoo I encouraged them to notice the careful planning: A house on every corner, and room enough in between the houses for gardens. I asked them to imagine the green fields and the quiet streets of yesteryear and to try to re-create in their minds what went on and then learn from it: to think of a child playing, perhaps with a few carved toys, or sitting in a small rocking chair lovingly fashioned by a father's hands; to stand in those small rooms and consider where the eight, ten, or more people slept; or to consider how they could have squeezed seven or ten people around the small table. Next I suggested they look at the warm, inviting, open fireplaces in the kitchens and think what it would have been like to have made that kitchen hum with the activity of cooking and the happy chatter of children; to smell spicy apples baking, and to see festive foods prepared during a holiday season.

The bustle ovens also fascinated Nauvoo visitors. They could smell the gingerbread or the golden-crusted bread piping hot from those ovens, or imagine the rice puddings filled with plump raisins. They could think of mothers scurrying around to keep things picked up and to keep picking up children so there would be room for all the other people.

We saw the cellars where the harvested potatoes, onions, turnips, and carrots were stored so that our sisters could better realize that the early Saints had to follow the ancient law of the harvest if they were to survive. Surely harvest did follow seed time. In order to harvest, the Saints had to plant seeds. Food had to be stored away for the wintertime. I wanted visitors to notice the smokehouses built to preserve the meat, and to imagine the apple trees hanging heavy with fruit. I wonder how many ways the mothers of those days found to fix that crunchy, wholesome fruit.

I didn't know how many visitors were aware of how important the courting lamps were in those days: If the father and mother liked the young man who was calling on their daughter, they filled the lamp full. If not, they just put a little oil in the lamp. I wonder how quickly their young people responded to the flickering flame dying out.

In the print shop, modern visitors could contemplate the important printing that was done.

At the blacksmith's shop, they could see the fascinating giant bellows and think of the virtual assembly line that had to be formed in order to build the wagons that the early Saints needed to evacuate the city in four months' time.

I wanted visitors to stroll with friends, and as they did, to think about the varied scenes of Church history that had taken place there, scenes that have affected your life and mine. By so doing, they could learn more of life's lessons from those Saints who came to Nauvoo practically penniless—because they had sold everything to purchase ship passage and gather to Nauvoo's Zion. The Saints in those days had very little with which to build provident homes, but I felt sure our modern visitors would be excited by their creativity.

I advised them to look up Mulholland Street and try to imagine how the Saints felt when the wagon bringing the bodies of Joseph and Hyrum rolled down its dusty length and turned toward the mansion house.

What of their wives? What of Emma? Emma who
mourned her husband's death and did not go west with the
Saints—she who was the first president of the Relief Society—
what were her feelings?

When Joseph told Emma he was going to give himself up
at Carthage, she asked a blessing from him. He told her to
write out the best blessing she could think of, and Emma
wrote the following:

> First of all that I would crave as the richest of heaven's
> blessings would be wisdom from my Heavenly Father be-
> stowed daily, so that whatever I might do or say, I could
> not look back at the close of the day with regret, nor ne-
> glect the performance of any act that would bring a bless-
> ing. I desire the Spirit of God to know and understand my-
> self, that I desire a fruitful, active mind, that I may be able
> to comprehend the designs of God, when revealed through
> his servants, without doubting. I desire the spirit of dis-
> cernment, which is one of the promised blessings of the
> Holy Ghost. I particularly desire wisdom to bring up all
> the children that are, or may be committed to my charge,
> in such a manner that they will be useful ornaments in the
> kingdom of God, and in a coming day arise up and call me
> blessed. I desire prudence that I may not through ambition
> abuse my body and cause it to become old and care worn,
> but that I may wear a cheerful countenance, live to per-
> form all the work that I covenanted to perform in the spirit
> world, and be a blessing to all who may in any wise need
> aught at my hands. I desire with all my heart to honor and
> respect my husband as my head, ever to live in his confi-
> dence, and by acting in unison with him retain the place
> which God has given me by his side . . . I desire to see,
> that I may rejoice with them in the blessings which God
> has in store for all who are willing to be obedient to his re-
> quirements. Finally, I desire that whatever may be my lot
> through life I may be enabled to acknowledge the hand of
> God in all things.

(Richard T. Bailey, "Emma Hale" [Brigham Young University, Master's Thesis, 1952], p. 112; a copy of the blessing is
also on file in the Historical Department of the Church, Salt
Lake City, Utah.)

While in Nauvoo, I encouraged each listener to think about Emma Smith's great virtues and her earnest desires.

I also urged them to stand on the edge of that mighty river which cuts America in two, to listen to the gentle lapping against the whitened driftwood; to look at the cheerful, yellow blossoms and the soft, purple wildflowers and to think about the lift that little spots of beauty can give to a troubled heart.

I asked them to ponder the mighty rumble of wagons, as hundreds rolled down and across the frozen river to the western shore; to think of those men and women looking back at their beautiful brick homes and their rich farms, with their abundance of all, left behind; to remember the temple they built to the Lord, so soon to be desecrated and destroyed; to try to feel the kind of faith and conviction that called and motivated the courageous women of that day, and then to recognize, perhaps, why it was appropriate to augment the Nauvoo Restoration Program with a monument. The purpose of the garden was to commemorate the past, but it was more than that.

The thirteen pieces of statuary in this lovely garden setting are designed to share what we know to be true about the essential and irreplaceable contribution of women to life. Only if we recognize the courage of the women of the past and confront the challenges that we face as women today, will we make possible the lives of fulfillment for the women and the men of the future. Hopefully the monument will cause all people who come to Nauvoo to stop and contemplate what they see, so they can recognize what noble people can leave to others.

Nauvoo was selected as the site for the monument because it was the place where the Relief Society was organized. The Prophet Joseph Smith indicated that this event marked the beginning of a new era for women, when light and knowledge would flow down to them from heaven. It was, and is, my conviction that the woman's role is vital and that the Lord looks upon each of his sons and daughters as beings of great worth. In fact, his is a gospel of hope, faith, and encouragement to all people who are converted and assume responsibility for their lives. Each individual will ultimately account to

God for his or her own actions and decisions. President David O. McKay once said:

> God made male and female; he established as distinct a difference between man and woman in temperament, in natural tendencies, and in the field of activity, as he did in sex; the most sublime beauty and the greatest harmony in life are attained when the man devotes his life to that for which nature has endowed him, and the woman puts forth her best efforts along the lines for which she is best fitted. It is a matter of deep concern that social and economic conditions today are enticing, if not forcing, women out of the sphere in which she herself can find the most happiness and can render the greatest good to mankind.

The Nauvoo Garden of Monuments can help women focus on obtaining the greatest happiness and on rendering the greatest good to mankind. The layout of the monument garden is significant. It has a series of overlapping circles representing a woman's influence at home, in the family, and in the community. The heroic figure of a woman in the center of the first circle signifies the limitless value of each individual woman; the figures that encircle her represent the important facets of her life.

The woman in prayer reminds us, "That we through our faith may begin to inherit the visions and blessings and glories of God." ("The Spirit of God," *Hymns*, p. 2.) Each woman has that great legacy and as she responds to the invitation of the Lord, she can communicate with him.

The woman learning signifies that "the Lord is extending the saints' understanding. . . . The knowledge and power of God are expanding; The veil o'er the earth is beginning to burst." We know that we can be inheritors of that knowledge and power. He has told us to be united even as he is one with the Father (see John 17:11). He also explained: "The glory of God is intelligence, or, in other words, light and truth" (D&C 93:36).

We want women to gain light and truth, to seek for it unceasingly throughout their lives. President Spencer W. Kimball said, "We encourage all of you to be abreast of the times, to be familiar with current events, to be able to read the signs of the times, to be prepared to direct your children in proper paths to guarantee to them a purposeful and eventful life."

The woman developing her talents depicts the development of our talents as necessary, if we are to help bring forth "the latter-day glory."

The compassionate woman embodies the promise that the "blessings of old" can return and bless countless lives, as they did when Christ walked upon the earth. He told his disciples: "Ye shall do the work, which ye see me do" (*History of the Church*, Vol. 5, p. 20). And when the Prophet Joseph Smith quoted these words to the sisters of Relief Society, he added, "These are the grand key-words for the society to act upon." (*History of Relief Society 1842-1966* [Salt Lake City: General Board of Relief Society, 1966], p. 22.)

In the second circle there is a recognition of the one totally essential role of the woman: to be a wife and mother and to rear and nurture children, that all of the spirit children of God might have the opportunity to come to earth for a period of mortal probation. There can be no human experience for anyone if women refuse to bear children.

The role of wife and mother in Zion is a great blessing and a challenging opportunity. It is a woman's responsibility to help create a home where children can be loved and taught in the ways of truth and light. Women must perform this essential function if the human race is to continue, and if we are to have the opportunity for exaltation.

One reporter there asked me, "Isn't your monument to women old-fashioned and traditional?"

"Yes," I answered, "if life is old-fashioned and traditional; if personal development, self-esteem, selflessness are old-fashioned and traditional. For it will be a statement in bronze about the essential, eternal worth of women as individuals and in the family setting. We consider these figures and their message as timeless. A woman is an essential part of the plan of life and salvation yesterday, today, and forever. There is no way to complete that plan without the woman."

The message of this garden is intended to help each person understand the essential concept of companionship of the man and the woman, walking hand in hand, counseling together, strengthening each other, working jointly to solve the problems of today, and rearing strong, competent children for the next generation.

I once heard a mother say, "No highlight of my life is more meaningful than seeing my children become contributing adults."

LDS women should want to see their children become contributing adults. It can happen if we seek to obtain some of the virtues possessed by the women of early Nauvoo, virtues such as wisdom, knowledge, understanding, cheerfulness, prudence, service, and obedience to God. A woman who exemplifies such virtues in her home will give a lamp of intelligence to her children forever.

As Relief Society sisters we seemed not only to pledge our full support to the monument project so that that beautiful garden could result, but also to pledge ourselves to becoming like the woman described in proverbs—a virtuous woman whose price is far above rubies, a woman of whom it can be said: "The heart of her husband doth safely trust in her, so that he shall have no need of spoil. She will do him good and not evil all the days of her life" (Proverbs 31:11–12). A woman who works willingly with her hands; who stretches out her hands to the poor; who has strength and honor, wisdom and kindness; who looks after her household; a woman whose children can arise up and call her blessed; a woman who fears the Lord (see Proverbs 31:10–31).

These virtues can be achieved by each of us. It was so for the prophetess Anna, who had lived so righteously that when the baby Jesus was brought to the temple she was able to recognize him, and she "spake of him to all them that looked for redemption in Jerusalem" (Luke 2:38).

Each woman must commit herself to recognize the Savior and praise him when he comes again to reign in the tradition of his father, a tradition that is the same yesterday, today, and forever.

The garden in Nauvoo yet proclaims the glorious message of the gospel. Each of us can proclaim that message with the same courage, faith, and conviction as did the women of early Nauvoo. We can create homes "without any ire" in anxious anticipation of the time when "Jesus decends in his chariot of fire."

We can commit our lives "to God and to the Lamb, [and] Let glory to them in the highest be given [by us], Henceforth and forever."

A United Press reporter, after covering the dedicatory services, wrote, "I had always thought Mormon women were slaves to their homes and to their husbands, but now I know it is out of a conviction that it is the best way to live. I only wish I had that same commitment in my life." (Personal letter to Charles Graves, copy in possession of author.)

Other nonmembers were affected by their involvement with the Nauvoo dedication. I had worried about taking the time of the missionaries in Nauvoo to assist, but their presence during those three days of the dedication was a blessing to many. Nearly every woman that I talked with told me stories of bus drivers or women who had really needed the love and spiritual insight the missionaries shared.

During their brief time in Nauvoo, most of the visitors repeatedly returned to the garden to see the monuments. An understanding of the work of women seemed to increase. One woman said, "I always thought the work my husband did was more important than my work, because he is a surgeon who could give sight to the blind; but after going to the Garden of Monuments I know that the work I do in giving life to children, and in nurturing them and teaching them, is the most important work of life because it is eternal."

After the services were over and all were home again, President Kimball asked one of the General Authorities if he had felt the Spirit of Christ there at the dedication services. He said he had. President Kimball replied, "Good, because it was there."

Much
Fruit

He that is faithful, the
same shall be kept and
blessed with much fruit.
—D&C 52:34

A short time after the monument dedication, a mail-o-
gram came addressed to me with the signature "Rosalynn Carter." It said: "I am inviting you to join me in Washington, July 27, 1978, for a day-long meeting of community
leaders from across the country to focus on how citizens can
improve employment opportunities in their towns and cities.
This "Seminar on Employment" will review not only those
federal resources directed toward employment, but, more im-
portantly, success stories from the private sector. It is my hope
that participants in this seminar; clergy, women, and business
leaders, will help me as First Lady address this issue." My
friend Jean Bradshaw had received the same invitation.

What did I, as the general president of Relief Society,
know about employment? "Well, you can learn can't you?"
were words from a remark President Joseph Fielding Smith
made to one who wanted more information. So I began to
learn. Thayne Robson, respected University of Utah business
professor, left his many duties at the University of Utah to talk
with me and with Jean W. Bradshaw. Professor Robson encouraged us by saying, "When the president of the United
States asks for your help, through his wife, it's up to you to get
back there and do the best job you can to inform him."

Both Jean Bradshaw and I found it almost unbelievable
that we had been offered such a once-in-a-lifetime experience.

We held local briefings on employment and job opportunities for days prior to our departure. But we still found it beyond ourselves when we entered the New York Presbyterian Church, just off of Pennsylvania Avenue, with three hundred other citizens from every state in the union for a day-long meeting with Rosalynn Carter. I thought she might make an appearance, but she did much more than that. She welcomed us all, went to each table where we were assigned, shook our hands. When she came to me, she remembered our visit together and the invitation I had extended to her to attend the dedication of the Nauvoo monuments. She spent the entire day with us at the seminar.

We noticed the predominance of southern accents among Mrs. Carter's staff members as we registered and received our engraved invitation for a White House reception to meet the president following the seminar. We then found our places at separate round tables in the fifth floor auditorium of the church, and we met many notable people from across the nation. All of them were community-minded people who shared a common concern: "What can we do as citizens to help America? Those at the same table at which I sat were religious leaders—Jewish rabbis, Catholic church leaders—and government employees who were assigned to find solutions to the problems related to employment.

I was impressed with Mrs. Carter's entrance, simple and without fanfare. She set the theme for the day's meeting. Her appearance was unpretentious. She seemed sincere in wanting to work toward a partnership of government and private citizens to meet the problems of unemployment.

The secretary of labor, F. Ray Marshall, and Ernest Green, assistant director of the Employment and Training Administration, presented an overview of America's employment problems and the battle of the Carter administration to put all citizens in America back to work. "The tragedy of unemployment," Secretary Marshall said, "is that we lose the person's output. Employment is a highly perishable product and it is inflationary to have people who want to work who are not working." He explained that from an 8 percent unemployment rate on election day 1976, President Carter, through his economic-stimulus package, had reduced unemployment to 5.7 percent. But despite this progress, major pockets of unemployment still existed nationwide, particularly among teenaged blacks and minorities. "Five out of six jobs are in the private sector," Marshall said. "It is the dedication, commitment, and single-mindedness of community efforts that can reach beyond government to help this country's unemployed." (*Deseret News*, July 31, 1978.)

My concern was mainly with the female heads of households. It seemed to me that their undesirable cycle of unemployment should be given careful consideration, because a mother teaches her children financial responsibility. In order to do this she needs to give them direction, and also the example of educating herself, dedicating herself to her family, and being loyal to her employer. The problems are many when a woman labors so much out of the home at a time when the children need her. I felt that it was a problem that needed solutions by our group that day. I suggested that homemaking be considered one of the great careers of our day.

I shared the Church welfare program as a possible solution to this problem of our day. I knew that through it people grew in self-reliance. When I told the group at our table about it, they were very responsive. I felt that the whole country could use it and that the people of the United States could be prepared to utilize all of its resources by receiving good training in the areas of financial management, intellectual and educational development, food and resource preparedness, and spiritual and emotional strength. They said, "It is most admirable. We wish we could do that for the people of the United States, but we can't. How do you control your people anyway?"

The answer was immediate: "We teach them correct principles and they govern themselves." (*Journal of Discourses* 10:57–58.)

They fully agreed that if we could but do those things, it would solve the problems of unemployment in America and give people the personal motivation and respect they need.

After a long day, Mrs. Carter's unflagging interest and concern continued in a question-and-answer period. Sometimes she would respond by saying, "I don't know, but I will ask Jimmy," or "Please see me after and we can talk more about that."

Later, at the White House reception, we asked Secretary Marshall about private business and its vital role toward job stimulus. "If private business could increase sales," he said, "sales would increase expansion, and expansion would create more jobs. Then we could look more to the investment side of business needs."

Merwin Hans, national director of the Office of Work Incentive Programs, was interested in the Salt Lake area WIN programs. In our preparation, we found that 270,000 women had been placed in jobs during that year. He also talked about the detrimental effects of taking the disadvantaged, unemployed mother out of her home and away from her children while she earned much-needed and necessary money. "I keep wondering," he said as he shook his head, "just what is happening to all those children." He was concerned about training mothers in parenting, health, and money management, and breaking the jobless cycle by teaching women in those circumstances the skills they lack.

Later, on the White House lawn, President and Mrs. Carter posed for picture-taking sessions with the representatives from each state. That meant that Jean and I talked briefly alone with the President and Mrs. Carter as we had our pictures taken. He spoke softly as he said, "Every person should be able to say 'I am a human being and I have the right to use my God-given life to my own advantage and to the advantage of those around me.' With the spirit of partnership you have created today, learning from each other, the great nation we already have can be that much greater."

Mrs. Carter invited us to the state dining room to enjoy the delicious party food prepared by the White House chef and to mingle with others through the first-floor reception rooms of the White House. How I hoped the efforts of that day could bear fruit!

An interesting letter including an invitation came to me through Carol Juchau, who wrote and asked me to speak at the Pleasanton California Stake women's conference. She also invited me to go with her to the Santa Rita Prison to see what work of the Relief Society sisters of her stake was accomplishing there. Our priesthood adviser to the Relief Society general board suggested that I meet with the prison officials rather than actually go to the prison. I did, and they could not thank me enough for the work that the Relief Society sisters were doing there. These officials appreciated their influence for good.

A few years later I received a second invitation from Pleasanton, California, along with an invitation from the Santa Rita Prison to inspect the program of Relief Society there. This time I was not only given permission of the Brethren but was also encouraged to go with their blessing and see what was being accomplished. On that trip, I ate with the prison officials, saw the living quarters of the women inmates, and watched their participation in a variety of sports events. I also went to the solitary confinement quarters for the women.

I listened to the lesson on friendship given by the Relief Society sister. Then, along with the inmates, I made a fabric picture frame. I sat between two women, one in prison for forgery and the other for using and selling drugs. Never once was the last name of any woman used; the Church members and the prisoners called each other by their first names. I was most impressed with the response of the inmates as the sisters shared their love, but I went away wishing the prisoners could be taught the gospel principles per se.

That evening a reception was held and I met many sisters from the Pleasanton area. One woman said, "Sister Smith, I understand you were a guest at the Santa Rita Prison today." I told her I was. She continued, "I was once at the prison, too, but not as a guest. I was an inmate. I attended the meetings held by the Relief Society sisters there. I was so impressed by the love and attentive concern of those women who came and taught us that when I was released, and Mormon missionaries came to my door, I listened to them and I joined the Church. Now I want to go back to the prison, not as an inmate but to teach the principles of the gospel. I knew how those women feel, and I am sure I can help them now."

I thought of the saintly women who had been influential with her. They had been going to the prison week in and week out for over five years, living and serving compassionately. Their kind words and deeds were no small part of their fruitful efforts. I better understood why the Lord tells us we must go to those who are in prison.

It was Easter time when our office received a telephone call from one of the women inmates of the state prison in Utah. She asked us if we could bring Easter baskets out so that when the children came to visit their mothers, the women inmates would be able to give them a basket.

When the inquiry came to me I said, "Yes, if it meets with the approval of those who administer the operation of the prison." However, when we talked with the prison officials, they rejected the plan because the children could receive Easter baskets elsewhere; the officials did not want the children to expect candy and gifts each time they came to see their mothers.

After thinking about their response we asked if it would be permissible to provide children's books to tell about the story of Easter. In that way, each mother had a gift for her child that she could read and that could perhaps touch her life with its story of Jesus the Christ. The officials agreed to this proposal.

Since I was going to Orem, I said that I would take the books down. When I arrived at the prison tower I saw a man signaling directions—I thought. We followed the direction to which he pointed and ended up in a field. We went back to the tower again only to find that the man's gestures were incident to his window washing. We interrupted his work long enough to get the needed directions.

At the entrance of the women's facilities, the electric doors were opened for me. I went in and left the books, but took away with me the sad and barren look upon the faces of those women. I could not help but think about the Savior and his great sacrifice so that no one need be imprisoned in such institutions. I thought of Jesus hanging upon the cross between two thieves. I remembered that the one challenged, "If thou be

Christ, save thyself and us." The other said, "We receive the due reward of our deeds: but this man hath done nothing amiss." (Luke 23:39, 41.) All the while, there between them, hung the Christ making his selfless sacrifice for them, and they knew it not. All of us, I realized, are somewhere with one of those three. We want to have all of the benefits of life given to us, however undeserved, or we are counting on the mercy of God—or we are following him who lived and died sinless, by choosing to live our lives in strict obedience to the laws and ordinances he came to proclaim.

Being asked to speak mid-year at the governor's prayer breakfast at a downtown hotel in Salt Lake City was an answer to my personal prayer. I had been the focus of so much public controversy because of my stand on women's issues that to speak to a group assembled to pray together was a pleasure, and I welcomed the opportunity. It was a uniting experience that we all needed. My hostess, the First Lady of our state Norma Matheson, and I had been together on many occasions: We had gone to visit the Job Corps training program; we had planned the annual Utah Territorial Ball; we had worked with the aging and the handicapped; and I had supported her effort to restore the governor's residence because I saw it as a symbol of the strength that a good home could represent for the families of our state. Our only real differences were on political matters. In the prayer breakfast we were united. It was a reverential time when differences could be laid aside. This was a time to pursue the most important action and ask for the help of the Lord for all of us.

At the prayer breakfast I quoted George Meredith: "Who riseth from prayer a better man, his prayer is answered." (*Bartlett's Familiar Quotations* [Boston, Toronto: Little, Brown and Company, 1980], p. 600.)

I referred to the time when, more than two hundred years ago, a group of men representing the thirteen original colonies gathered in the city of Philadelphia to try to come to a consensus which would facilitate the government of the newly established United States of America. The records they left tell us that there was not an easy outpouring of agreement, but a genuine upheaval of thoughts and a long and tedious debate that took place between them. Finally from that gathering, so many times near to hopeless wrangling over differences as monumental as any we have subsequently experienced, resulted the Constitution of the United States of America.

That Constitution did not come easily, nor, in my opinion, did it come without the help of God. Benjamin Franklin was one of the men most influential in bringing the delegates together and insuring the drafting and approval of the Constitution. He worked quietly but tenaciously to see that this group of men, who had it in their power to create the necessary union of the colonies, did not turn away from their historic work.

Norman Cousins, in his book *In God We Trust*, reports that "Once, when breakdown in the constitutional debates seemed imminent, Benjamin Franklin cooled the passions and restored the perspective of the delegates." He said:

> Our different sentiments on almost every question . . . [are] methinks a melancholy proof of the imperfection of human understanding. We indeed seem to feel our own want of political wisdom, since we have been running about in search of it . . . I have lived, Sir, a long time, and the longer I live, the more convincing proofs I see of this truth, that God governs in the affairs of men. And if a sparrow cannot fall to the ground without his notice, is it probable that an empire can rise without his aid? We have been assured, Sir, in the sacred writings, that except the Lord builds the house, they labour in vain that build it. I firmly believe this, and I also believe that without his concurring aid we shall succeed in this political building no better than the builders of Babel: We shall be divided by our little partial local interests, our projects will be confounded, and we ourselves shall become a reproach and a byword down to future ages. And what is worse, mankind may hereafter from this unfortunate instance, despair of establishing governments by human wisdom and leave it to chance, war, and conquest.

I therefore beg leave to move, that henceforth prayers imploring the assistance of heaven, and its blessing on our deliberations, be held in this assembly every morning before we proceed to business. (*In God We Trust: The Religious Beliefs and Ideas of the American Founding Fathers* [New York: Harper and Brothers Publishers, 1958], pp. 17–18.)

I have no doubt that this appeal to heaven for assistance, which Benjamin Franklin urged the delegates to undertake, was one of the factors that helped them find an accommodation and a consensus that would allow their differing ideas to work together.

Significant and controversial issues loom ahead of us in our day. The dream of the America they envisioned in Philadelphia has not always been able to accommodate the realities of our failures, as individuals and as groups, to live up to their ideals.

Our set of problems, while different from those of the founding fathers, is equally difficult and equally important to the survival of our country and of all mankind. We, too, need to take Benjamin Franklin's pleading to heart and daily implore the "assistance of heaven, and its blessings on our deliberations" in order to find solutions to such deep and difficult problems.

We need to seek the order and purpose that comes from accepting God as the creator of the universe and all that is in it. He is the source of higher law which can give us direction and consensus as we deliberate.

As I say this, I am aware that there are many differences among believing people and even greater differences between the believer and the nonbeliever.

I glimpsed this difference as an Indian medicine man offered a blessing upon the food served at a luncheon held in connection with a state conference on the family. He began by addressing God as "Grand Father." I had heard the term "grandfather" so many times and used it myself with my own grandfathers that, at first, I was repulsed at the familiarity of the term used to address God. Suddenly my understanding was enlarged. I recognized not only the high honor being paid to God, but the praise given to mothers, fathers, and grandparents who live worthy of adulation.

In a similar context, my study of the Constitution impressed upon me that our founding fathers have given us not only a remarkable document but one which both advocates and preserves our rights to diversity and unity. Both can enlarge our understanding as a people.

The debate at the beginning of this nation, it is obvious to me, created a Constitution that was to preserve for us our right to worship as we choose. It was not designed to deny the existence of a Supreme Being but to fully support that belief.

Because those men were conscious of the oppression often suffered under a state-enforced religion, they wrote into the Constitution the right to worship as one chooses. There can be no other correct way to make a people free. One does not come unto God by force and coercion. Mary L. O'Hara said it well in four thoughtful lines she entitles "Kneeling."

> It matters not how oft you kneel
> In attitude of prayer so true,
> Unless inside, where no man sees,
> Your very soul is kneeling, too.

We know that the Lord can only accept the devotions of those who pray with such a sincere and contrite heart.

It seems to me that the Constitution is written to prevent religious abuse by not allowing the imposition of a politically enforced religious belief; but at the same time, it is worded to preserve the right of sincerely religious people and religious organizations to contribute meaningfully to the discussion which forms our governing laws.

I believe our nation benefits greatly from the input of good people whose perspective is shaped by a faith in God and the attendant framework for life supplied by that faith.

Consider three specific principles:

First, the world is based upon universal laws which govern in the eternities. We have the agency to determine our actions here and now, but the result of those choices will be in accordance with the everlasting laws which exist. At the conclusion of our lives we will be the sum total of our actions, no matter what our pretenses. The same is true for nations.

The Chinese say, "If a man plants melons he will reap melons; if he sows beans, he will reap beans." The Spanish proverb is, "Take what you want and pay for it." The scriptures tell us: "Every good tree bringeth forth good fruit; but a corrupt tree bringeth forth evil fruit" (Matthew 7:17), or, good will beget good and evil will bring evil. Our choices do not alter the laws of the universe.

Second, we are all children of God. My faith in God leads me to understand the real brotherhood we *all* have with each other. That common birthright puts us in direct relationship to God and to each other. This common heritage should help us reach out and try to lighten each other's burdens.

Third, each individual is of infinite worth to God. I believe that the continuing growth and development of each person is a fundamental eternal right and we need to find ways which will allow this fertile growth to continue.

We all need to understand that every person is unique. Our society, our world, needs the best each man and woman has to give. We need to create a climate of hope and faith in which the spirit can develop. Norman Cousins writes:

> The American Founding Fathers, to the extent that they can be regarded as a group, believed deeply in the ability of a human being to learn enough in order to take part in self-government; in the capacity of people to make sense of their lives if given reasonable conditions within society itself; in the responsive power of men when exposed to great ideas; in the people to stand upright spiritually without *ornate* or *complicated* props; in man to live under due process of law; in *man* to make basic decisions concerning his religion or his politics or anything. . . . Not all the founders acknowledged the formal faith, but it was significant that their view of man had a deeply religious foundation. Rights were "God-given," "Man was endowed" by this creator, there were "natural laws" and "natural rights"; freedom was related to the sacredness of man. The

development of a free man was not divorced from the idea of moral man, any more than religious man could be separated from moral man. There was also strong spiritual content in the confidence of the American founders in the capacity of man to govern his own affairs, to hold the ultimate power in the operation of his society, and to be able to decide correctly when given access to vital information. (*In God We Trust*, p. 8.)

From time to time each of us should review this magnificent heritage, for in the deliberations of these great men lies a simple, meaningful foundation for purposeful accomplishment in each life. Upon this framework of faith and truth they created a government which can be responsive to our needs, providing we, as individuals, retain the source of controlling power and use it wisely.

Therefore, we need to be guided by the light of heaven in our deliberations so that we can find the areas of our accord; discover truth; eliminate ignorance; and find working combinations for all the magnificent ideas of which men and women are capable as they deliberate to find solutions to problems.

It required time, commitment, energy, and prayer, then, to make our people a free people and make our government work. Those same things are needed today.

I recall a story that came from the pen of Lowell Thomas, author and world traveler, about Abraham Davenport, a member of the state senate of Connecticut. He described an incident which occurred on May 19, 1790. On this day darkness came at noon. Because of some meteorological phenomenon, blackness enveloped the area of Hartford, Connecticut, in the middle of the day and panic broke out. People then knew much less about the laws that govern the universe than they do now, and they thought the end of the world had come.

In Hartford, the Connecticut legislature was meeting. The lower house meeting broke up in alarm. In the state senate a motion for adjournment was made. The motion suggested that adjournment was necessary so that the legislators could meet the day of judgment with whatever courage they could manage to summon.

But Abraham Davenport arose in opposition to the motion. This is his statement: "I am against adjournment. The day of judgment is either approaching or it is not. If it is not, there is no cause for adjournment. If it is, I choose to be found doing my duty. I wish, therefore, that candles may be brought."

We must importune God every day to bless our work in our communities, in our nation, and in our world. We must seek his direction and continue our work with the same steadfast diligence of Abraham Davenport, "doing our duty" daily and consistently. We must seek the enlightenment of God in personal and in public prayer. In this way we will be able to find those positions of working consensus that will allow us to make headway against the difficult problems we face in our times.

As William Adams Brown wisely reminds us, "Prayer introduces us to the great companion who meets our human needs with divine response."

17

Good Seeds
Are the Children
of the Kingdom

The field is the world; the
good seed are the children
of the kingdom.
—Matthew 13:38

I noticed as I worked with President Kimball that he often gave deference to women. I recognized that when, at the beginning of my administration, he blessed me that I would be able to help the women of the Church understand their feminine roles. He continued with courtesy and with that reaffirming consistency he accorded to me and other women. I think of the day he called me to his office and asked if I could foresee any problem for Relief Society if he called my counselor to serve with her husband and help open the African mission. Of course my answer was that we would sorely miss her, but that we would manage. I knew President Kimball was free to issue the call without consulting me, but it was obvious that he respected the position of responsibility to which he had called me.

My hope is that President Kimball was equally aware of the love and respect I held for him and that I always did my best to serve him faithfully, even as my early predecessor, Emmeline B. Wells, had done when, in 1876, President Brigham Young asked her to direct a mission to save grain against a day of need. She did, and that wheat was used in Europe during the First World War, during the San Francisco Fire, and later when local farmers needed the wheat for seed. The Relief Society had managed that wheat as a sacred trust. But after consultation with the administrators of the Welfare Department of the Church there was a consensus that the Relief Society had fulfilled its responsibility with the wheat and it was time to include the Relief Society wheat with the Churchwide grain storage program. President Kimball responded affirmatively to our proposal that we make a presentation of the Relief Society wheat at the welfare session of general conference on Saturday, September 30, 1978. There, I officially proposed that the 266,291 bushels of Relief Society wheat be made part of the grain storage plan of Welfare Services for the benefit of all the members of the Church and that the wheat fund be used exclusively for the purchase of more grain.

After a sustaining vote of the women present in the tabernacle that day, President Kimball accepted the wheat in behalf of the Brethren of the Church and the Church membership in general. He expressed gratitude and appreciation and indicated he was aware of the sacrifice and diligence of the Relief Society sisters who, for over a century, had faithfully discharged the sacred wheat trust fund. He then counseled, "We ask you also to support the Brethren, and we ask them to support you and to work together as partners and companions in furthering the work of the Lord and your own salvation. Let this gift of the Relief Society today be an example of the cooperative effort and harmony that can enrich our lives in the Church and in the home." ("The Fruit of Our Welfare Services Labor," *Ensign*, November 1978, p. 77.)

As the chairman of the Committee on Child and Family for the National Council of Women, one of my major responsibilities was the kick-off event for the International Year of the Child, a project of the United Nations for 1978. The workshop was held in New York City on December 7, 1978, in the Church facilities across from Lincoln Center. More than two hundred delegates as well as Relief Society members from the five New York stakes attended the day-long workshops, which highlighted Jean Childs Young, wife of the then United Nations Ambassador Andrew Young, as the keynote speaker. Four former presidents of the National Council of Women, as well as former Relief Society President Belle S. Spafford, attended the workshop sessions.

All of the presenters were brilliant. Their workshops were informative. In fact, the whole day came together in a very harmonious blend of intelligent action and friendly response. Many of those present said they had never participated in such an intellectually stimulating meeting. At noon we invited all attendees into the cultural hall for a luncheon. The room was perfectly beautiful. The red tablecloths made the lighted, candy-covered gingerbread houses more prominent. The candles and giant poinsettias that adorned the head table were breathtaking. The lights were low, and the glow of the Christmas tree on the stage shed its light on the many gifts at its base.

"Annie," from the broadway hit musical of the same name, was there at the workshop luncheon as our guest. She brought with her the dog that played Sandy in the show. The young star had been invited to come and accept gifts given by members of the National Council of Women and take them to orphanages in New York City. These gifts were piled bountifully under the tree. I had just entered the hall when Annie marched right up to me. "Where is Sandy to sit?" she wanted to know. Then she added, "I want him right next to me at the head table!"

My reply was, "I'll see what I can arrange."

I went to Phyllis Kimball, stake Relief Society president who had been responsible for the preparations and transportation of all the food and decorations, and relayed the message of our young Broadway star.

Sister Kimball said, "I can't do it. I just can't. It is repulsive to me to put a dog at the head table; we have worked very hard to make this a lovely event and I can't humor a spoiled child by putting her dog up there." She quickly added, "I'll do it if you tell me to, but might I suggest instead that we get a little table and extend our head table, let the dog eat at it, and let Annie sit right next to her dog?"

That very special sister had a good solution to a difficult problem and the conference continued on flawlessly.

Wouldn't it be nice if all difficult situations could be handled
with such grace?

I readily accepted an invitation to speak at a Grantsville,
Utah, ward sacrament meeting on January 1, 1979, because I
wanted to feel again the spirit of President J. Reuben Clark. I
knew it had been long years since he had lived in Grantsville,
but I hoped the aura of his boyhood days still lingered there.
As my husband Douglas drove me in a heavy winter snow-
storm toward Grantsville, I told him of my anticipation.

The fact that President Clark had been born in Grantsville
had endeared him to many people there. I wanted to know
more of that great man. His daughter, Marianne Clark Sharp,
had been the education counselor under Belle S. Spafford in
the general presidency of the Relief Society. As a member of
that general board, I had been under her tutelage for the four
years prior to my call to serve as the general president. Sister
Sharp had always made me feel my work on the board was acceptable, effective, and important. I appreciated her and
loved President Clark for the good seeds he had planted in his
children and for this daughter of his whom I knew had integrity and decisiveness. She was dear to me because of her closeness to the Lord and her intelligent approach to life. I wanted
to be there where her noble father had spent his childhood. I
thought it might help me to know how her strength had been
derived and how he had raised his children to bring an abundant harvest of blessing to the whole Church. He always delivered wise counsel in his conference addresses, as well as at a
Relief Society conference in 1940. Speaking of the home, he
said:

> The Latter-day Saint family, in a Latter-day Saint
> home, has three great functions to perform.
>
> First, it must bring its members such lives as will enable
> them to return to the inner circles of that celestial home
> from which they came. A dwelling with the Heavenly Fa-
> ther and Mother throughout the eternities.
>
> Second, it must so carry out its duties, rights, and func-
> tions as to enable it, in turn, to found a celestial home that
> shall, in some eternity hereafter, be equal in power, oppor-

tunity, and dignity with the celestial home from which we came and to which we shall return.

Third, it must so live its life as to provide for the spirits yet waiting to come to this earth for their fleshly tabernacles, both bodies and minds that shall be healthy, for the spirits coming through them are the choice spirits, which have earned the right by their lives in their first estate, to the righteous homes—to the families of greatest promise and opportunity; and this family must provide for this spirit which it invites to come to its hearthstone, an environment that shall meet the strictest requirements of righteousness.

("Our Homes, *Relief Society Magazine*, Dec. 1940, p. 808.)

I did much traveling before July of 1979 when I was appointed to serve on the National Advisory Committee for the White House Conference on Families. That committee consisted of twenty-one men and nineteen women. We were selected to represent the diverse political, racial, and ethnic backgrounds of people in the United States. Various members of the committee were experts in education, psychology, economics, health, law, welfare, and family policy. Others were leaders in business, religious groups, social services, and neighborhood organizations.

Some members of that committee may have considered the opportunity to be just another everyday appointment, but I recognized it as a great honor to be asked to serve our country and its families in that manner; I always made it a matter of prayer. Our task was to "examine the strengths of American families, the difficulties they face, and the ways in which family life is affected by public policies." (*Listening to America's Families* [Washington, D.C.: White House Conference on Families, 1980], p. 234.)

As a committee member I journeyed back and forth across the nation as I participated in fourteen days of hearings, as well as attended the three White House conferences in Baltimore, Minneapolis, and Los Angeles. I invited my brother, who lives in Baltimore, to attend the one in his city. We sat near the front of the auditorium and he could not believe that the president of the United States would come down and talk to those of us who were near the front of the room. When President Carter came to me, he called me by name and said, "Hello, Barbara, how are you enjoying the conferences?" *That* surprised my brother even more!

Listening to the hundreds of individuals who related their concerns and needs for their family took a great deal of time, but it was a very rewarding experience, and one that we knew needed our attention. Other forums and activities took place during that year of recognizing the American family. It was after our year-long effort that the committee published a full report of our findings and listed the recommendations that came out of the conferences.

Of course, the ERA battle was still very much with us. I was given the responsibility of traveling throughout the Midwest to help women understand the position of the Relief Society against the amendment. I admired women like Vivian McConkie Adams, who gave so much of themselves and their time to protect the families of America against the possible effects of ERA. Another dedicated woman was Patty Kemp, a mother of young children, who felt an overwhelming need to fight the amendment and thereby protect the future of America. She studied and became very knowledgeable. She arranged forums in which women could discuss the problems inherent in the ERA.

As I traveled with her to attend some of those meetings, another very attractive woman who was a model told me that before she joined the Church she did not have a clear understanding of the implications ERA could have in her life. A short while after her baptism she had attended a homemaking meeting. As she listened to the counsel given there, she sank lower and lower in her chair; they talked about clean, neat, orderly homes. She realized that her home was a disaster. Her children had difficulty finding two matching shoes to put on. She decided it was time for her to begin to manage her household, not just participate in interests outside the home. During that meeting she determined to talk to the bishop's wife and ask for her help. She did. She explained that she knew how to dress, but that she didn't really know how to keep a good home. The bishop's wife said she would be happy to help her. She made a list of things she recommended that the woman do every day. The woman tried to do those things, but she couldn't seem to stay with the list. Finally, in despair, she went back to the bishop's wife and said, "I can't do it. I've tried, but there is just no way I can manage to have that kind of a house. Now what do I do?"

The bishop's wife said, "If you really think you can't do those things, the only thing you can do is go to the Lord and pray that he will change your heart. When that happens, you will find you are able to make the necessary adjustments to maintain a neat and orderly home."

That sister really wanted to be a model mother and a model homemaker as well as a fashion model, so she began to fast and pray for help. Finally she felt that she had a "change of heart." She went back to the bishop's wife and said, "I think I can do it now." She was given a shorter list this time and, in addition, the bishop's wife talked to this woman's husband and told him of the things she had suggested that his wife do. She then told him that his approval and help to do those things, and to work with the children to do the same, was essential. Together they worked. The mother was incrementally given additional chores until the family learned to work together and accomplish the goal of a clean, neat, orderly home. The model said to me, "We aren't perfect yet, but we have come such a long way. I am pleased and happy and know the joy of keeping a good home."

The surprising, insightful conclusion to her story came when she then explained that experience had made her realize that the ERA was not an amendment that she or other women needed. For women to feel equal to men, they but needed to plant good seed—a clear gospel perspective—and realize who they are and the power and potential they possess. Within the home takes place the vital work of the world, but wherever women, married or not, wield influence with that intelligent vision, they will ultimately develop themselves and their po-

tentials. Home is where women can wield a strong, positive influence on generations yet to come.

How I wished I had taken her with me when I attended
the National Council of Women seminar and gala award
luncheon on careers and professions, held in New York City
that year! Linda Johnson Robb, chair of President Carter's
Advisory Committee for Women, spoke on "new goals for the
public and private woman." Among other things, she said that
women were intentionally left out of the Constitution in spite
of the appeals by Abigail Adams to her husband and in spite of
petitions bearing signatures of hundreds of women. Even
though women had helped settle the country, the feeling was
that they belonged in the home and they shouldn't want to
compete with their husbands in the labor market, in politics,
or in the community.

She pointed out that a woman was receiving only fifty-
seven cents for every dollar a man earned, and that we needed
to find ways to compensate women equally with men for the
work they do. The intent of her remarks was to advance support for the then proposed Equal Rights Amendment. While I
have always felt women should receive equal pay for equal
work, her comments did not sway my belief that the blanket
approach to correcting such inequities was erroneous.

18

Their Seed Shall Be Known Among the Gentiles

And their seed shall be
known among the
Gentiles: . . . that they
are the seed that the Lord
hath blessed.
—Isaiah 61:9

E ach year of serving in the presidency seemed more mo-
mentous than the last. The year 1980, for example,
would be filled with the Sesquicentennial celebration, a major
change in the Church meeting schedule, a new Relief Society
General Board structure, a plan for adapting Relief Society to
the developing countries of the world, my hour-long appearance on a nationwide television show, and many other matters
of consequence.

As we contemplated what the Relief Society's contribution
to the one hundred and fiftieth anniversary of the Church
might be, we acted on several possibilities that emerged
clearly. Since the Nauvoo Garden of Monuments had proven
such a strength to the sisters who were able to attend the dedication or to later visit Nauvoo, extending that experience to
more members seemed a worthwhile endeavor. Consequently,
we had four full-sized, bronze replicas of the Nauvoo statues
cast and placed in the plaza of the Church Office Building as a
gift to the Church. There they continue to be viewed and enjoyed by visitors from all over the world, including many
women who contributed to the original statuary in Nauvoo.

In researching the Relief Society's history, we found that
the sisters in other generations had commemorated every fiftieth anniversary of the Church with a Jubilee Celebration in

the tradition of those mentioned in the Old Testament, in which the children of Israel held year-long commemorations. To echo the significance of that tradition, those former-day Relief Society women wrote letters to families yet to be born and collected interesting papers and artifacts. These they sealed in a jubilee box that was to be opened fifty years later. We were disappointed that the box we were to have unsealed had been opened prematurely, but we had a box made in which we placed letters from each member of the Relief Society General Board; copies of current Relief Society materials; and pictures of the Nauvoo monument, of building displays, and of the board members themselves.

Trying to determine what materials might be of value to preserve for future generations was cause for considerable thought, but we felt a sense of real satisfaction as it was all sealed in the box and the key put in safekeeping for the next fifty years. The ceremony gave us a sense of having responded to sisters who, like us, were endeavoring to create a living legacy that would help tie women of all generations to the "something-better-for-them" ideal that the Prophet Joseph Smith had promised when he organized the women that March day so long ago. In a similar manner, throughout the wards and stakes of the Church, Relief Society jubilee boxes were filled and sealed.

The idea of a jubilee box was given further significance that year when the Brethren, too, observed the same practice at a large Sesquicentennial banquet held at the Church Office Building. General Authorities and organizational presidencies and their spouses watched as President Gordon B. Hinckley closed a jubilee box containing important documents marking the progress of the Church at that milestone in its history.

I was thrilled with the Relief Society's participation in the Jubilee Celebration, which included not only the statues and boxes, but a float in Utah's Twenty-Fourth of July Parade and the planting of thirty-five redbud trees in the Church Office Building plaza. The latter two events were, again, a response to a request from the sisters of an earlier day. Fifty years earlier they had ridden in a carriage in the Twenty-Fourth of July

Parade and had requested that the Relief Society presidency of 1980 might also ride in the parade. They had planted a tree in hopes that the Relief Society women of 1980 would plant another.

While we were not obligated to carry out those wishes of our predecessors, we felt that in doing so we would honor them and the work that they did. We also found, as we carried out their requests, that we were establishing a link with the past—a hand of sisterhood which we hoped would provide strength for the generations who followed us. When we asked about planting a tree, the Brethren agreed but referred the matter to the landscape personnel so that whatever we did might fit into the long-range plan for the grounds. We learned that not one tree but a group of thirty-five would best fit those plans. This seemed only reflective of the increasing number of sisters in Relief Society, and we were pleased to fill that need. The planting ceremony was a delightful one. Even the First Presidency joined in with shovels and brief comments. Press and media coverage made the occasion complete.

All of the events surrounding this celebration helped us to realize that the work we were doing had long-term implications that power in the past can give greater impact to the present. By taking heed to the past, we really can stand on the shoulders of those who have gone before.

I endeavored to find in the Jubilee Celebration some corresponding expression of that event for our family. Utilizing Church programs as a pattern for family activities had helped our family develop many meaningful traditions. I went to our Mills family records and found a letter from my grandmother which began, "To the one who may open this fifty years hence." She then gave a short history of her life, bore her testimony that she belonged to the Church of God, and indicated that she had received her endowments and patriarchal blessing. She had graduated from Brigham Young Academy at sixteen years of age, and went on to teach in Hoytsville, Utah, a small town on the Weber River. Shortly after that she returned to the academy and taught in the primary department. She expressed her concern that, at the age of twenty, she was "as

commonplace as anyone could think." (This is the same grandmother who later became a physician.) Two things she mentioned brought tears to my eyes. "Well, every heart knoweth
its own bitterness." I wondered about her problems. The other
was a prayer that God would guide and direct the feet of those
who followed her in the path of right. "Do not trifle with
edged tools. If you know or think anything to be the least bit
wrong, shun it!" It was a thrill to read the message she had left
my children and me.

The Relief Society participated in the International Conference on Records in 1980. That year the conference was held
in the Salt Palace in Salt Lake City, which afforded ample
space for the charming model home which was the setting for
the Relief Society exhibit. The structure was quaint and appealing and designed so that those viewing it could walk in the
front door, through a homey family living room, past a working kitchen, and out the back door. The theme, "History,
Made Fresh Daily," was expressed by an array of family pictures hung on the walls, albums and histories displayed on
tables, and memorabilia preserved in various ways—all giving
ideas of how to preserve history-making moments in our families. The message was further punctuated by the aroma of the
large sugar cookies being baked continually in the ovens of the
kitchen right there in the house, and being served to each person who walked through.

The exhibit was an immediate success and was constantly
accompanied by a line of people waiting to enter. We could
have fulfilled the assignment of a booth at the conference more
simply than by constructing a house, perhaps, and many
would have understood the message. But when I think of the
hundreds of people who passed through that charming house
and saw how items they currently had in their own homes
could have lasting historical value, each tasting the sweetness
created by such a home, I was pleased we had chosen to put
forth the extra effort.

History was truly being made in the Church in 1980 with
the area conferences that took President Kimball, President
Romney, members of the Quorum of the Twelve, and the gen-

eral auxiliary presidents of the Young Women and Relief Society to the Philippine islands, Taiwan, Korea, and Japan. It was my intent as I traveled to those conferences to help both the brethren and the sisters better understand the importance and benefits of Relief Society. As I prepared I had prayed that I might effectively present my assigned talks, but after I delivered my first message in the Philippines, I could see I had not been as convincing as I had hoped.

I began to fast and pray more diligently than before. When I spoke in Taiwan, I gave my information about Relief Society, then asked each of the Brethren to stand, in turn, if they would like every woman of Relief Society age to attend Relief Society meeting every time she possibly could. President Spencer W. Kimball, President Marion G. Romney, Elder Gordon B. Hinckley, Elder Mark E. Petersen, Elder Marion D. Hanks, and Elder Yoshihiko Kikuchi all stood. Then the whole congregation seemed to come alive. It was what I had prayed would happen. As we traveled to Korea, I decided to ask President Kimball if he would feel all right if I followed that same procedure again. He said, "I think you have been inspired. I certainly would encourage you to do it."

It was raining when we arrived in Korea. The Saints had been praying for good weather, but it snowed during the night, too. We held the meeting in the chapel and cultural hall instead of out of doors as had been planned. When I spoke there, I again asked the Brethren to stand and even make brief comments regarding their feelings about Relief Society. I was very pleased with their affirmation of the Relief Society.

As the morning session concluded, President Kimball stated that he would go out and shake hands with those who could not find room in the building. To his surprise, hundreds were waiting outside for him. At lunch, President Kimball announced that if those Korean Saints could be out in the cold weather during the conference, so could the rest of us. The rest of the group then delivered their addresses outside. All arrangements were quickly finalized.

After delivering their talks the speakers sat down, shivering with cold. Some said they had never spoken under such difficult circumstances. The wind was blowing and it seemed to blow the words away. When President Kimball stood to speak, however, he didn't seem cold. He was calm and confident, and he spoke with great clarity. When he concluded his talk President Romney quietly said, "That was a miracle. We have just seen a miracle. That was a miracle."

I listened afterward and many people said those very same words to President Kimball, "That was a miracle."

Later I asked President Kimball how he felt about that talk and he smiled and he said, "I felt very good about it." For the rest of the conference he seemed to get stronger with each talk he delivered. I knew I had witnessed a miracle.

My trip to the Far East was especially valuable in bringing perspective to our efforts to adapt the Relief Society curriculum to all areas of the Church. It was increasingly apparent that the standard program was not suitable for every unit of Relief Society. The differences in the numbers of sisters, gospel readiness, and availability of materials all made trying to use the same program a daunting challenge. When I returned, a further effort to understand what the circumstances of the sisters were in the far-ranging areas of the Church, both in the United States and in countries abroad, was initiated. We called in sisters who had lived or served in many different areas of the world. They shared with us their knowledge and experiences regarding many locales of the world.

Utilizing their input, we were able to develop a three-phase organizational plan for implementing Relief Society worldwide. First-phase involvement was simplified to include only a Relief Society president and two counselors who completely directed the compassionate service, teaching, and homemaking experiences. The second phase expanded the organizational structure to facilitate developing programs. The third phase continued the full Relief Society program with many additional women called to share the responsibilities, allowing every woman the opportunity to have part in the three fundamental areas of Relief Society work. I then met with Brother Preston Nydegger from Church Translation Services and requested that the Relief Society materials be translated into the various foreign languages. He was most agreeable.

On the heels of a nationally publicized attack on the Church by a former member of the Church who strongly advocated ERA, a telephone call came from the program director of Phil Donahue's show. She said that Phil Donahue had invited Sonia Johnson, by then excommunicated from the Church for maligning Church leaders and policies, to be a guest on his show; she also asked if I would be interested in appearing on the program with Sonia Johnson. I told her that I would not. She asked me why. She said, "This is your great opportunity to tell the world what you think, as opposed to her opinion." I tried to explain that Sonia Johnson was already, although inaccurately, considered a martyr for women's rights and that if we appeared together on his program, what I had to say would not get proper attention. I suggested that Phil Donahue give Sonia Johnson the full program time, and then later give me a full hour. That way we could both be heard. The program director said that Mr. Donahue would never consider doing that. She then said, "Can you suggest anyone that would go on the show with Sonia Johnson to represent the Mormon Church?" I asked her to let me think about it.

I called her back about a day later and suggested that Beverly Campbell would be an appropriate person to ask. Beverly belonged to the same stake to which Sonia Johnson had belonged, and had been actively working against ERA. The program director thanked me and said they would probably ask Beverly Campbell, which they did.

Sister Campbell was at the beauty parlor getting her hair done for the appearance when she was contacted by the people from Phil Donahue's show. She was told that Sonia Johnson had refused to appear with her, and that they consequently did not want Beverly to come. Phil Donahue did give the full hour to Sonia Johnson, and he made the false statement that no woman from the Mormon Church would appear with his guest, Mrs. Johnson.

Mormon women all over the nation began to call in. Telephone calls were made to Beverly and she was asked if it was true that she had refused to appear. A great deal of media coverage ensued, explaining that Beverly Campbell was practically on her way to the airport when she was told not to come.

Angry and irate calls to Phil Donahue continued. Finally, I received another call and was told that if I would appear on Phil
Donahue's show, I could choose any one of three dates and I
could have the full hour. They would be happy to have me as a
guest. I asked if I might take Beverly Campbell with me. I told
them I thought they owed it to her to let her appear. They said
they would talk to Phil and get back with me, but they
thought it would be all right. When they called back again
and told me that Beverly could go on with me, they said, "The
only difference is that now only one date is available because
Phil is going to be out of town on the other two dates.

That didn't matter. We would be there, but we did expect
a public apology from Phil Donahue because he had said no
one would go on the show with Sonia Johnson, and that statement was not accurate. They said that would be fine. The date
and time were set.

I asked Elder Monson what he wanted me to say when I
appeared on Phil Donahue's show. His response was that I
should just be myself—be humble, but not let Phil Donahue
walk over me either. Elder Monson would be satisfied if I just
said one thing, "Tell them that we are for equal rights for
women, but against the Equal Rights Amendment as the way
to achieve them." That was no problem; I had said that so
many times before. President Monson's counsel, however, did
free me from the responsibility I was feeling of trying to explain all about the Church in those few moments before the
television cameras.

Elder Packer's response to a similar question was that I
shouldn't be unduly concerned: there would be millions of
people out there supporting me. The Church was a vital,
growing group who knew the truth, and many others would
want to hear the truth as well. He said, "Give them the answers to the questions they should have asked."

President Benson answered my question of what I should
say, with a question. He said, "You will go fasting and praying, won't you?" I said I would. He then said, "And we will be
praying for you, and the Lord will bless you." The advice of

those three members of the Quorum of the Twelve Apostles was enough to help me, and yet not enough to overwhelm me.

I called and talked with Utah's Senator Orrin Hatch for his insight regarding the Equal Rights Amendment. He spent over an hour talking with me, and then asked to be excused to cast a vote on the Senate floor. Later he called me back and we continued our conversation. I was humbly grateful to him.

I also talked with local media people in Salt Lake City. They all were generous and thoughtful with their time and suggestions for an effective guest appearance. These kinds of conversations continued with people from all walks of life right up to the night before I was to leave for Chicago.

It was then that our next-to-youngest daughter, who was expecting a baby, became seriously ill with toxemia and had to go to the hospital. She asked the doctor what toxemia meant as far as she and the baby were concerned. The doctor said, "It could mean that you'll get along fine. Then again, it could mean that you will go into convulsions, or it could mean that you will have a heart attack. We hope to prevent those from occurring and so we want you here where we can watch you." My daughter turned to her husband and asked him and her father to give her a blessing, which they did. Then I asked them if they would also give me a blessing before I went the next day to be on the show, and they did.

Douglas and I went home, and early the next morning we called the hospital and found that Catherine's situation had worsened. I hurried and put a few things in a small suitcase. My husband backed the car out. Running out the door with suitcase in hand, I slipped on the ice on the top step, and slid down about seven steps to the bottom. I ached and could have cried, but there was no time. I tried to catch my breath on the way to the hospital. We visited with Catherine until it was time to catch the flight. Douglas drove me out, then hurried back to the hospital. The plane was delayed. I waited for nearly two hours before it took off.

I was so concerned about Catherine that I nearly forgot that I had promised to go out to Naperville, near Chicago, to speak at a fireside that night. They were expecting a prepared address on the Equal Rights Amendment and had invited their legislators to attend.

Upon my arrival in Chicago, Steve Coltrin, the director of Church Public Communications in New York, Beverly Campbell, and I met for a few minutes to discuss what we wanted to say over national television about Mormon women. It was then time to go to Naperville.

On the way Brother Coltrin asked the stake Relief Society president to tell me about the tickets to Phil Donahue's show. She said that tickets had been really hard to acquire. But a block of fifty tickets had been given to one individual, not a member of the Church, to disperse, and this woman felt she had no use for them. So fifty tickets had been given to Mormon women. That was a wonderful surprise. We knew that at least some of the audience would be supporting us.

A very large audience was waiting when we arrived in Naperville. I asked the Regional Representative if he would like the meeting to last about one hour. He said, "I originally thought so, but there are so many people here and they are so anxious to hear what you have to say, that perhaps you'd better go an hour and a half." There were times during the years of my presidency when the direct intervention of the Lord was so obvious as to be unmistakable; the talk I gave that evening was one of those times. I felt my lack of specific preparation, but I had been talking about this subject constantly for a year. Sister Campbell talked to the audience for a short time, not wanting to detract from what I might want to say. I followed, shared some information and statistics, and then told them about my strong feelings on that vital subject.

As I concluded, I told them about my anxiety over my daughter back in the hospital. The benediction included a mighty plea to our Father in Heaven in behalf of my daughter and our about-to-be grandchild. When I arrived back in my hotel room the message light was on. I called home to find that the baby had been delivered. It was in distress, but also in the hands of a skilled pediatrician who had every hope that all would be well. My daughter's condition was very good. What a blessed relief!

That night, as might be expected, was a restless one. I was up early praying for divine help that I would not ruin the Church's image. I did not want to embarrass anyone; I wanted to be helpful in explaining what then appeared to be a very unpopular stand.

The next morning Sister Campbell and I met and went down to the lobby of the hotel to wait for the driver from the Donahue show to pick us up. We waited and waited, but he didn't come. Sister Campbell talked to the desk clerk. He told us not to worry; the driver always picked up the Donahue guests on time. After more waiting, she had the desk clerk call the television station. They said, "We didn't send him. We thought they would be coming with their own people." We quickly called a taxicab. Fortunately, the driver knew exactly which door to take us to. When we arrived at the studio, we had only minutes to spare before show time.

We were ushered into a board room and Phil Donahue came in. After asking us to identify ourselves, his conversation went something like this: "Welcome. Just a little advice. It seems like you have a long time when you think of an hour show, but with the involvement of the audience and the time out for commercials it goes by very quickly. The best counsel I can give you is to keep your answers short. Say what you want to say in as few words as you can. And please remember, this is not a show when you raise your hand if you want to talk. If you want to interrupt me, you do it. If I want to interrupt you, I will do it. But please, keep your answers short."

He went on the set to a burst of rousing applause. It was obvious that the audience loved him. He told them about his guests. Backstage, my arms had been full of books and tapes as evidence of things that Mormon women could do, and do well, but someone deterred me with, "Please don't take those things on. You look like a salesman." We made our entrance. There was some applause, but not at all with the warmth that Phil Donahue received.

I was so nervous that when I tried to talk it was as if my mouth were full of cotton. I was already dry from fasting, but with those hot lights and the tension of the situation I could hardly get enough moisture to speak. The stage crew noticed

the problem and kindly brought me a drink during the first
station break.

Phil Donahue did apologize to us as the program began,
for giving a false impression about Mormon unwillingness to
appear with Sonia Johnson, and he did offer us the opportunity to present our position. Ordinarily, his shows from Chicago were call-in shows. Ours was taped for later presentation
and so the interaction was with the audience. I liked it better
that way because we could look directly at those who questioned us and tell them of our convictions.

I could not talk fast enough. As the show came to an end he
gave each of us a chance to make a closing statement. I tried to
tell the audience about five things they should know about us
and our beliefs, but time went too quickly and I didn't get all
five points explained. However, I must admit that if I'd had
my way the program would not have been as effective. In the
time frame of the program Phil Donahue had asked questions
that were on the minds of many people. Those people would
not have been nearly as receptive if I had only told them what
I thought they should hear. After that television appearance, I
had a new perspective on the scripture that states, "Their seed
shall be known among the Gentiles" (Isaiah 61:9). I never sus-
pected that being known among the Gentiles would include
my appearing for the Church on a nationally syndicated television talk show.

About two years later, Phil Donahue came to do a broadcast from Salt Lake City. I debated whether to call him, but
decided I should take the opportunity to introduce him to
some of the fine Mormon women in the valley and give him a
tour of the Relief Society Building. I did call the hotel telephone operator who checked with Phil Donahue. Immediately
she called back to indicate that his schedule was too tight to fit
anything else in, but he requested that I come to a private reception being held for him that evening. He invited Douglas to
accompany me.

Douglas and I had no tickets for the reception, but when
we arrived, one of his staff recognized me and said that Mr.
Donahue wanted us to be brought into the private reception
then in progress. Phil was there with his delightful wife, Marlo

Thomas, and a few other people I did not know. When Phil greeted me, he exclaimed, "You have no idea how many thousands of letters we received after your appearance on the show."

I responded, "I received a few thousand letters and telephone calls myself!"

"Why didn't you tell me of all the problems you were having when you went on the show?" he continued.

"There really wasn't time, and you wouldn't have been interested in my family problems, anyway," I replied.

"But I would have," he protested, "and I would have treated you much nicer on the show."

We visited for a short while, and he then asked if I would accompany him into the grand ballroom for the formal reception. He said he wanted us to be seen together. I walked beside him, and Douglas escorted his wife, Marlo. With the ballroom packed full of people, I found it amazing how few in the room I knew. We talked a short while longer, and I indicated I had to leave. In mock dismay he said, "Don't leave me alone with all these people!"

I laughed and, giving him a knowing smile, said, "People are your business."

We did talk a bit more and, as he bade me good-bye, he said, "Don't let this be the end. Write me, call me, do something—keep in touch."

On his television show the next day he said that he continued to have ongoing conversations with Barbara Smith, who lived in Salt Lake City and who had been his guest on a program originating in Chicago.

There had been some question about the value of having the general president of the Relief Society appear on such a controversial talk show. I thought I should do it primarily because many women of the Church wanted to have someone speak up for them. The telephoned and written responses both Phil Donahue and I received after that appearance seemed to validate my reasoning.

19

Gleaning in His Fields

And when ye reap the
harvest of your land, thou
shalt not wholly reap the
corners of thy field,
neither shalt thou gather
the gleanings of thy
harvest.
— Leviticus 19:9

J anuary 30, 1981 . . . Met with Elder Petersen and Elder Larsen regarding the restoration of the Sarah Kimball Home." Those lines from my journal reminded me of how many months we had been engaged in the restoration project before it was finally dedicated in March of 1982 to honor the 140th anniversary of the Relief Society's founding. The Sarah Kimball Home means something special to all women of the Church because it was there that the idea of Relief Society was conceived. Seeking a way to help with the work on the Nauvoo Temple, Sarah and others determined to organize the women to sew for the men and give compassionate service. While our intent in restoring the home was focused more on Relief Society than on Sarah Kimball herself, it is interesting to note that the project also helped to fulfill a promise made by the Prophet Joseph Smith to Sister Kimball.

Sarah Melissa Granger was just fifteen years old when she went to Kirtland to join the Saints. The records indicate that she was interested in Church doctrines and revelations and that she used to discuss religious matters with her father. Later she attended the School of the Prophets. In her early twenties she married Hiram Kimball. Sarah was a member of the Church, but Hiram was not; he did join the Church later. When their first baby was born, the Nauvoo Temple walls were only about three feet above their foundation. The Saints lacked the money they needed to complete the building. Sarah wanted to make a contribution to the temple project, but she wanted it to be her contribution alone, not her husband's; and even though he was financially well off and could afford to give generously to the Church, contributions from her husband didn't meet her needs as she saw them. She thought a great deal about how she could fulfill her responsibility. Then she had an idea. She had a baby boy just three days old. When her husband came home later that day and came to her bedside to admire the baby, she asked, "What is the boy worth?"

"Oh, I don't know," he said. "He's worth a great deal."

"Is he worth a thousand dollars?" she queried.

"Yes, more than that if he lives and does well."

"Then," she said, "half of him is mine, is it not?"

"Yes, I suppose so," he replied.

"I have something, then, to help with the temple," she said.

"Have you?" questioned her husband.

"Yes, I think I'll turn my share [of the baby] in as tithing," she responded.

"Well, I'll see about that," said her husband.

Soon after that conversation her husband met with the Prophet Joseph. Hiram said, "Sarah proposes to turn over the boy as Church property." He then related their entire discussion to the Prophet.

President Joseph Smith seemed pleased with the joke: "I accept all such donations," was his reply, "and from this day the boy shall stand recorded as Church property." He turned to Willard Richards and directed, "Make a record of this, and you are my witness."

Turning to Hiram, Joseph said, "Major, you now have the privilege of paying $500 and retaining possession, or receiving $500 and giving possession," to which the new father responded, "Will you accept the reserve block of property north of the temple [as payment]?"

"It is just what we want," said the Prophet.

The deed was made out. Later the Prophet said to Sarah, "You have consecrated your firstborn son. For this you are blessed of the Lord. . . . Your name shall be handed down in honorable remembrance from generation to generation." (See Augusta Joyce Crocheron, *Representative Women of Deseret* [Salt Lake City: J.C. Graham and Co., 1884], pp. 23–24.)

Perhaps the restoration of the Sarah Kimball Home was part of that "honorable remembrance" that the Prophet promised.

However, this was not the only thing worthy of note that Sarah Kimball did, for her commitment to the cause of Zion was unflagging and she continued to demonstrate this in myriad ways as a remarkable example of devotion and independent strength. After she came to the territory of Deseret she became the Relief Society president of the Fifteenth Ward. The sisters, under her direction, made woolen cloth, carpet rags, spools of cotton, baby stockings, crewel, and braid. They dried fruits, made shoes and moccasins, and sold them all to earn money to build a Relief Society hall. They helped buy a ward organ. They built a granary and stocked it with grain. They also helped build the Salt Lake and Logan temples and the Deseret Hospital. They provided carpet for the ward meetinghouse. They purchased a knitting machine and set up a tailoring establishment within the ward. They sent assistance to those who suffered in the Chicago fire.

They mailed the *Woman's Exponent* to sisters in England too poor to subscribe. They founded a ward library and sponsored quarterly parties for the widows and aged of the ward. Under Sarah's leadership they began a ward kindergarten, financed a professional teacher, and also paid the tuition for needy students.

We felt that the spirit of Sarah Kimball seemed particularly appropriate for the women of the early 1980s, many of whom were having difficulty resolving the messages they were hearing in the cacophony that was the "women's cause."

Typical of the concerns raised by the women's movement for the Latter-day Saint woman was a letter from a twenty-five-year-old woman in New Mexico: "The reason I am writing this letter is because I have a question which I hope you will be able to help clear up in my mind. You see I really do not understand the role of a woman in the Church or in this life."

It is a question I had been asked before by many people, both those in the Church and those not of our faith. It was a difficult, important, and significant question.

The "role of a woman" has become one of the most-discussed questions of the last decade. Many trivialize the traditional role of women; many defend the traditional role of women. The gulf between them is wide and deep.

Part of the difficulty encountered in answering that question resulted from trying to describe a woman's mission on earth in terms of a woman's "role." The word *role* is very limiting. It suggests a part, like a part in a play, and requires definitive statements that cannot be applied to all women everywhere.

In a play each role is carefully fashioned to depict certain human beings in specific situations. These roles consist of carefully crafted moments upon the stage as the audience sees one or two characters grow and change under the fire of the given forces that have been set into play by the author.

Writing a play is one of the most demanding forms of human expression. Good playwrights cut thousands of words and hundreds of lines from their work before it is finished, so that each scene carefully builds toward the play's climax. There is no time for extraneous lines or the whole fabric of the play is lost. The playwright cannot indulge in exploring unnecessary byways to reach the human heart.

Each role being played is defined and, in a good play, skillfully designed. The time devoted to the role is limited. The emotional conflicts to be viewed are carefully arranged.

However, no matter how great the moment on the stage, and many great ones have illuminated understanding, the role is nevertheless a skillfully crafted one representing the limited view that we see.

Women do not fit into such carefully crafted roles in everyday life. Their lives cannot be successfully molded into a "role." To consider all women in terms of one role is a mistake, for each woman has many roles and often plays them simultaneously with no scripted, pre-designed endings.

The people she meets are not selected and controlled characters. She must walk the streets of a city or the paths of a countryside quite uncertain as to who will walk into her life from day to day. Certainly in some situations she will control with whom she will spend her time. But at other times she will face the unknown and confront problems and situations she has never before thought of.

All of us come into this world as a one-of-a-kind person with unlimited potential for growth and development. We have agency. We have talents. We have to increase "in wisdom and stature, and in favour with God and man" from day to day (Luke 2:52). We will have times when our days feel as Shakespeare described them: "Tomorrow, and tomorrow, and tomorrow, creeps in this petty pace" (*Macbeth*). And we will have times when Maxwell Anderson's line is most appropriate: "I came here seeking light in darkness, running from dawn, and stumbled on a morning" (Maxwell Anderson, *Winterset*, [New York: Harcourt, Brace, Jovanovich], p. 127).

Life for each of us is like that. It has highs and lows. It has mountains to climb and valleys to cross. It has light and it does indeed have shadows. Just as in plays, good people and bad people come into our lives. Some of them wield enormous power over us. And, just as in plays, there are sequences of events which profoundly affect our lives.

Life is an amalgamation of many things. We do not select eighteen or twenty scenes to play and then proceed to act out those scenes. Each day to us is a fresh new start and our choices during that day will shape and influence not only that day but our entire lives. Lack of good choices will also have a profound influence upon us eternally.

When our Heavenly Father chose his Beloved Son, Jesus Christ, to come to earth, he rejected Lucifer's proposal because our life here had to be much more than a carefully orchestrated series of scenes and roles. All souls needed this time on earth to learn to walk by faith, to choose good over evil, and to live a mortal life—because mortality is essential to each one of us if we are to develop our full capabilities.

President Spencer W. Kimball very carefully explained that the words of the scriptures apply to all of us. In one conference he closed his remarks by stating: "I hope you have taken copious notes, not so much on what the speakers have said, because you can always reread them in the *Ensign*, but notes on the thoughts that have come to you individually and the way their messages apply to each one of you." (Conference Report, October 1975.)

We must individually apply to our lives the words given to us both in the scriptures and by the prophets and Apostles. Both urge us to look to the life of the Savior as our perfect example.

Look to our living prophet. He holds the keys of the kingdom at this moment in time. Listen to his words and believe. Remember the basic assignments which the Lord has given us to help us in our time on earth: First, that we need the experience of mortality in order to prepare for the eternal life we aspire to attain. Second, we are here, in the world of mortals, to learn to walk by faith. Once we commit ourselves to walking by faith we must continue that quest as we practice faith and learn to make it a significant power in our lives.

This instruction is not for only certain of God's children; it is for all of us. If we need role models, we should turn to the scriptures and find the great women of faith who preceded us. They are there, recorded in holy writ. Read of Eve's elevating words spoken after the Lord had explained the error of Adam and Eve and what must result. She said, "Were it not for our transgression we never should have had seed, and never should have known good and evil, and the joy of our redemption, and the eternal life which God giveth unto all the obedient" (Moses 5:11).

Think of Mary, the mother of Jesus. What greater example of a woman blessed of the Lord could we have? Think of her response to the angel: "Behold the handmaid of the Lord; be it unto me according to thy word" (Luke 1:38).

Sarah, the wife of Abraham, became the mother of nations. She was blessed of the Lord because of her obedience to his direction.

Elisabeth, Mary's cousin, understood that, as the angel said, "With God nothing shall be impossible" (Luke 1:37). Her son, John the Baptist, given life and training because of his mother, could then fulfill prophecy. It was also by obedience that Sariah and Lehi came to the American continent. I can't even begin to imagine how hard it must have been to leave a house of plenty to travel in the wilderness. It was also by adherence to the restored truth that Sarah Kimball received her promises from the Lord. Life was not easy for any of them, I am sure, but they understood the importance of faith and obedience. It was the way pioneer women helped to build cities. It was the way Zion was built in the tops of the mountains.

Finally, we are here to learn. From the very beginning Adam and Eve were told to replenish the earth and to subdue it. We know that we can only subdue the earth by discovering and learning the laws which govern the universe and then by living in accordance with those laws.

Eve, Mary, Elisabeth, Sarah, Sariah, the pioneer women. Women of those times worked with the great men of God, and we still benefit from their work.

We had to understand the laws of gravity before we could learn to suspend them and fly. But that has been done. We had to understand the laws which govern this earth before we could break through the barriers which kept us from the moon. The Lord has told us that there is a law that governs all things both on earth and in heaven. If we would return to live with him, then we must be willing to abide by the laws of heaven.

The Lord has explained these things through the scriptures and through his anointed servants. We will also open our understanding if we will but knock. He even offers to reason with us as one man reasoneth with another. I hope each of us will put herself in a position to have her mind opened to his plan and purposes.

My mind was opened to a greater understanding of God one day as I merely walked through the cactus garden at the Huntington Art Gallery. As I was told of the hundreds of varieties of cacti which grow upon the face of the earth, I suddenly realized that I could not create one plain blade of grass. I was overwhelmed with the power and majesty of the Lord, who could create almost endless varieties of intricate cacti. How that thought filled my soul with wonder and appreciation for the Lord. I could then read each line of the scriptures with more reverence, greater understanding, and deeper appreciation than before.

A simple experience perhaps, yet profound to me. It enabled me to understand, from that time on, that if we learn a principle of the gospel and live it, we can prove to ourselves that, with each law we accept, we grow in wisdom and in knowledge and increase our vision of life and its purposes. Our vision and insight then expand so that we may receive new insights and new growth. Through the plan of life and salvation we grow one step at a time.

All should seek understanding on the question of a woman's role in the Church and in society through this same process of discovery and insight. Fundamentally, a woman not only needs to seek understanding and live all of the principles of truth which the Lord has revealed to his children, but must also realize that he excludes no one; there are no qualifying factors for either men or women when the Lord teaches.

Now, I would not want you to think that no differences exist between men and women. They do. I just want you to know that it is very easy for me to understand that each soul is of infinite worth to our Heavenly Father. Douglas and I have seven children, sons and daughters, and each one is loved profoundly, personally, fully, and completely. In the infinite wisdom of the Lord, there is no other way than this for him to look upon his children. They are all of great value—his sons and his daughters. He wants us to understand that, and so he has said, "Neither is the man without the woman, neither the woman without the man, in the Lord" (1 Corinthians 11:11).

His plan is that we join together, men and women, in the great creative work of bringing children into the world that they, too, might profit from the mortal experience. Their highest good and growth are dependent upon our learning to work together as one. In the infinite wisdom of God it is necessary for all to do their assigned work and to make themselves worthy to continue to grow endlessly in his presence.

Some women think, because they have not married, that they are outside of the Lord's plan. Don't think for one moment that the Lord did not plan for those who are single in this life. He has enabled them to grow in love and in service even though they do not have immediate access to personal family experiences as a parent. The single woman prepared by life's opportunities and responsibilities should remember the words of Mary, the mother of Jesus, and of the angel, Gabriel: "Be it unto me according to thy word" (Luke 1:38), and "With God nothing shall be impossible" (Luke 1:37).

Consider one of the major assignments from the Lord to his sons: to function in the administrative responsibilities of his Church here upon the earth. He has called prophets, Apostles, Regional Representatives, stake presidents, branch presidents, bishops, home teachers, and mission presidents to serve in these positions. It is true that he has delegated assignments to women through these priesthood leaders in the governing councils at various levels of Church administration, and the sisters' work in the kingdom is important; but the power under which women operate is the priesthood power given to men to act in behalf of the Lord. We must honor and respect and claim the blessings of that power.

To women he has given a vital assignment. He has fashioned us biologically in such a way that women alone must carry out this task: the right, responsibility, and opportunity to bear children and nurture them through their tender years of infancy and youth, to be with them, to teach them, to protect them, to prepare them for that which is to come, to love them—this is a great work. It is fundamentally the work for which the earth was created. It should be viewed by all as being of singular importance in the plan of the Lord. A human race would not exist if women were to abdicate their assignment in this regard. In order to become as God is, we must have a mortal body. We must have the opportunity to prove ourselves. We must be tested and tried in mortality. We must experience life, with its vital teachings and training, however long or brief our stay.

Someone once said, "Next to God himself we are indebted to women, first for life and next for making life worth living."

A young college man decided to earn some extra money for his schooling by working with only men for the entire summer in an Alaskan shrimp cannery. There he gained an appreciation for the ability of women to make life worthwhile. After the three months were over, he came home and said, "I had no idea how desperately I would miss women. It wasn't just dating women that I missed up there, where I never saw a woman, but their refining influence, the gentle, kind words they speak. Vulgarity and profanity became commonplace there. The atmosphere deteriorated to the lowest level of living. Without women, men no longer dressed to look their best. Most of them never shaved. Their homes were sloppy. I can truly testify that it is not good for man to be alone."

That young man would have likely agreed with George Hermes, who avowed, "A beautiful and chaste woman is the perfect workmanship of God, the true glory of angels, the rare miracle of earth, and the sole wonder of the world." (*The New Dictionary of Thoughts* [Standard Book Company, 1960], p. 732.)

When the beautiful and chaste woman brings forth children and raises them in the ways of the Lord, in obedience and faith, they can grow toward their divine potential. Only then can women fulfill their essential, invaluable responsibility. It is sad when women do not understand their important part in the plan of life. Dr. James Dobson suggests:

> If I could write a prescription for the women of the world, I would provide each one of them with a healthy dose of self-esteem and personal worth (taken three times a day until the symptoms disappear). I have no doubt that this is their greatest need. . . . If women felt genuinely respected . . . they would not need . . . something better. If they felt equal with men in personal worth, they would not need to be equivalent to men in responsibility. If they could only bask in the dignity and status granted to them by the Creator, then their femininity would be valued as their greatest asset, rather than scorned as an old garment to be discarded. Without question, the future of a nation depends on how it sees its women, and I hope we will teach our little girls to be glad they were chosen by God for the special pleasures of womanhood.
>
> (Joyce Landorf, *The Fragrance of Beauty* [Wheaton, Illinois: Victor Books S. P. Publishers, Inc., 1981].)

The future of any woman or her family depends upon how she views her womanhood. I interpret the "special pleasures" of womanhood to be those I have just mentioned: "Bringing forth life and making life worth living." I think I recognize the challenges women face as they make decisions regarding their lives. Let me share with you the choice made by one beautiful, young, single returned missionary.

Almost two years after her mission she decided to depart from the traditional job opportunities most often accepted by women. She didn't want to be a teacher, a secretary, a nurse, or a clerk. She took instead a marketing position that required her to sell, and to contact many heads of firms in their Eastern city offices. To her surprise, most of the business executives with whom she worked were transacting business not in the office, but in a more informal setting. They combined business with pleasure, and each day seemed to her like one big party.

She soon found that the morals of the men and women in the world she had entered were not the same as the morals in her carefully protected situation of the past. Many married men made improper advances to her. She learned quickly how to say no while smiling and saying, "That's sheer culture shock to a young Mormon girl from Utah." Often her response would result in a religious discussion.

She found that some things were imperative if she was to earn the money she needed, be effective in her job, and still maintain her standards. She learned that she had to:

1. Work hard, know her product, and make a great presentation. It was challenging, demanding, and exciting.

2. Work hard to keep her faith strong. She took her scriptures with her, prayed faithfully, sought LDS singles groups in the cities where she worked, and attended Sunday services. She also welcomed invitations of families to attend their family home evenings.

3. Constantly remember that having a family of her own was the most important direction of her life. Because of

that she determined she would always be a beautiful, chaste woman—it would be her priority first, foremost, and forever.

She learned to focus on her objectives by doing creative handwork which helped her to remember who she was and what her standards were. One sampler she completed featured a beehive with the motto "East or West, Home is Best." Under those words she embroidered in counted cross-stitch, "Trust in the Lord with all thine heart; and lean not unto thine own understanding. In all thy ways acknowledge him, and he shall direct thy paths." (Proverbs 3:5–6.)

There is no question but that the challenge is to remain morally clean; with the promiscuous life-styles displayed by the media and the high acceptance of immorality by worldly standards, it is difficult now and it will become increasingly difficult.

But the law of chastity is simple and direct. No sexual relationships should occur before marriage and only strict fidelity should exist afterwards. Thus the Lord can help us sanctify our lives and build a cornerstone of trust upon which eternal families can be built in the hereafter. Adherence to the law of chastity will save us from enormous pain and sorrow and permit us to become the blessed of the Father.

A young mother of five children became involved in some rather demanding political activities. Every day she left her children to go to her newest interest. Her mother counseled, "Dear, you must stay home and tend to the needs of your children," to which the young mother replied, "Oh, Mother, you are so old-fashioned. We live in a different generation from the one you lived in. I'm organized. I can do what the children need to have done in one hour. When I leave they are well taken care of. Our generation has to be up and doing. We are progressive. We are here to accomplish worthwhile things, not to spend our time wiping noses and doing housework. Really, we are beyond dishes, dusting, and diapering babies. Someone with less ability can do those menial tasks."

It was never intended that home become a prison for a Latter-day Saint woman, or for any woman. It was never anyone's intent in the Church to circumscribe the ways in which a woman might contribute to society or to the world in which she lives. On the contrary, women have been encouraged to utilize and expand their abilities—but not at a time when we would threaten the potential of those nearest and dearest to us. Women must understand the purpose of the home as a great learning center where the nurturing and training of children take place. There have always been mitigating circumstances that make it necessary for some women to leave their children and work outside the home; but for the majority of homes, the responsibility for the care of the children must be carried out by mothers who give their children their time, their full concern, and their loving attention.

Statistics are piling up which indicate that more and more mothers of small children are either working out of the home or becoming involved in out-of-the-home projects. More and more children are being left alone in empty houses. More and more children are being given to others to care for from early morning until late at night.

Where will the children learn the moral foundations for their lives? Where will children learn of God and his ways? Where will children get the tender and individual love they need? We simply cannot ignore the implications of these questions. We must not fail to recognize the destructive ramifications resulting from lack of adequate love and care for our children.

Any woman who bears or adopts a child is responsible for the care and the training of that child. Very quickly the moments of childhood go by; they will not come again, and all too often children are left facing life alone, unprepared. They look back at their home life and find—what? Life without the essential tender, loving care to which they are entitled. They must be taught of love and of God if they are to have faith and testimony. They need an example if they are to have the firm foundation necessary to set and achieve eternal goals. The saddest time for anyone is when he or she feels unwanted. As for the mother, her opportunity to help her children grow and develop in favor with God and man, as did Mary with her son Jesus, is short-lived. It is but a brief few years. I remember my mother's counsel, "Spend every minute you can with your children; they will be grown and gone before you realize it." I thought, "Mother, you have forgotten how tied down you can be with seven little ones." Now I know she was right.

Our Heavenly Father constantly reiterates in the scriptures the great value of the individual soul, each a unique individual, unrepeated and unduplicated in all of creation—a uniqueness existing not just in cactus, or in trees, or in flowers, or in birds, but in his children as well. He had provided a gospel plan. It is the plan of salvation for each human soul. The struggles are fundamentally the same for all of us. The ordinances of salvation are the same for all of us. Each human being is given different assignments from time to time, but all of the blessings of the priesthood are available for each of his children.

Perhaps the most significant and deepening insight I gained during my term of office is that the key factor in salvation and exaltation is individual choice, a principle we have the opportunity to live by. Will we choose to live by eternal principles and climb mountains and cross valleys and come into an eternal morning where truth and light await the faithful and obedient? Will we determine to devote our lives to this eternal quest and search diligently for the truth, no matter how different or difficult our circumstances?

To my young friend in New Mexico who wrote, asking me to define the role of women in this life, and to all who ask, let me urge upon each an understanding of the rich potential for growth available to us in this mortal experience; if we are not diverted from our path, we too will become the blessed of the Father.

The Prophet Joseph Smith left a message with the sisters that I believe is important for all of us today, when he said: "After this instruction you will be responsible for your own sins. It is an honor to save yourselves; we are all responsible to save ourselves." (Joseph Smith, *Teachings of the Prophet Joseph Smith*, sel. Joseph Fielding Smith [Salt Lake City: Deseret Book Co., 1939], p. 227.) To do that we need to listen to the right voices and make our choices in light of the Lord's plan for us.

Being Fruitful

That ye might walk
worthy of the Lord unto
all pleasing, being fruitful
in every good work.
—Colossians 1:10

During my first seven years in office, an important aspect of the Relief Society responsibility had been the supervision of the creation and distribution of temple clothing. Sister Marian Boyer had worked with Reba Aldous and they had done an excellent and tasteful service in guiding the design and operation of the distribution centers set up in Tokyo, London, Sydney, Sao Paulo, Bern, and in many locations throughout the United States. That was a time in which we consolidated 177 stake and mission garment- and temple-clothing outlets into a convenient mail-order department, thus enabling members living at a distance to have easier access to the clothing. The responsibility for this work had been assigned to the Relief Society by President Joseph F. Smith. With the changeover, the work was assigned on April 8, 1981, to the management of the Presiding Bishopric, who had the stewardship for Church temporal business operations within the system.

If we were sorry to give over the work of sacred clothing (for we had afforded it loving attention), we surely had no difficulty in utilizing the extra time that the shift created. With the growth of the Church an ever-present challenge, we continued to urge the implementation of the three phases of Relief Society, which would enable the essential elements of service —visiting teaching, lesson instruction, and homemaking—to

operate in any Relief Society group in the world, regardless of
its size and its leadership abilities. The flexible three-phase
program afforded the organization of local presidencies to
oversee every unit and to add additional parts of the program
to it as the group enlarged. There were service opportunities
and interest groups which could respond to the needs of the sisters and still allow growth within the context of Relief Society.
A response to need was the guide, and a fruitful Relief Society
experience for every woman was the aim of this innovative
step.

To help sisters understand the nature of this flexible plan
and the board member positions that functioned within it, we
offered orientations by appointment to presidency groups who
came to the Relief Society Building. Many did come, and this
became a significant part of the work of our office. We were
pleased with the close association this setting afforded us with
stake Relief Society leaders.

Other groups also came to the building. We invited working women so that we could hear their story. Of course, we
found that they did not have "a" story, but that there were as
many different situations and feelings described as there were
women. We did find them of one voice, however, in concern
for their children. Although they did not resent working outside their homes—and many were doing so by choice and because they liked it—those who still had children in their homes
did have anxieties for them and their welfare, knowing that
those children were not always getting the measure of attention from them that they felt was needed. Meetings like these
with the women of the Church were most helpful to us as we
attempted to effectively respond to concerns, and express those
responses in ways that could be beneficial to the individuals in
need.

One group I met with had problems so complex as to almost defy solutions. These were the handicapped. I visited
their centers and learned of the kind of help being offered to
them in the form of clothing, learning materials, and appara-
tus. But the most heartening realization I gained was of the
potential within handicapped persons themselves—the un-

tapped strength within them to help themselves and others. I know now how important it is that we all develop an awareness within ourselves and within our society for the tremendous potential that exists among those who live with handicaps.

I continued to learn more about their challenges and about the conditions in which they live when Maree Kolendar took me to a red, rambler-type home where some of Utah's mentally handicapped lived. I was very impressed with the cleanliness of the institution and the love that all who worked there showed to those who were institutionalized. Maree said that it would be most helpful if volunteers would come forward who would give the men and women who lived there some assistance. If a volunteer could take one of those persons on a city bus and teach him how to ask for directions, it would make the handicapped person a little more independent. "Training sessions could be arranged to suit the time of the volunteer," she said.

Soon after that my nephew invited me to go to a rest home for elderly men and women. It was enlightening and, at the same time, heartrending. Some of the elderly were up and around, others were contented to lie in bed. Some wanted to be waited on, and still others were trying to help one another. I wept when I met five women who were former Relief Society presidents. No longer could they reach out in compassion. The time of their service had passed, and now—day in and day out —they were dependent upon the service of others.

I was interested to find in the dictionary this definition of the word *handicap:* "Any encumbrance or disadvantage that makes success more difficult." These words call to my mind the bottom line of the problem. Some living among us have problems that make their success more difficult. Therefore, the most appropriate thing we can do for a person with a handicap is to accept the responsibility of doing all we can to make "success" possible for each of them—even if his struggle is greater and longer and more intense than that of others.

We should remove from our thinking and feeling those attitudes and actions which make so many of us turn almost automatically away from them. Those who are handicapped sense it when we turn away or walk around them so that we do not pass close by. They feel it when we pity them but do not reach out to comfort and love them. We miss so much when we allow ourselves to have such feelings of prejudice or discrimination—even if they occur because we don't know how to respond appropriately.

As I listened to a panel composed of people in wheelchairs I heard them discuss the problems of the handicapped. They said, "People often look at us *as* wheelchairs. We are not wheelchairs. We are people. If you get to know us, a small miracle will happen in your lives. You'll learn to like us."

The truth of their appeal seemed to flower in my own life and was later brought to my attention by one of the stake Relief Society presidents who accompanied me to the meeting. She reported that after the meeting she walked into a shoe store and found herself face to face with a man in a wheelchair, whom she did not know. She said, "Normally I would not have stepped forward to speak to him, but this time, because of the panel I had attended, I did. A very interesting twenty-minute conversation followed, and we left feeling that we were the best of friends." She was really excited by her experience and wanted to help others know the same joy she felt.

Often we rob ourselves when we fail to take the time to get acquainted with people who struggle with handicaps. Sometimes the very intensity of their efforts gives them insights and experiences we will never know unless we can learn from them. They actually shed a new light and understanding upon our own lives. I would hope that we all would try to be more sensitive and much more responsive every day to the people around us who struggle for success with handicaps, handicaps as constant as they are disabling. Four guidelines may be helpful in this endeavor:

First, being genuine in our responses requires us to understand the real problem. For example, Marianne Fisher told me, "I was born blind to parents who loved and wanted me. There are those who would say that a handicap is merely a 'nuisance.' But in reality, a handicap is an existing, real thing

—something to be surmounted. How true the old adage, 'Where there's a will, there's a way.' Success has come to me because I have been selective in my goals; I have studied the best methods for reaching those goals, and I have had the determination and perseverance to attain them; but my goals have required that many people help me. These people have recognized me as a person, and they have found out that my blindness is only a difference."

In the Relief Society Resource Center many teaching displays were prepared. One display gave those who took the time to look and listen a sense for what it meant to live with limited vision, tunnel vision, cataracts, or even blindness. Another display invited participation in the simple exercise of trying to button an article of clothing with one hand, zipping a zipper with a stroke-numbed body, or lacing a shoe without the use of fingers.

When my father was almost eighty years old, he had an aneurysm in his abdomen. In order to save his life and give him better blood circulation, his doctor determined that my father must have his leg amputated. It was decided that my father alone should make that decision. While he was still in the intensive care unit, he was asked to give his permission for the surgery. He said that he really wanted to live a little longer and if the only way he could do it was to have his leg amputated, they must go ahead and do it. My heart ached for him in the subsequent weeks and months that followed, as I watched him struggle to regain his health and learn how to balance his body on only one leg. It was wrenchingly difficult. Time after time, before he learned to adjust his balance and compensate for his missing limb, he fell heavily. I learned more of courage from him than I had ever learned before.

I came to know President J.R. Larsen when the Relief Society dedicated the Garden of Monuments in Nauvoo. He had been injured in a jeep accident when he was serving in the armed forces. He determined, however, that he would not be relegated to a minor role in life, and he struggled to live a normal, demanding life without the use of his legs. He was fortunate because he had a patient, devoted, tender, loving wife to care for him, so he was able to continue his schooling. He became the dean of the College of Life Sciences at the University of Illinois and president of the Champaign Stake.

President Larsen manages to get himself in and out of his car and in and out of his wheelchair with a skill that belies the seriousness of his handicap, and all the while he directs major projects. He became the executive producer of our *Because of Elizabeth* commemorative pageant in Nauvoo. Later he orchestrated a single-adult area conference that he wanted carried out with excellence. He helps his coworkers understand that his problem is just a touch of inconvenience in getting about, but has nothing to do with the vigor of his mind, with the quality of his spirit, or with his immense capacity for doing and serving.

Those of us who do not have obvious disadvantages need to become aware, when we see the great capacities of the handicapped, of the struggle they have. We must help them fulfill their desire to use and develop their strengths.

The second guideline is to understand the great value of human life. People who come to mortality with handicaps can often teach us great lessons about that.

Life offers problems of aging, and of handicaps even in children. Some children must be taught, through a laborious process called patterning, what for most children are the simple skills of crawling and walking. Time and time again therapists patiently move the little bodies through motions that they hope the child's muscles and mind will eventually learn to do on their own. So like that patterning are the processes of family living. Over and over, patiently we lead children in the pattern of gospel living that we hope will eventually be learned and adopted as their own. Humility, thankfulness, concern for others, and integrity are but a few of the attributes we hope will someday function naturally, given time with these fledgling fathers and mothers, bishops, home teachers, visiting teachers, and primary presidents. As with the patterning for the handicapped child, the hope of success in patterning such a life-style lies in our own sure grasp and our consistency in daily living. Even so, each maturing child must eventually choose, making an independent choice of how to live this life.

At a luncheon where the coveted award of the Woman of Conscience for 1981 was presented, I met the recipient of the award. Her name was Anne Carlsen. She manages a school for the handicapped. She works with children from four to twenty-five years of age and says, "The work is hard, but we get special joy when we hear of our graduates in today's highly competitive world finding employment as teachers, computer programmers, accountants, radio announcers, mechanics, physicists, and in other vocations."

An article written about the day when Anne H. Carlsen was born reads:

> Laughter and joy greet most births. This time, mother, father, and the doctor cried. Before them lay an infant with only stumps for arms, six inches of thigh for one leg, and a withered, twisted stump for the other leg.
>
> Finally Alfred Carlsen, the father, picked up the small bundle wrapped in a warm blanket. "We will thank God for this new life," he said. "We shall wrap our love around this little girl and do everything we can to bring happiness to her."

And they did—father, mother, four brothers, and one sister. She was loved and she was educated, and she has gone on to give a lifetime of love and education to many others who have needed her.

I left that luncheon with a profound conviction that when the miracle of life is blended with the miracle of love, both the person with the handicap and the person desiring to give help can bring to pass greater miracles than this world has dared to envision.

The third guideline is to become fully cognizant of the great importance of attitude. The topic of a conference held in Chicago was "Serving the Handicapped Child." The panelists there constantly recommended and referred to two key words —*attitude* and *treatment*.

One of the great concepts advanced during this century is that when men and women change their attitudes, they can change the course of their lives. The experience of handicapped people certainly verifies this. Time and time again, accounts of handicapped people tell us that a positive attitude has allowed them to find success even on their jarring road of disadvantages and seeming disasters.

A boy in Oregon plays the organ for a group to which he belongs. It's a stunning achievement, because he was born without hands.

A woman who has a disabling disease that has been slowly robbing her of her ability to walk has nevertheless received many appointments to major state committees because she continues to achieve against numbing odds.

A woman whose arms hang helpless because of a fall on the ice has found that she can accomplish certain things with her life that she didn't know were possible. She is a blessing to all who know her.

With a positive attitude people with handicaps can often remake the world to fit what they insist it can be. However, almost always that positive attitude has to be inculcated by a loved one, a friend, or a teacher who believes and who loves endlessly.

The fourth guideline is to love enough to reach those who need us; to love enough to help another person climb over the rocks and through the rough places. What greater joy can we know than to be a part of the journey of discovery that a handicapped individual must make! Watching the play *The Miracle Worker*, one experiences the magic moment when Anne Sullivan, the teacher, finally helps Helen Keller, the blind and deaf child, make the connection between the word and the substance—water—by tapping the letters into the little girl's hand. At first, word associations were difficult to make. But that day, after Anne poured cold water over Helen's hand and then spelled out w-a-t-e-r, the connection between things and their names abruptly became clear.

"That living word awakened my soul," said Helen Keller. "It gave it light, hope, joy, set it free! There were barriers still, it is true, but barriers that could in time be swept away." (Helen Keller, *Story of My Life* [New York: Airmon Publishing Co., 1965], p. 21.)

A whole new life opened for Helen Keller.

In all that we do to transform any newfound awareness into a meaningful action, we must remember that the best help is the kind that allows the one being helped to develop the ability to do what he can for himself.

A psychiatrist once told me that parents of children with polio must learn to let their children walk alone. If the child falls when he tries to learn to walk again, the parent must let the child struggle to get up; and if he falls again, he must struggle up again and again. Unless children take those new steps on their own, he said, they will never walk again.

A dear friend with muscular dystrophy wrote: "I have realized I have a renewed responsibility to be a good example to my family. Often love and a good example are the best things a person like me can give. I now realize that patience is very important in a family. I find that with patience, more doors are opened because I don't get discouraged so easily, which could lead to hurtful situations, especially with those that are closest to me. I am ever thankful for having opportunities to help me continue to develop patience and those qualities that come with it."

Not only too much help but also too little help can be detrimental. A very necessary guideline for all of us who want to help is that everything we do individually and every program we support collectively should be designed to do for others what they cannot do for themselves, but should first let them do all they can do for themselves. Gaining mastery over difficulties gives one a sense of peace and well-being with each hard-won achievement, mastery that stimulates further growth.

George Eliot said, "What do we live for if it is not to make life less difficult for each other?" (Richard L. Evans, *Richard Evans' Quote Book* [Salt Lake City: Publishers Press, 1971], p. 174.)

As a result of my experience with handicapped people, I know now that we can have the sensitivity to care. We can have the presence of mind to become aware. We can have the empathy to share life with our thirty-five million brothers and

sisters with handicaps. And we can have the good sense to utilize the will, the spirit, and the hearts of everyone around us,
those with visible handicaps and those with hidden handicaps,
that we might build an even better society in which to live.

Always a high point of any Relief Society year is the general women's meeting, and this one was another rewarding experience. The Tabernacle was filled with faithful women; the
songs were beautiful and the flowers gorgeous. President
Hinckley spoke for the First Presidency in his typically stirring
way, and President Benson, president of the Council of the
Twelve, represented that body. It would be difficult to esti-
mate the force of these meetings and their impact upon the
lives of the women; but the sisters' continuing request for Tabernacle attendance, their demand for copies of the recordings,
and their growing numbers in local gatherings held throughout the Church to receive the broadcasts, attest to the need the
meetings fill. Women seem to hunger for a word from Church
authorities that confirms their faith in the path they have chosen, that tells them that the Lord knows and cares and understands the sometimes difficult way that is theirs.

I hope women do have a clear sense of how much the Lord
cares about them. Nothing has come as a clearer testimony to
me of his concern than in working in his daughters' cause, and
feeling answers to my prayers in their behalf. The stronger my
conviction grows, the greater my desire to reach out to the
women to try to communicate his love.

As I have received telephone calls and letters and have visited with women, I have concluded that there is nothing we
need more than a sure testimony to help us solve our problems
with courage and strength. But before we can know the truth
with more than mere mental assent, we must go through the
same process as have our prophet leaders. Our testimonies
must be a conviction of the heart and of the knowledge that
fills our souls.

President Harold B. Lee said, "Testimony isn't something
you have today, and you have always. A testimony is fragile. It

is as hard to hold as a moonbeam. It is something you have to recapture every day of your life." (*Church News*, 15 July 1972, p. 4.)

Many people say they would like to have faith, to be able to believe, and they wish for a testimony; but Alma tells us that we can have a testimony if we really *want* to know the truth. We must want it enough to be willing to *search* and *study* and *listen* and *pray* and *fast* for it.

We must be sensitive enough to recognize the swelling in our hearts or the responsive tears in our eyes as the *beginning* of understanding, when light comes. We must be honest enough to accept and appreciate it.

This is only the beginning, but when we really taste the sweetness of truth and know that it is *good*, we must build on those beginnings and nourish our faith with diligence and patience and trust. Then the truth will take root and "spring up" unto eternal life for us.

His Seed Shall Inherit the Earth

His soul shall dwell at ease; and his seed shall inherit the earth.
—Psalms 25:13

January 1982 found my counselors, Sisters Marian R. Boyer and Shirley W. Thomas, and me working toward the March completion and dedication of the restored Sarah Granger Kimball Home in Nauvoo, Illinois. Actual restoration had been directed by an archeologist from Brigham Young University working in concert with the Church Historical Department. Tibby Simmons and her sister, Oma Wilcox, coordinating with Paul Anderson of the Church Historical Department, had undertaken an extensive purchasing trip to obtain furniture for the home that would be appropriate to the period. Sister Luacine Fox had prepared a sound and slide presentation describing Nauvoo during that early period, to be viewed by visitors touring the home. Authenticity was thus ensured at every step. Sister Ann Reese, member of the general board, had organized the work of the Relief Society sisters in preparing food and programs for the dedication celebration.

We were pleased we had been given permission to carry out the restoration of that structure as part of the rebuilding of old Nauvoo, because in that small but elegant home the first plans for the Relief Society had been discussed. It had been a scene from that house, too, depicting that conversational beginning of Relief Society between Sarah Kimball and her seamstress, that had made such an impact on me when I saw its reenactment at the first Relief Society meeting I attended as a young married woman.

The dedication itself took place on March 11, 1982. The skies were only partly clear, but the purpose of the event remained unclouded. We had a sense not only of restoring the beauty of the home but also of having renewed the aim of those early sisters who had established the work of the women in the "cause of Zion." As the Prophet Joseph Smith had said, "The Church was not perfectly organized until the women were thus organized" ("History of the Relief Society," *Relief Society Magazine*, March 1919, p. 129). The other buildings already restored in Nauvoo created a visual statement of early Church organization. We hoped that the addition of the Sarah Kimball Home to those buildings would help others recognize that the work of women has always been an integral part of the Church.

Relief Society women in stakes near Nauvoo participated in the dedication services held at the Nauvoo Visitors' Center by preparing the food and by providing a lovely choir. Elder Dean L. Larsen, executive director of the Priesthood Department and adviser to the Relief Society, offered the dedicatory prayer, and talks were given by members of the Relief Society General Presidency. Also adding color and excitement to the day were continuous dramatizations performed in the restored cultural hall, musical presentations in the ward meetinghouse, and the slide and sound production shown in the visitors' center.

Although we had originally planned for the restoration of the Sarah Kimball Home in Nauvoo to be a part of our activities for the commemoration of 140 years of Relief Society, we knew that relatively few sisters would be able to attend the dedication service. Consequently, we arranged to have the services carried by a television broadcast, which many sisters viewed, with the hope that the program might have lasting value to members and nonmembers. We hoped that those who visited Nauvoo would feel the spirit we recognized there and be led to know of the Lord's regard for women.

In addition to the Relief Society's dedication of the Sarah Kimball Home, a combined effort of the Relief Society, Young Women, and Primary organizations generated in 1982 a tribute to women as a "legacy remembered and renewed." We met as presidencies to plan and allot the work that, by the time the idea was fully conceived, needed to be accomplished in a very short time.

The tribute turned out to be a varied and full program: an exhibit of women's art shown in the Salt Lake Art Center galleries, and later in the Relief Society Building; and a walking tour of downtown Salt Lake City that included the Beehive and Lion houses, the Relief Society Building, the art exhibit, and the Promised Valley Playhouse. The playhouse featured special shows for the tribute to women. Major concerts were held in Dallas, Los Angeles, Oakland, Washington, D.C., and Salt Lake City. Performing were vocalists, instrumentalists, and even a ballerina—Mormon women who excelled and were chosen by experts in each field for their outstanding ability.

Included also in the "legacy" events of the Relief Society were lectures given in the Relief Society Building. Once again, women were chosen for distinguished contributions in their particular fields. A stimulating and worthwhile series of talks resulted that were reproduced both on tape recordings and in a book, so the lectures would have a wider distribution. Another book compiling the best of the *Relief Society Magazine* articles from 1914 to 1970 was also published.

The events continued for an entire week in March and included a large reception held in the Church Office Building to which seven thousand women came to meet the general presidencies of each of the women's organizations, as well as some of the General Authorities. They enjoyed seeing the outstanding displays and were served refreshments that represented the worldwide influence of the women's organizations of the Church. The high point of the tribute to women was the women's meeting held in the Tabernacle and broadcast via satellite to sisters throughout the world.

The overall effect of "A Tribute to Women" was a unifying one for the three women's organizations. We found there was great power in unity of purpose.

We all knew we were blessed in a most remarkable way throughout the events. The undertaking had not been the result of long-range planning and so we found ourselves with an overwhelming amount of work to accomplish in an alarmingly short period of time. Elder Dean L. Larsen requested that the women's general presidencies and their boards meet together so that he could pronounce a blessing on our efforts that we might work under the authority of our callings. He promised us that doors would be opened and that the way would be provided to accomplish our seemingly insurmountable task. He said that as we worked under the Spirit and power of the Lord, success would be ours.

We saw the fulfillment of that blessing in the splendid events that transpired. I feel certain those events could not have happened without that special help. I also believe that blessing had implications beyond the tribute to women and legacy events. That time signaled a new day and a new day for women to accomplish, under the priesthood, the work the Lord would have them do.

Another uniting of forces came during the year 1982 as the officers of Lambda Delta Sigma, formerly under the umbrella of Relief Society, actually became associate members of the general board of Relief Society and accepted general board assignments. This, too, brought the women's organizations together in a closer working relationship. Lambda Delta Sigma had long served the young women of college age in a necessary way, but now it would also serve in the context of the larger picture of Relief Society. With this change their work became better integrated with the work of women as a whole. The union served not only to better establish Lambda Delta Sigma in the Church's overall sphere, but also to enhance the work of Relief Society through the women who came onto the board, serving as they did on general board committees and lending their strength and input. I felt the hand of the Lord in each change that brought the women closer. I could sense a kind of "circle-the-wagons" strength being built. It suggested to me that we were quietly being led to mobilize in order to thwart the forces that will eventually accelerate their efforts to destroy our mounting influence of righteousness upon the world.

We always tried to influence other women's groups whenever the opportunity arose, as it often did through the National Council of Women and the American Mothers, Inc. We had that opportunity when we hosted the American Mothers' Convention in Salt Lake City and provided family enrichment seminars. Many of our guest speakers were Latter-day Saints with professional expertise in family counseling and family enrichment. Gospel principles were an integral part of their approaches for effectively healing or nurturing the family unit.

I was serving as an executive officer of the American Mothers, Inc. when its annual convention was held for the first time in Salt Lake City. Each year at the convention an American Mother of the Year and a Young Mother representative were named. I had served on the committee to help select the Mother of the Year, and grew in respect and admiration for the mothers as I read their portfolios and distributed copies for other judges to read. I enjoyed my tenure with that organization because they maintained as their purpose the strengthening of the moral and spiritual values of the home. It was also particularly rewarding to note that a significant percentage of the states' representatives were Latter-day Saint women. I was proud that they were consistently recognized as outstanding mothers and that they made a major contribution to the moral and religious fiber of the nation. The hundreds of women who came to Salt Lake City for the conference seemed genuinely impressed with the influence of the Church.

I felt a continuing desire, even a need, to reach out to women in many different settings. When I was first called as the general president I had a strong testimony of the Relief Society as a gift of the Lord to the women of the Church. As I served and worked in that position, the realization came to me that this blessing was not intended for Latter-day Saint women only, but that the Relief Society organization was a gift of God to all women.

What far-reaching influence the programs of the Church could have became clearer to me after Muriel Dobbins of the *Baltimore Sun* came to my office. We spent an entire day together as she endeavored to learn why the president of the United States had such an interest in the welfare plan of the Church. President Ronald Reagan had toured several of our welfare facilities and thought that the governmental structure of the nation should implement a similar welfare program.

I often thought about how the Church and its programs could affect others in the world and in the Church. An experience of Sister Eliza R. Snow came to mind and I saw a parallel between her experience and that available to all women. Of her remarkable experience she wrote:

> Following my baptism I retired to my bed. . . . As I was reflecting on the wonderful events transpiring around me, I felt an indescribable, tangible sensation, if I may so call it, commencing at my head and enveloping my person . . . producing inexpressible happiness. Immediately following, I saw a beautiful candle with an unusual bright blaze directly over my feet. I sought to know the interpretation, and received the following: "The lamp of intelligence shall be lighted over your path." (*Eliza R. Snow: An Immortal* [Salt Lake City: Nicholas Morgan Foundation, 1957], p. 6.)

Beginning early and continuing to the end of her life, Eliza R. Snow received divine direction in deeply significant ways. Hard work, study, and faith were a part of her training. Her faith in the cause she espoused never seemed to waver, and the "lamp of intelligence" did guide her many and varied endeavors. Her work included being instumental in organizing the Relief Society during its inception in Nauvoo, and organizing it once again after the Saints settled in the Salt Lake Valley. She was the first general secretary of the Relief Society and its second general president. In 1878 she also organized the young women of the Church as the Young Ladies' Mutual Improvement Association.

Eliza R. Snow was instrumental in establishing a home industry outlet for the handwork of the Saints. She knew that if the Saints were to prosper, home industry was essential. She presided over the board that established the first Latter-day Saint hospital. She was among the sisters who commended the territorial governor for signing the legislation which gave women the vote in Utah, and was active in the subsequent activities which won for Utah women major civil rights not enjoyed by women in other states.

She knew the women she served. They had been instrumental in the establishment of the settlements in the Rocky Mountains. She believed they deserved to be part of the decision-making process in the government of the state and its communities. In her published articles she wrote to teach as well as to express those deep feelings.

As I consider the "lamp of intelligence" afforded Eliza R. Snow, I am deeply convinced that the many women who have committed themselves fully to the gospel and received the attendant blessings received as well that candle's light, that "lamp of intelligence" that enables them to see their way in knowledge and faith with its divine light and inspiration.

Through that light women are able to live and serve well because they can distinguish and choose that which is the "good part," in accordance with the Savior's counsel to Mary and Martha. That option of choice is not only one of our great privileges; it is also a requirement. Consistently right choices are the means to exaltation. We each must rightly choose that good part for ourselves, but in our own pursuit of righteousness we also have an obligation to help others make meaningful, righteous choices.

The Church endeavors in all its programs, as we do through the Relief Society, to help people understand that each person has agency, a God-given privilege that daily needs to be wisely exercised. The ancient prophet Joshua declared to Israel, "Choose you this day whom ye will serve; . . . but as for me and my house, we will serve the Lord" (Joshua 24:15). In later times President David O. McKay explained to us, "Next to the bestowal of life itself, the right to direct our lives is God's greatest gift to man" ("Free Agency . . . A Divine Gift," *Improvement Era*, June 1950, p. 366).

Women who study the gospel of Jesus Christ become more and more aware of the law of agency. There is no more profoundly important doctrine than this in the whole structure of gospel teachings. It is critically important that we each understand our choices between good and evil in this mortal life, because those choices ultimately affect our spiritual and eternal life.

The gospel teaches us that there is responsibility in choice, and the essential elements of choice which lead us to a oneness with eternal things are available to all, no matter what the circumstances of their lives. Too often it is suggested that choice should be accompanied by freedom from consequences. To perpetuate such a notion is no service.

We do not live in a capricious world of mere chance; rather we belong to a universe governed by law. Natural happenings and human behavior are both subject to the rule of law. If we throw a ball into the air, it will come down in response to the law of gravity. If we give love, love will be returned to us— perhaps in ways we least expect, but it will come back to us. As we recognize that this undergirding to human experiences exists which is based upon universal and eternal laws and their natural consequences, the essential and eternal nature of choice becomes apparent.

Sister Belle S. Spafford died on February 4, 1982. I had visited her that evening in the hospital. Later, after I had returned home, her family called to say that she had passed away. I reflected upon all that her life had meant to mine. I was grateful the Lord had allowed me the privilege of knowing her in the depth I did, for she had given me not so much shoes to fill as shoulders to stand on and vision to see afar.

One of the sweet experiences occasioned by her death was the next scheduled board meeting, to which we invited her counselors, Sisters Marianne Sharp and Louise W. Madsen. They joined in as we each paid tribute to Sister Spafford. It was amazing to realize the many ways in which one person can touch the lives of others. We bore testimonies, and the phrase "a crown of righteousness" took on a new meaning for all of us in contemplating Sister Spafford's service.

I thought of her in September of that same year as I presided at the nineteenth anual Woman of Conscience Award ceremony held at the Waldorf Astoria Hotel in New York City. The award for 1982 was given to Ethlyn Christensen, an eighty-year-old woman who had been active in efforts to secure the rights of senior citizens. The award also noted the contributions of the United Nations Assembly on Aging, a conference that focused attention on how perceptions regarding the aging were changing.

As chairman of the Woman of Conscience Award ceremony, I, along with a wonderful group of experts I called to act as a committee, arranged to solicit resumes on possible recipients of the award and to coordinate all of the details for the presentation. In order to do this we asked the governors of all fifty states to present a Woman of Conscience nominee. The committee produced a videotape entitled "Look, America, Aging Is Changing." I never cease to marvel at the selfless service of the old and the young, the professionals, and the nonprofessionals. Thanks to them, the aging citizens of each state are better recognized and more often given needed assistance.

Leaving that project and being informed that Brigham Young University had asked me to speak at a devotional assembly, and that I had been chosen by the students to receive the Exemplary Womanhood Award, was most humbling. I knew that the award was given, on alternate years, to men and women. I looked at the list of recipients that included Presidents Harold B. Lee, Spencer W. Kimball, and Marion G. Romney, as well as J. Willard Marriott; the sisters included Belle S. Spafford, Camilla E. Kimball, Florence S. Jacobsen, and now me. I felt highly honored just to have my name listed there.

I recognized the singular distinction such an award represented. I needed the backing of my family, and they were there. They had sustained me in many ways with their time and efforts; often they came to support me on short notice or to gather together as a family because I had limited time between assignments. Loyally Douglas had taken me to the airport and met the plane upon my arrival home. These kindnesses and their sacrifices in so many ways had made it possible for me to serve in my calling without restriction; my appreciation was immense. However, nothing that they did helped me more than the goodness of their lives. The righteous, exemplary lives they still lead honor their father and me as no other recognition could.

22

Yielding
Seed

And God said, Let the
earth bring forth . . .
yielding seed . . . and it
was so.
—Genesis 1:11

J anuary 1983 was a month for sadness as the Church
mourned the death of the beloved Elder LeGrand Richards
of the Quorum of the Twelve. Relief Society lost a good friend
in his passing. In tribute to him, the Relief Society General
Board handled the floral arrangements for the funeral service,
which was held in the Salt Lake Tabernacle.

At the end of that month Sister Shirley Thomas, the general Relief Society education counselor, my loyal, competent
friend, and one of my mainstays, was called to serve, with her
husband as mission president, in Melbourne, Australia. I certainly wished her well, but I knew I would miss her able hand
in the work of the Relief Society. Sister Thomas had deep spiritual insights and was gracious, feminine, and caring. The response of her little four-year-old granddaughter represented
my feelings and those of others closely associated with Sister
Thomas. The granddaughter had cried uncontrollably at the
airport. A few days later her mother asked the little girl if she
would like to go shopping with her. Still missing her muchloved grandmother, the little girl had replied, "Yes, but let's
not go by the grandma dresses. It makes me feel too lonesome."

Sister Ann Reese was called and graciously accepted the
position of second counselor in the Relief Society General Pres-

idency. Because Sister Reese and I had been called to the general board the same day, we had sat next to each other at board meetings for four years. I knew she was very well prepared to assume that responsibility. Although her service as an executive officer was brief, she was a strong, supportive, productive, and intelligent counselor. She followed in the footsteps of her noble mother who had served as the general secretary-treasurer of the Relief Society under Sister Spafford.

In February I received a call from Elder Boyd K. Packer. He suggested that, as a member of the Church Board of Trustees, I meet Sandra Day O'Connor, who was giving an address at Brigham Young University. Justice O'Connor had been newly appointed to serve on the Supreme Court, the first woman to serve in that position. In her address she indicated that she had not expected the appointment, but felt that a qualified woman should be under consideration for such appointments. She was moved to tears by the record of her genealogy that was given to her as a gift from the university; she had not known of her family history before that presentation was made.

Shortly after meeting Justice O'Connor I left for Las Vegas in response to an invitation to address the North Las Vegas Stake for a Relief Society conference. At the reception held afterward, one woman related a humorous interchange that she'd had with her young daughter. The mother had told her daughter she was going to the meeting in which I would be speaking. The little girl had responded, "She's the lady who doesn't have any children, isn't she?"

"Why do you say that?" her mother queried.

"Because the program said no babies or children under twelve!"

Actually I had seven children at the time and thirty-five grandchildren—most of the latter being under twelve.

After my stay in Las Vegas I returned to the work waiting for me at Church headquarters. It seemed as if each day became more pressing, yet the work needed to go forward with increased vigor, enthusiasm, and understanding. As a presidency, we felt the need to unite the women of the Church in that effort, to have them further assist the Brethren with their strength, support, and work. We went to the temple seeking direction from the Lord so that we would be wise and diligent in our own efforts to serve him as we endeavored to be a vanguard to the sisters in facilitating a further unity of the faith.

That evening I read again the book of Enos from the Book of Mormon. The scriptures, which ever sustained me in my joys, remained for me that well from whose waters I quenched my thirst during times of searching or distress. My reading that evening helped renew my inner strength and spirit.

Addie Fuhriman, a member of the Relief Society General Board, and I met with women whose request was that the Relief Society take an active part in encouraging legislators to enact stiff laws against child molestation and abuse. It saddened us to know that increased immorality had necessitated the introduction of such laws. Our meeting was the beginning of my involvement to curb this violence directed at innocent young people. The combined efforts of many concerned Utahns later culminated in the enactment of rigorous Utah legislation against child abuse in the year I served as president of the Utah Chapter for the Prevention of Child Abuse.

About this time Douglas and I responded to an invitation to the Christian and Jews dinner where Barney Clark, the first artificial heart recipient, and his doctors were to be honored. It was a unique experience to be at that celebration of medical progress, but even more impressive was the indomitable will of the human spirit he displayed.

During a flight to Fayetteville, South Carolina, for a Relief Society conference, I enjoyed a warmhearted and memorable conversation with two Relief Society sisters. One sister made the statement that she liked to be home when it rained. When I asked her why, she explained that she then built a fire, put on music, cleaned the house, and baked bread. When her family came home it was wonderful and cheery inside, even though it was unpleasant and difficult outside. I wished for her and her family a great many such rainy days.

While I was in Fayetteville, the stake Relief Society president took me to the homes of three members. I particularly remembered visiting with Sister Lillian Money. She had a beautiful little home with Early American furnishings. In the bay window were three thriving, red geraniums.

Even though she had cancer, Sister Money had a happy, wonderful spirit. Her husband had been in an accident and had become a paraplegic just four days before they were to marry. They postponed their marriage while he learned how to handle his legs. Sister Money studied and became a botanist. She told me that when she was a child, her mother used to take her for nature walks. As a result of that early exposure, Sister Money had become intensely interested in plant and animal life, later making botany her profession. As I visited with her I realized that her life must have been far from easy, but one would never have known it from her appearance, attitude, or bearing.

On June 16, 1983, I was in Cape Canaveral, Florida, to witness the space shuttle launch scheduled for two days later. Along with women leaders from across the nation, I had been invited to represent the women of the Church as Sally Ride, the first female astronaut, participated as a flight crew member in this launch. The invitation was not extended to my husband, nor could I take anyone else, so I went alone.

Not wanting to spend my forty-second wedding anniversary alone that evening, I had asked my hosts to accompany me to dinner to celebrate that occasion. We had toured the area during the day. Upon arriving back at my hotel to prepare for our dinner engagement, I was told it was important for me to return a phone call, received in my absence, from President Gordon B. Hinckley of the First Presidency. I was not prepared for what followed when I complied with the request.

"Are you tired? Do you want to be released?" I heard President Hinckley's voice ask from the other end of the line. My feelings at that moment would be difficult to describe. How should I answer his inquiry?

If anything, my schedule had become more involved. Countless hours and minutes continued to be filled with demands upon my mental, emotional, and physical resources. From the beginning of my term I had been convinced of the importance of being available to anyone wanting to talk to me. For that reason I had established and maintained an open-door policy. Still, not all concerns could be resolved immediately. Occasionally I had to seek answers from those with knowledge and expertise in specific fields, answers that demanded time-consuming follow-up. Board meetings, conferences, media interviews, out-of-town and in-town assignments: the bulk of the hours available to me every day was spent in such undertakings.

In all honesty I had to admit that I had worked through many moments of fatigue; no one escaped those—but was I truly ready to be released? Was anyone ever ready for the season of adjustment such a step invariably brings with it? I had observed others go through it. I well remembered my own sense of loss when I was released from my first Church position as a Social Relations teacher. This transition would not be different.

Nearly ten years earlier, shortly before President Kimball visited my home asking me to serve as general president of the Relief Society, I'd had a premonition that he would ask me to serve. But nothing had prepared me for President Hinckley's call.

Since I was not alone in the room, it proved difficult to carry on a coherent conversation with President Hinckley, and we decided that I would meet with him when I returned to Utah. After I hung up, I needed to concentrate solely on my thoughts, but it proved to be impossible; my prior arrangements had claimed the next few hours.

Released. On the way to the restaurant I mulled the word over in my mind while the ebb and flow of conversation washed around me. A new sister would be called; the mantle of stewardship worn by someone else. *Released.* It had a strange ring and elicited strange emotions. Was it because I had not expected it, even though when I accepted the position I was told that my term in office would not be as lengthy as that of my predecessor, Sister Spafford?

During the meal, not really aware of what I was eating, I forced myself to socialize and to talk about things that were taking place in the space program and, therefore, in the history of our nation, but my thoughts continued to travel other roads. Beyond the turmoil of my emotions, there were practical matters to consider. Would I still carry out my present assignments, since I had not yet been officially released? Which projects could I still complete, and which should receive priority? Exactly how much time did I have left?

Some of my questions and concerns would be resolved in the near future, but my mind, whirling like a merry-go-round, was demanding answers at once. All I knew with certainty was that throughout my life I had always accepted in total faith decisions made by any of the General Authorities. To them fell the major responsibility of administering the affairs of the Lord's kingdom here on earth. The decade I served under their direction had been a labor of love, diligence, and total commitment on my part. Having done that which I was asked to do, was I now to learn that the acceptance of a release was as important as the acceptance of a call? Was the fruition of my nearly ten years' labor such that it had yielded seed sufficent that I be released? I prayed for the strength and ability to bring my term of office to a close with a measure of grace.

When I awoke the next morning, the peace which had so eluded me was mine once more. During the night I had received an assurance that all would be well. The gospel entailed both the hot sun and the gentle rain which help produce a rich harvest; I was grateful for both in my life. Filled with the peace that passes understanding, I was ready to face the days ahead.

As the plane touched down back in Salt Lake City, Douglas was there to meet me. There really was no place like home, where one's roots were deeply embedded and entwined with those one loved most dearly.

"Counting time is not as important as making time count," James J. Walker said. My counselors and I followed that counsel as we put ourselves to the task of completing our assignments. No one else knew we had but six months remaining to do so. Experiences during that period burned upon my soul with greater intensity, for I knew those opportunities would not come my way again.

I looked at my counselors and general board members and nearly wept with love for them. They were my friends, my sisters in the gospel, in love, and in unity. They were the ones who had so ably helped me carry out my responsibilities by pooling their talents, ideas, and imagination, but above all, through each one's unfailing willingness and desire to serve. All of them, at one time or another, had sacrificed personal needs in order to thus serve. The past years had forged a strong bond of appreciation between us for the divine heritage and gifts each had so unselfishly shared. I knew I would miss the close association we enjoyed. However, I did find considerable solace in knowing that those who would follow us would also have as their goal the advancement of the Relief Society, the Lord's gift to his daughters.

One highlight of July 1983 was when I was invited, as one of 120 guests from across the country, to attend a formal state dinner at the White House. The occasion was a formal reception for the emir of Bahrain, Shaikh Isahim Salman Al-Khalifa. Bahrain is an Arab state made up of a small group of islands in the Persian Gulf. I was delighted that my husband could attend the dinner with me, and I was especially honored when I found that I had been seated at President Reagan's table! President Reagan quickly put all of his guests at ease, and the conversation at our table was most enjoyable, including that with Sally Ride, astronaut, Moses Malone, basketball player, and Betty Heitman, co-chairman of the Republican National Committee, among others. I believe that was the first time a Relief Society general president had been asked to a state dinner. I was honored, and also felt that my invitation was a recognition of Mormon women as a significant force for good in society.

23

Joy in the Harvest

They joy before thee according to the joy in harvest.
—Isaiah 9:3

I met with President Gordon B. Hinckley after my return from Florida. It was determined that my release would take place at the upcoming April 1984 general conference. Throughout my years in office, I had tried to do all that needed to be done each day. Now, with my tenure soon to be over, which tasks were of prime importance to yet accomplish became apparent to us.

At the next executive meeting I informed the other officers of our pending release and we then spent time recounting the marvelous experiences that had been ours. Next, we discussed what we hoped we would still accomplish during our term of office. We compiled a list of projects and gave out assignments for each member to complete.

The number of women serving on the general board had diminished, so we asked the Brethren if it would be possible to call six additional board members to assist us with our projects for those last few months. Approval was given. Among other goals, we wanted the written history of the Relief Society to be completed. That project was assigned to Jill Mulvay Derr and Janath R. Cannon, with Deseret Book Company serving as publisher upon completion of the manuscript. We also wanted to have the grounds of the Sarah Granger Kimball Home completed, with gardens and auxiliary buildings established that were representative of the Early Nauvoo period. We felt that a time-line display in the Relief Society Building would help visitors see in perspective the great gift of Relief Society given to the women of the Church throughout the ages. We wanted the displays that were current to be updated, so they would all be ready for the new presidency. We wanted to plan a commemorative Relief Society birthday social for March 17. We thought, too, how special it would be to have all of the recipes we had served at socials in the building combined into a book and given to those attending this, our last, social. It seemed appropriate to have sister Mayola Miltenberger, the general secretary, compile a book on the history of social services for the period that the department was under the direction of the Relief Society. Of course, we wanted all of our records up to date, desks cleared out, and the office in top shape.

Invitations to give speeches continued to come in, since no one else knew of our pending release. Board members were assigned some of the addresses and the members of the presidency accepted others. I am certain that when I delivered the Brigham Young University devotional assembly address on February 14 and talked about love, no one there could have even begun to comprehend the great love I felt for my listeners and for the sons and daughters of God worldwide. For all of us, officers and board members alike, our hearts were filled to the brim with love and service; all were involved in a maximum of activity. We were so busy with our final projects, as well as routine work, that we didn't even pause to assess the abundant blessings of our work—except as we counseled women with difficulties, or when tender memories from our past Relief Society days would surface. But with the quickly passing weeks, we all eventually felt the effect of ten years' culmination of Relief Society planting, nourishing, and harvesting.

It was such a sad time for us when Elder Mark E. Petersen passed away. He had been a friend and mentor for Relief Society for many years. We were honored to help select his burial clothing and to arrange with his home ward for the flowers to be displayed in the Tabernacle. We remembered his counsel that "Relief Society is vital to the welfare of every Latter-day Saint woman." ("Why Every Woman Needs Relief Society," *Ensign*, March 1976, p. 74.) We agreed when President Gordon B. Hinckley said, "He was a man of tremendous industry, great loyalty, and unshakable faith" (*Church News*, Jan. 22, 1984).

The snowy, blizzard-like weather that prevailed on March 17 as we celebrated the one hundred and forty-second anniversary of the Relief Society did not daunt the Relief Society women. Hundreds came to participate in the commemorative activities held at Church headquarters in the Relief Society Building. Speeches and songs, dances and dramas, and a final open house were among the varied events of the celebration. The *Relief Society General Board Favorite Recipes* cookbook had been published and was there given to stake Relief Society presidents who were in attendance from throughout the Salt Lake Valley.

Of particular interest to me was the musical dramatization, *From the Pages of Relief Society*. It was staged three times that day, the anniversary of the organization's first meeting in Nauvoo in 1842. The dramatization presented sketches of Relief Society history portrayed in dance and song. It reminded me of that first Relief Society meeting I had attended many years previous. Then, those sisters had presented a dramatization in commemoration of the one hundredth anniversary of Relief Society. I never thought for a moment then that I would later watch the one hundred forty-second anniversary presentation of the organization I had learned to love so well as its general president.

The *Ensign* requested an interview with me shortly before my release. The reporter wanted to know if, as members of the Church, we should look beyond our own circles of family and friends in our efforts to serve. I replied that while we must be careful not to make family the boundary for our ministrations, we should begin with those closest to us. Women should serve first within their own spheres—with their children at home, among adult friends, in their extended families, and then in their professions, reaching out in love to serve someone daily. Love is never wasted—whether it is extended to a little child,

a lonely sister, or an elderly couple. The power of love to refine our own souls does not depend on whether the one we love
reciprocates or appreciates our affection. When we love, we
grow. Each member, and Relief Society as a whole, can experience that growth as we dedicate our efforts to strengthening
women in their homes and families, helping women to become
better educated, encouraging them to give charitable service
in their communities, and helping them to learn to live peace-
fully and joyfully in today's world.

Too soon all our days were gone. It was conference week-
end. Emptying out my desk, taking that last look around my
office, I thought of all the events that had taken place in that
beautiful Relief Society Building, events again so fresh in my
mind as part of a soul-searing, soul-soaring experience. I
wanted with all my heart to make the last ten years mine forever, with their innumerable, priceless moments I had shared
with my counselors, the board, our staff, and women from
near and far.

At the opening session of general conference, I sat in the
place assigned to me alongside my counselors and looked out
over the Saints gathered in the Salt Lake Tabernacle. I knew
there were thousands of others watching the proceedings on
television and still others tuned in by radio. As the conference
proceeded, I was called upon to address for a final time the audience of people I loved. The walk to the podium, long even
for speakers not hindered by emotion, seemed especially
lengthy to me that day. I felt a rich outpouring of love from
my heart for the brothers and sisters of the Church. I had felt
their support; I had been inspired by the love and dedication
of their lives. I had witnessed their compassion and loving
ministrations for their families and their neighbors; I had sa-
vored their creativity, rejoiced in their achievements, and
shared many moments of happiness with them. I had seen
their nobility emerge as they dealt with sorrow, disappoint-
ment, and personal tragedy.

Even so, I could not help but ask myself if I had really
helped meet the needs of the women of the Church. I knew my
calling had been not only a great responsibility, but also a

wonderful privilege. My farewell remarks were but a feeble effort to convey the joy I had felt in that intensely rewarding work that had been so sweet to me. That near-decade of service seemed to be but a fleeting, beautiful moment of time. I was filled with gratitude for that work that had been mine to do and for the opportunity to touch the lives of so many women. I deeply hoped I had helped my Relief Society sisters to feel strengthened and encouraged and filled with more faith in the Lord Jesus Christ. I did know of a surety that these years had been a very fruitful season and that the Relief Society would continue to grow and move forward, blessing the lives of all who would accept it as a gift from the Lord.

Seedtime and Harvest

Seedtime and harvest . . .
shall not cease.
— Genesis 8:22

Now I have a new assignment in the Relief Society—one which may well be the most challenging I have ever held, including my ten-year odyssey as general president.

With my lifetime of acquaintance and service in my much-loved Relief Society, I now face the responsibility of going with my husband while he assists in the administration of Church responsibilities to people whose cultural backgrounds are entirely different from mine. He will serve the Lord as a member of the First Quorum of the Seventy, and his assignment is in the Area Presidency in the Far East, where most of the millions who live there have never heard of The Church of Jesus Christ of Latter-day Saints and have little or no contact with Christianity.

I will be set apart as an area general board representative to teach the women who have accepted the gospel more about the Relief Society, the Young Women's program, and the Primary organization. Though I have had more years of service in Relief Society, I have also served in the other organizations. The seeds planted in my youth and young womanhood must be fruitful and be harvested in this new calling. I believe the Lord can guide me if as a servant in his vineyard I help plant the good seed in these faraway lands.

Looking back on my heritage, I am aware that the most important seeds of personal testimony planted are those planted in the hearts of God's children everywhere. The scriptures are very specific in telling us that such seeds when planted, if not cast out by unbelief, will begin to enlarge souls, to enlighten understanding, and to be delicious. The intimate connection between heaven and earth comes with this wisdom and understanding. The fruit of the seed must be nurtured with the love given to one another. We can then let the power of the nurturing and renewing force of love find expression in our daily activity. The sweet harvest of peace comes as we live the teachings of the Lord.

I know that going forth to live among strangers to teach the ways of the organizations of the Church is a very small sacrifice compared to the travails which others went through to plant the seed of testimony in my life. Recently I was reading again a remarkable letter from my great-great-grandfather. As a new convert to the Church, he was called to help Saints who were strangers to him. Those saints had recently been forced from their homes by persecution. He left this account:

Quincy, Illinois
February 1, 1839

When the Saints were crossing the Mississippi River in their exodus from the state of Missouri, I was appointed by the Authorities of the Church who had crossed over, as one of a committee of three to reconnoiter the upper river country in the state of Illinois, the then-territory of Iowa.

In order to ascertain if there was any chance for the Saints to find shelter from the inclemency of the season, Brother S. Bent and Brother Israel Barlow were to be my colleagues. Brother Bent was taken sick a few hours after we started, and returned home. Barlow and myself went on nine days in our exploration and found in the towns of Upper and Lower Commerce about forty empty dwellings, for which we made conditional arrangements. We then crossed over the great "Father of Waters" into the territory of Iowa and there we found the barracks of the old Fort Des Moines, erected in the Black Hawk War, with accommodations for about 40 or 50 families. We then found Dr.

Isaac Galland. He proved to have possession of the buildings and a right to sell 20,000 acres of land, known as the "half-breed reservation," formerly belonging to the Sac and Fox nations of Indians, and also proposed his terms of sale. After obtaining this information and documents showing what we had done and what could be done in that direction, we returned to Quincy, where a conference or meeting was called and we made our report.

After it had been deliberated upon for a while, it was decided and agreed that an express with the papers be sent to Joseph Smith who was then in Liberty Jail in Missouri. After several fruitless attempts were made to obtain a person from among the Saints who had come out of Missouri, Bishop Partridge came to me and asked me if I would accept the appointment. Although I had heard of the threats that the Jackson folks had made against the Mormons in case they should come there to sell or take possession of their lands (I was a stranger in Missouri and also to the Saints, having just arrived from the city of New York on my way to gather with the Saints) notwithstanding, I was not intimidated and therefore replied, "If it is the will of the Lord and the decision of his servants who have the authority to appoint and endow me with the power and let me have your faith and prayers, then I will go and do the business or be found dead trying."

Accordingly, the necessary power of attorney was made out and the directions written. On the 10th of March, 1839, I left Quincy, Illinois for Jackson County, Missouri. On the 15th I arrived at Far West, where there was a committee that had been appointed to assist the brethren in disposing of their property and making up their outfit preparatory to leaving the state. To this committee I was recommended for assistance and counsel if I should need it. They thought I ought to have some person with me, and sent Brother Charles Bird, who was acquainted with Jackson County.

We left Far West on the 20th, I having visited the brethren in Richmond Jail in the meantime. On the morrow we visited the Prophet Joseph Smith in Liberty Jail, and then and thereafter I made my report of the up-river mission and delivered to him the documents and papers sent by the authorities in Quincy. Having received his

sanction and blessing, we crossed the river into Jackson
County and went to the city of Independence, a distance of
some 20 miles and put up at the city hotel, then kept by
Spotwood Knowland. The next morning we went to the re-
corder's office and got my power of attorney registered and
paid up all the taxes that had accumulated on the land for
the five years past. We then advertized the several plots of
land for sale. Just at this time, a young man by the name of
Mason, from Kentucky, arrived in town in search of a
place to locate a farm and seeing the notice, came to me.
He wished to see the land. I went and showed him the largest pieces and he made choice of a quarter section known as
the Whitmer Farm and paid me $700 in cash, and gave me
a horse, saddle, and bridle worth $100.

The next morning, as Brother Bird and myself were
crossing the public square, we met a posse of about forty
men, who coming up to us, opened to the right and left,
forming a hollow square, with ourselves inside. On looking
around, I saw the people on every side coming until the
crowd would have numbered some three hundred. One of
the first posse, a tall slim man by the name of James King,
a brother of Thomas King, sheriff of Jackson County, informed me that I must deliver up to them the money and
property for which I had sold the land, and that I must
leave the county before sunset, or I would be found a dead
man, as I could not remain another night in Jackson
County and live.

"And," he said, "we mean what we say, and you need
not presume anything else."

After he had finished, and a pause of about one minute
occurred, I observed, "You have pronounced sentence
upon me. Can I be allowed the privilege granted to con-
demned criminals in courts of law? They are asked if they
have any cause to show why the sentence of the law should
not be executed upon them."

He said he had no objection to my saying a few words,
but would not hear any long preamble. Several of his party
sang out,

"Let him speak, let him speak."

He said, "Say on."

After about a half a minute I commenced by saying, "A few years ago, the God of Israel sent a few of his servants to settle in Jackson County, Missouri. He had but few at that time on the earth who would acknowledge themselves his servants to obey. They came forth, and in conformity with the laws of the United States and the state of Missouri, they made selection and entered some 20,000 acres upon which they settled some 1400 or 1500 souls in the space of three years, at which time the people of the country arose simultaneously, almost en masse, and drove those servants of God from their homes and from the county in violation of all law. Those servants of God then settled in other counties, and subsequently were driven from the state, under the exterminating order of Governor Boggs. Among those servants of God there were some who were very old, some cripples, some sick, some widows, and many orphan children, who are destitute of means to convey themselves out of the state. And the Lord will not that they should be exterminated. And, therefore, the God of Israel has ordered that the lands from which his servants were first driven, shall be sold, and the means used in helping those helpless ones out of the state. I am sent here to perform that business, and in the name of Israel's God, and by his power, I shall accomplish the work. And in no way can I be prevented, only by committing willful, cold-blooded murder. And, if anyone present is prepared for that, now is the best time you can ever have, in the blaze of this beautiful morning sun and in the presence of this large concourse of witnesses, that the honor and glory of the deed may descend to the latest posterity. That is all I wish to say."

On looking around I saw nothing of Brother Bird, I heard nothing said by anyone and soon the people began to leave and I was alone, without anyone near enough to speak to. So I went about my business and sold all the land I was authorized to sell, except six acres of prairie, lying alone. The amount in all sold was about $2,700.

I was in that state of Missouri about 40 days. On my way from Jackson County, I stopped a few days at Far West, and while there, Lael Maynard, an apostate, swore out an attachment for some $350 levied on five yoke of oxen, three horses, and a wagon, and some $300 worth of dry goods; and in order to have the use of the property to help the brethren out of the state, I paid the amount and costs in money. Just at that time, Joseph Smith the Prophet was taken from Liberty Jail to another for trial, and from there sent Brother Ripley to Far West for some cash, and the committee saw fit to take $150 of the money I had and sent it to him. About that time the Prophet Joseph and his fellow prisoners left their keepers and went to Illinois.

When about 100 miles from Far West on my way home, I saw Sheriff Brasfield, who had the Prophet in charge when he left. The sheriff had a posse with him and while he was acquainting me with the particulars of their escape and how they stole two of his horses, one of his posse said, "And would have stolen more if they had had more money." The sheriff was a fiddler and had a fiddle in his hands at the time and said to me, "When you see Smith, tell him for me, if I ever find him, I will play him the tune Jo Smith."

On my way out of the state, I met Brigham Young and several more of the Twelve on their way to Far West to lay the cornerstone of the temple. And I let Brother Young have twelve dollars cash.

When I left Far West, I brought the family of Parley P. Pratt, Brigham Young's wife's mother Angel and daughter Caroline and Sister Bosley. When I came to the Mississippi, the water was so high that I had to go several miles down the river to find a place where the bottom lands along the river were not overflowing, and where there was a ferry to cross. There on the Illinois side was a large slough to ford where the water came up to the wagon bed. As I drove up the banks out of the water I looked back and saw something in the water about the middle of the slough, which I thought was a bundle of clothes which had fallen off of the back end of the wagon, and called out, "There is something lost off in the water," upon which Sister Pratt cried out, "It is Mary Ann!"

(She had fallen into the water. A wheel had run over her and crushed her fast into the mud at the bottom of the stream, but as it rolled over her she caught the spokes, and the wheel brought her, Mary Ann Sterns, to the surface.)

I jumped from the wagon and sprang into the water and brought her out. She was nearly drowned, but we brought her to, again.

In the meantime, my horse, being somewhat spirited, took to the timbers and ran afoul of the trees and stopped until we were ready to start. And from there we went on to the city of Quincy, Illinois without anything occurring worth noting here.

This is a truthful account of the transactions and occurrences of the mission to Jackson County, Missouri, and the business done.

Attest: D. W. Rogers

The facts of history do bring sensitivity to our souls and, in my case, the stalwart examples of both men and women whisper to me the spirit of testimony in the Restoration. I cannot read their stories without understanding that the early converts who heard the Prophet teach were touched by a profound confirmation of the Spirit, for they gave up everything they had in order to move the work forward for the blessing of all the children of men.

I am constantly finding an interplay between current events and history. That which is recorded impacts the next round of events and thus becomes an important factor in shaping what yet lies ahead. So it is that the stories of my progenitors profoundly influence me. The seeds planted as a result of that influence have shaped my whole life, even as the seeds sown by missionaries around the world change the lives of the people they teach.

Since my release as general president I have come to realize that I am part of history, as we all are. Now I go to this new calling, praying that I can make a contribution to a new page in the history of the Church. I hope that same confirmation of the Spirit which allowed my great-great-grandfather Rogers to complete his mission will sustain me in this new calling.

After my release I was invited to Naperville, Illinois, for a Relief Society anniversary social. All of those participating in the program represented, in costume, women of the past. They had studied a great deal about the women they represented. They gave workshops about an area that had been of special interest to the individual woman. They maintained their portrayals all day long. Then came the concluding session of their conference, and they presented the history of the Relief Society.

It was very much like the historic vignettes I watched as a young woman; the difference was that this time, as they talked about the general presidents of Relief Society through the years, the spotlight was turned on me and there I stood as part of that history. There was an audible gasp as the sisters realized that we are making history and the record of our lives will be an ongoing guide to those who follow us. I, too, gasped at that poignant moment as I realized my part in the history of Relief Society.

The work now ahead of me will be to see if I have the vision to take what I know and share it with others who have had less experience with the principles and practices of the Church. The value of individual souls will enlarge my understanding if I learn to respect and love my Asian sisters, and teach them organizational and leadership skills of the Church without trying to force them into a Western mode of Relief Society. I hope I can let the principles upon which Relief Society is founded find expression in their lives through the patterns of their cultural heritage.

Service in the Church should be a schooling by which we are able to give greater service. Now as I go to be with my Relief Society sisters in new places, I will demonstrate what they mean to me through my willingness to serve them. Initially I will be the stranger, hearing strange languages and strange-sounding names in this organization the Lord has given for the blessing and benefit of women everywhere. But I truly believe that Joseph Smith turned the key for women for their advancement throughout the world. I believe the Lord wants his daughters to have all the blessings promised in this period of mortality. I know from my experiences in Relief Society and from the manifestations of the Spirit that he loves his daughters, and it is his intent that they should have life, and have it more abundantly. I am privileged to be able to use my experiences in helping make a worldwide sisterhood a reality.

The insights I have gleaned with each new calling from ward, to stake, to general assignments tell me that as I serve in Asia I need to start at the very beginning, with the individual, and then, through organizational programs, facilitate the individual's ability to effectively incorporate gospel teachings so that the harvest will be abundant for the individual and for the kingdom. Even as a child, I learned that Relief Society was people—individual women, each with her own set of needs, each with challenges, and each wanting to be loved and accepted. This organization is a place to help women utilize the gospel, to find friends and commonalities, to help women feel the joy and the importance of their unique contributions. It is a place to help them verify the great gospel teaching of the value of the human soul. Decisions that are made that will affect these Asian women's lives must be made with consideration for the individual, because nothing is more important in the scheme of things than the individual soul.

Very early I found that Relief Society was a place to learn such valuable, eternal lessons—lessons of gospel principles and truths that are not to be left at church but are to be applied in day-to-day living. These lessons I learned from my mother. For me, compassionate service has become one of the most significant of those principles. My desire is that my service to my Asian sisters be hallmarked by compassion.

I look forward to this new field of labor in the Far East, firm in my conviction that the organizations of Primary, Young Women, and Relief Society are given by the Lord to help us care for the needs of all his children. The effect of that key, turned by the Prophet in behalf of women, is expanding to all the world, and women's lives everywhere are destined to be immensely enriched, to partake of the abundance the Savior offered, if we are not diverted from our goal of becoming the blessed of the Father.

The Rights
of Women

I am for the rights of women. Let me make that perfectly clear.

I am for the rights of women. I could not in good conscience head an organization of a million women if I were not for women's rights.

In the realm of women's rights, the history of the organization I represent is an illustrious one. The Relief Society organization was in the forefront of the fight for the right of women to vote. In addition, as early as 1890 the *Woman's Exponent*, a paper put out by the early Mormon women, documented the need for equal pay for equal work, a most revolutionary and progressive point of view for that time. The expansive and enlightened point of view of the *Woman's Exponent* is indicated by its subtitle: "The Rights of Women of Zion and the Rights of Women of All Nations."

From the beginning of the suffrage movement our women attended national and international suffrage meetings, where we were active in securing rights for women.

I repeat: I stand as a representative of an organization that is in favor of rights for women. However, we may differ with

Address delivered in Coeur d'Alene, Idaho, January 15, 1977.

some people on the best way or ways to achieve these rights. In my opinion, the Equal Rights Amendment is not the way.

It is interesting that so many seem to be misled by the title that has been given to the proposed Twenty-seventh Amendment: "the Equal Rights Amendment." These words, as wonderful as they sound, do not truly equate with fairness and insightful justice.

So, I repeat, the Equal Rights Amendment is not the way.

I say this sadly. I wish it were possible to pass one amendment to the Constitution that could make everything right for both men and women. History gives me no such confidence, however. In fact, recent history fills me with extreme anxiety and with deep concern. In a newspaper article, Professors Harrison M. Davis and H. Carleton Marlow explained: "On June 23, 1972, Congress approved Title IX of the Educational Amendment Act." By June, 1975, the Department of Health, Education and Welfare had prepared the regulations to implement Title IX of that act. In early July 1975, the same month in which the regulations became effective, Representative Edith Green, author of Title IX of the Higher Education Act, admitted that she herself would not have voted for the act had she known how HEW would interpret the congressional intent in drafting the regulations."

She "has claimed that some of the HEW regulations really *subvert* the congressional intent."

> After *futile* efforts in Congress to change the regulations, to bring them into harmony with the intent, Title IX finally became effective on July 21, 1975.

> A moral, legal, and educational entanglement has resulted from a well-intentioned attempt to end sex discrimination.

> Since October 1975, the Office of Civil Rights rulings on the HEW Title IX regulations have outraged President Ford and local school board members, who regard the "maze of regulations and administrative interpretations" as a potential "nightmare of irrelevant governmental intervention in an area of education policy which traditionally has resided with the people at the state and local level."

President Ford labeled as *unreasonable* the ruling in Scottsdale, Arizona, which forbade father-son/mother-daughter school-sponsored activities. By charging that the unelected bureaucrats of the Office of Civil Rights and HEW have overstepped their statutory authority, critics are diverting public attention from the *real* culprits—those congressmen and public officials who approved the act in the first place without clearly defining the meaning of the terms of the act or without assessing fully the impact that ambiguous laws will have on individuals and social organizations when they are implemented.

In a *U.S. News and World Report* of March 1975, U.S. Supreme Court Chief Justice Warren Burger is quoted as follows: "Increasingly, Congress legislates in broad general terms. Sometimes the legislation is not as thoroughly considered as it might be, or because it goes through natural processes of compromise, with resulting ambiguity, the courts are compelled to do the best they can to try to discern the intent of Congress."

In view, then, of what has happened to Title IX, I cannot in good conscience support a constitutional amendment that is even more powerful and more ambiguous. I do not wish history to accuse me of not perceiving how calamitously laws that are not definitive may be interpreted.

At this point in time it seems to me we are trying to *suppose* what the proposed Equal Rights Amendment will do, but we don't really know. *If,* and I stress the word *if,* we were all of one mind and one philosophy and united absolutely in our values, we might dare to pass an ambiguous amendment; but we are a pluralistic society, whose members have many backgrounds and perspectives, and this results in differing and often conflicting opinions.

We must, therefore, be especially wary and thoughtful when we do not know what interpretations *will* be made of any piece of legislation. And so I repeat, one of the strongest arguments for opposing ERA, or for rescinding its passage as is the case for you here in Idaho, is that we do not know what it will do!

Proponents agree with opponents on this: no one knows what it will mean in our lives!

But the consequences now unknown will most certainly be far-reaching. We can base this statement, in part, on what is happening in states where an ERA provision has been enacted into state constitutional law.

An example could well come from your neighbor state of Washington, which adopted a state Equal Rights Amendment in 1972. In the case of Darrin vs. Gould, the *Pacific Reporter* (2nd series, starting on p. 882) reports the following:

> Parents of high school girls brought class action claiming illegal discrimination against females in the field of high school interscholastic football competition.
>
> The Grays Harbor Superior Court denied relief, and plaintiffs appealed.
>
> The Washington Supreme Court, on September 25, 1975, held that the school could not constitutionally deny two of its fully qualified high school students permission to play on the high school team in interscholastic competition solely on the ground that the students were girls; . . . the denial constituted discrimination based on sex.
>
> Justice Hamilton stated this: "With some qualms, I concur in the result reached by the majority. I do so, however, exclusively upon the basis that the result is dictated by the broad and mandatory language of . . . Washington's Equal Rights Amendment.
>
> "Whether the people in enacting the ERA fully contemplated and appreciated the result here reached, coupled with its prospective variations, may be questionable.
>
> "Nevertheless, in sweeping language they embedded the principle of the ERA in our constitution, and it is beyond the authority of this court to modify the people's will. So be it."

I call to your attention some of the words used by Justice Hamilton relating to the Washington State Equal Rights Amendment and this particular case: "with some qualms," "I concur," "broad and mandatory language," "prospective variations," "sweeping language." These, my friends, may sound like "scare" words, but they come from a state Supreme Court justice's ruling.

Justices Finley, Wright, Utter, and Bracktenback in their majority decision wrote: "Presumably the people in adopting Constitutional Article 31 intended to do more than repeat what was already contained in the otherwise governing constitutional provisions, federal and state, by which discrimination based on sex was permissible under the rational relationship and strict scrutiny test. . . . Had such a limited purpose been intended, there would have been no necessity to resort to the broad, sweeping, mandatory language of the Equal Rights Amendment."

Again, may I call attention to words used by the State Supreme Court justices: *broad, sweeping, mandatory language.*

The decision rendered in this case in the state of Washington is indicative of far-reaching consequences not envisioned by the people when they ratified the amendment.

If ambiguity and the very possible unforeseen extreme interpretations of the law were the *only* reasons I had for being against the Equal Rights Amendment, they would be sufficient. However, I have other equally grave reasons to consider its passage unwise.

First, the proposed amendment, which I hope you in Idaho will rescind, might very well create severe difficulties in families by abruptly and adversely upsetting role patterns of men, women, and children. For example, in a marriage relationship there would probably be loss of legal responsibility for one partner to another.

Second, many proponents of the ERA seem to be disappointed that women do not play a more prominent role in public life. They attribute this condition to legal obstacles, when actually it is mainly due to social prejudices and pressures, and to certain widely held values that I think are positive. Frequently women who value the role of homemaker and parent do not have the desire or the time to pursue a visible public role.

I believe that building stable families, which will produce able, dedicated citizens, is the best possible service women can give to a community. Traditionally, the law has made note of this as it has tried to build safeguards to protect women not only as individuals but also as essential family leaders of prime importance. To destroy these protections and safeguards would be calamitous. No gains would outweigh such losses.

I feel certain that removing safeguards and redefining roles would result in many unworkable situations and frequently in the disruption of family relationships and accepted social practices.

Stable families constitute the heart and core of society. The need to rear children in security, love, and understanding has never been greater. Thus any changes in the traditional safeguards for homemakers should be carefully evaluated as they relate to the optimum growth of children and the stability of the family. The woman's role in the family will never be wholly the same as a man's—it can't be. We should protect the family—indeed all members of our society—while working effectively for any necessary changes to benefit women.

Third, under ERA it might be ruled in a divorce that neither spouse would be responsible for the children if each of them didn't wish to be.

Fourth, the amendment might not only legalize a homosexual union but also make it legally permissible for persons living in such a union to adopt children. I do not think that such an arrangement for children would give them a good chance to prepare for normal family living, but rather would perpetuate personalities that are poorly equipped emotionally and would lead to further breakdown of normal family patterns.

Fifth, the probable legal morass resulting from the amendment is frightening. In the legal complications, we might find that each issue would have to be litigated at least until each state has amended its laws, and then a great deal of litigation would have to go on to interpret the amended laws.

The national ERA is so broad that I am convinced it would bring us much more trouble than has been envisioned by even the most pessimistic of its opponents. And in many instances women would be hurt, not helped.

A very substantial concern for those of us who care about helping women is that the ERA would, in fact, cause women to lose previously hard-won rights. For example:

1. Preferential admission to professional schools would be in jeopardy.

2. Job preference for women would be changed or eliminated.

3. Athletic opportunities for girls in public schools and colleges could be greatly limited if girls must compete physically with boys on equal terms.

If sex could no longer be a consideration in legal interpretation, boys and men would most likely be given preference in many areas, and this preference could not come under the scrutiny tests on the basis of sex. Contrast that with our present arrangement. Under the Fourteenth Amendment the strict scrutiny test must be applied to determine whether there really is a compelling reason for allowing distinction because of sex. Under ERA this test could not be applied, and any help that women might need beyond that granted to men could not be given.

We are going to need piecemeal corrective legislation whether ERA is enacted or not. We'll have to go to court anyway. But I suggest that by going the ERA route we will lose much more than we can gain. The better way is to move effectively to enforce present laws and enact others that are needed.

I am pleading today that we use reason, not emotion, in resolving this issue. The words *equal* and *rights* sound so full of hope that there is danger of our being deceived by false impressions; hence we need to pay strict attention to how the amendment has twisted the real meaning of those words.

I hope you never forget that we are for the rights of women. I hope you can see that while we are against the ERA, we are for individual legislation which would bring equality under the law to men and women.

We all tend to get impatient when changes need to be made. I often wish the changes could be made instantly in this case, but experience has taught me that the creation of laws that free people from repressive traditions and ignorance requires careful study and reflection. Each law, each step in correcting wrongs, needs to be carefully considered so that the process of righting wrongs does not create worse problems.

Time does not allow me to explain all the changes we would like to see brought about to help women. However, I would like to discuss examples of areas in which provisions for women need to be changed or strengthened. These changes can be made if we will work at them consistently and vigorously.

Laws need to be changed where necessary to ensure that a homemaker's contribution to the family is equal in value to the spouse who works outside the home, and laws should be passed to protect the woman's contribution.

If a state has discriminatory tax laws, they should be changed. For example, if equal-inheritance protection is not given to husband and wife, such laws should be corrected.

Laws have recently been passed giving women equal opportunity to obtain credit and sign contracts. Strict enforcement of these laws is necessary.

The laws regarding equal pay and equal job opportunity must also be enforced to guarantee all individuals their rights.

Social Security laws are another area in which reform is required.

Widowers, as well as widows, should be able to claim their spouse's benefits.

Government pensions should be equal for men and women performing the same work.

A close look should be taken at the laws governing unemployment benefits for women; and where inequalities exist they should be corrected.

When that protection is not already provided for, we need to find legal means by which communities can assist a wife who is physically abused by her husband.

The whole area of women and children's rights in divorce needs to be reexamined urgently. Where injustice occurs in the areas concerning equitable division of property, maintenance, and child custody and support, we should work to change the laws.

We need to work to find much better ways to enforce laws on alimony and child support. While alimony and child support are sometimes abused, many responsible women need the support they give.

If these supports were eliminated, as they well might be under ERA, we would probably see an increased number of divorces in this country, which is already troubled with too many divorces. If alimony were to be done away with, it is probable that more husbands would seek divorce.

I truly believe that women would suffer greatly under new interpretations of divorce laws under the ERA.

The above are just examples of areas that need urgent attention. There are other areas we need to work on.

But bear in mind that that ERA cannot and will not meet these needs. Individual corrective legislation is needed.

Where do we go? What do we do?

First of all, we need to understand that no blanket piece of legislation can take care of all of our problems.

I have tried to explain our opposition to this proposed amendment and why we are so concerned. We need to work vigorously using our time, strength, and means, as much as is reasonable, to defeat the amendment or, as in the state of Idaho, to rescind it.

This will take a lot of work.

Your state legislators should be brought to know how strongly you feel that they should vote to rescind the previous vote on ERA.

For me, as an American, an unusual situation has arisen. In the midst of this struggle over how best to secure equal rights, it has been suggested that Mormon legislators should not have the right to vote on this issue.

What strange advice to give in a democracy that is devoted to freedom of speech and religious freedom! Surely legislators are elected by people who want them to represent them! Surely legislators are duty-bound to vote! They *must*, if they are responsible. They do not represent just themselves; they represent their constituency, particularly the majority of the constituents.

There is much for all of us to do, much that calls for vigor, courage, and understanding, if we are going to do as our ancestors have done for us—leave this world a better place for our children.

Concerning this proposed amendment and all laws, especially those laws aimed to help end discrimination for both men and women, there are positive things we can do:

1. We can devote part of our time as citizens to patriotic duty and study these proposed laws carefully.

2. We can identify issues and problems that need attention and urge our lawmakers to introduce corrective measures.

3. We can studiously reexamine our laws to make sure we root out discrimination.

4. We can, then, not only initiate those laws that are needed but also personally lobby for their passage.

5. We can join groups that exhibit good judgment and share our point of view. Group effort often seems to have greater impact than individual efforts.

6. We can work actively to support and reelect state and congressional legislators who will strive to eliminate discrimination.

7. We can exercise sensitive and watchful concern as part of our citizenship roles. We can note violations and help to see that the laws are enforced. And surely we all should periodically examine our role as citizens and ask ourselves if we are obeying the law, helping to enforce it, or trying to change it when necessary. In other words, are we truly law-abiding citizens?

8. We can continue to encourage women to participate in public life when their family life permits it. Their understanding, insight, and sensitivity are needed, and the need will grow.

9. We can actively support legal or legislative action in instances where laws are not being enforced or where misunderstandings as to the interpretation of a law has arisen.

10. We can complain less and do more. In this case, particularly, move vigorously and intelligently to let your legislators know that you want to have this measure rescinded.

America is a wonderful country. Our form of government has been good to its men and its women. There is still much to do and I don't wish to minimize the task, but even with all our problems I'm glad I'm an American woman, a citizen of the United States.

I hope we will always protect the blessings we have and not pass laws that are unnecessary, that are ambiguous, or that will jeopardize our present laws protecting women.

Let us unite, strive, and work forcefully for what we believe is right and is needed in the law. Let us strive with equal vigor against that which is wrong.

I'm pleased to be among the people of Coeur d'Alene. Coeur d'Alene recalls French trappers; explorers; men and women who were brave and daring; men and women who explored unknown worlds; men and women who were rugged, determined, and lived with hope, courage, vision, and determination.

This area of Idaho is grandeur itself—beautiful lakes, timber, mines, the riches of the earth. But the fruits were not to be had without much planning and work. Although it is my first trip into your Panhandle, I realize that your pride is well founded.

The victory over poor legislation, like the winning of the West, calls for the same mettle, the same dedication, and the same spirit and work as was required to make Coeur d'Alene possible and Idaho possible.

This spirit is still here. I can see it. I can feel it.

It is my hope that you will be able to rally the support of the people and the legislators of this state and rescind its ratification of the Equal Rights Amendment.

In conclusion, I hope you will remember two significant quotations. Joseph Conrad said, "Being a woman is a terribly difficult task, since it consists principally in dealing with men."

But then, as the late, famous Hattie McDaniel said, "They are the best opposite sex we have."

Let's work to make the laws better for all of us, by making them good for both men and women.

Your Promise
to the Land
of Promise

I t is a thrilling experience to stand before this vast audience this morning and realize that you are the children of God chosen to come forth in these last days to do his work. I learned during my recent visit to your campus that you are well aware of the world's problems: disease, poverty, hunger, immorality, and man's inhumanity to man. I saw that you are seeking solutions, thoughtfully considering the opinions of others, using scientific methods, and interacting in ways that can prepare you to declare unitedly and boldly that you will follow Jesus Christ to a final victory. This is not to be a game that ends in a tie, or one which contains a strategic plan for a last-second shot; it is to end in a victory that binds evil and unrighteousness and frees the Lord's people that they might be safely gathered into his kingdom.

To some this victory may seem an impossible dream at this point in time, but I assure you it is possible and it will happen. However, it can come about only through honest men and women who are willing to dedicate their lives to its accomplishment. I feel sure that to some it may have seemed impos-

Address delivered at Brigham Young University Devotional Assembly, February 17, 1976.

sible that George Washington could ever free the colonies from the great power that controlled them. It may have seemed impossible that those colonies would ever unite after the battles of Lexington and Concord. The Congress had studied and debated for nearly a full year. I'm sure that it was a weary but happy John Adams who, after his tireless efforts in the Congress, wrote to his wife, Abigail, as follows:

> Yesterday the greatest question was decided which ever was debated in America, and a greater, perhaps never was nor will be decided among men. A resolution was passed without one dissenting colony "that these united colonies are, and of right ought to be, free and independent states."

Notice his insight in this addition:

> You will think me transported with enthusiasm, but I am not. I am well aware of the toil, and blood, and treasure, that it will cost us to maintain this Declaration, and support and defend these states. Yet through all the gloom, I can see the rays of crashing glory. I can see that the end is more than worth all the means. (*The Book of Abigail and John* [Harvard University Press, 1975], pp. 139, 142.)

And they were not just idle words in which those men pledged their lives, their fortunes, and their sacred honor:

> For their dedication to the cause of independence, the signers risked loss of fortune, imprisonment, and death for treason. Although none died directly at the hands of the British, the wife of one . . . succumbed as a result of harsh prison treatment. About one-third of the group served as militia officers, most [of that group had] seen wartime action. . . . [Five] of these men . . . were taken captive. The homes of nearly one-third of the signers were destroyed or damaged, and families of a few were scattered when the British pillaged or confiscated their estates.
>
> Nearly all of the group emerged poorer for their years of public service and neglect of personal affairs. (*Signers of the Declaration* [U.S. Department of Interior, National Park Service, 1973], p. 31.)

It was not a flamboyant or glamorous gesture, then, when they signed that document that declared to all the world that compelling reasons made it necessary for them to break from Great Britain.

The move for independence occurred in an age of mental enlightenment, as recognized by Norman Cousins in his book, *In God We Trust:*

> The seeds of the free mind seemed to sprout at the same time. . . . Ideas have a life of their own. They can be nourished and brought into active growth by a small number of sensitive, vital minds which somehow respond to the needs of a total organism, however diffused the parts of that organism may be. (*In God We Trust* [Harper Brothers Publishing, 1958], p. 7, p. 6.)

And so it was with the ideas that brought men to pledge all they had and, in fact, life itself to the founding of this nation. Concepts and even phrases of the Declaration of Independence seemed to occur to various men at almost the same time. The framers of the Declaration of Independence experienced the thrill of recognizing that what they were thinking, other great minds were thinking as well. In writing the Declaration, what Thomas Jefferson did was to bring the words, the need, and the moment together.

We know from revelation that the Lord raised up these good men to do this mighty work. It was no accident. The remarkable and joyful thing is that these young men and women who lived two hundred years ago accepted the challenge of their times so effectively. Laced throughout their writings is the evidence of their reliance on divine guidance. In the Declaration itself, they appeal to the world court on the grounds that they acted in answer to that higher law of God which provides that all men are "endowed by their creator with certain unalienable rights." Norman Cousins describes the founding fathers' faith in man:

> The American Founding Fathers . . . believed deeply in the ability of a human being to learn enough in order to take part in self-government; in the capacity of people to make sense of their lives if given reasonable conditions within society itself; in the responsive power of men when exposed to great ideas; in people to stand under the due

process of law; in man to make basic decisions concerning his religion or his politics or anything else. (*In God We Trust*, p. 8.)

This is the provision that our Heavenly Father has made as to the potential in all of us. Inspired by the Lord, the Prophet Joseph Smith said, "I teach them correct principles, and they govern themselves." In the mighty struggle before the world was, God stood firm for the resolution that mankind had to have their agency so they could progress. Our Heavenly Father has continued through the ages to offer us knowledge and wisdom, and also to allow evil as well as good to exist so that we might have options necessary for the exercise of our agency.

A sense of destiny seemed to be with Americans even in their earliest encounters with this continent, as evidenced by John Winthrop's words as early as 1600. He wrote: "For we must consider that we shall be as a city upon a hill. The eyes of all people are upon us. So that if we shall deal falsely with God in this work we have undertaken and so cause him to withdraw his present help from us, we shall be made a story and a byword through the world." (*Britannica Library of Great American Writing*, vol. 1, p. 36.)

In Louis Untermeyer's foreword to the *Britannica Library of Great American Writing*, he supports this fact and yet recognizes the great diversities in America as he describes it and its people:

> This is a country of contradictions. Restlessness, a love of movement for its own sake, is distinctly an American trait, but so is the love of the land and the desire to get one's roots deep into it. Americans are avid for experiment. They will buy and try anything new. But they are also devoted to the status quo, to things as they are and to letting well enough alone. They are nostalgic about the last (and lost) frontier; they lament the passing of the past; yet they believe in an ever-expanding, limitless future. They are isolationists, and they also see their country as the pivotal force of the world. They are a hybrid product of many kinds, creeds, and colors from every possible racial group, and yet they are a race apart, a polyglot people to whom

the letters U.S. mean not only United States but personally "US."

The typical American cherishes his contradictions. He is both proud and complacent about the size, vigor, and variety of his country, a country intensely devoted to ancient doctrines and the Good Book. And yet he knows that within less that fifty years, this same country produced two new Bibles: *The Book of Mormon* and *Science and Health*. He is likely to seem naive, apt to regard his nation as the New Jerusalem and himself as one of the specially privileged elect, one who echoes the declaration of John Adams, "I always consider the settlement of America as the opening of a grand scheme and design in Providence for the illumination and emancipation of the slavish part of mankind all over the earth." Yet his very boastfulness stems from a sense of wonder; he shares a gigantic vision which in the midst of vast prairies and breath-taking plateaus rears skyscraping cities of incredible industry and luxury. (*Britannica Library of Great American Writing*, foreword, Louis Untermeyer.)

So here we are—you and I—Americans of diverse backgrounds, trying to understand our destiny, celebrating the significant event of the founding of our country, and looking at the two hundred years of contradictions and magnificent events side by side. Our view of history is tempered by revealed truths. This country came forth with divine help and planning to provide a climate in which the gospel could be fully restored. Men of all nations were brought together as a melting pot so that they might be prepared and ready to hear the word of God. And at this crossroads in time, you stand quite naturally ready to examine our country's history. Take care how you look. History is not an easy thing to understand. Therefore, read widely, think deeply, and judge wisely.

We cannot alter the pages of history, but we need to understand what was done in the past, even if it was not all praiseworthy or of good report, so that we might avoid mistakes in the future. Errors should not blind us to the good that our nation has contributed to the progress of mankind. As a country, we have contributed much in the field of government. No other constitution acknowledges that the source of power reposes in the people and that only that power which they delegate belongs to the state. The sober, thoughtful system of checks and balances has stood the test of severe and traumatic challenges. This principle of checks and balances stands as a torch in the night. We need to keep that torch burning. The idea of democracy itself must have new champions. Only about one-fourth of the nations in the world are functioning as democracies. The temptation to wield power is great, and most of the world is still struggling to be free from the fetters of oppressive government. No matter how benevolent the dictatorship, control of human life is a terrible price to pay.

A free country is an American dream. Keeping that dream alive in your minds and hearts is a continuing responsibility. Don't be discouraged by error, foolishness, or selfishness. Don't be cynical when you observe that not everyone has found opportunity in the America you know. Liberty, freedom, democracy, and trust in God—these are, as John Adams said, our "rays of crashing glory," worthy of our ongoing support whatever the cost. They can be ours. We *can* be free if we *will* be free.

The Lord has told us in the scriptures that this blessed land will be free only so long as its inhabitants serve the God of the land. Remember the words in 2 Nephi:

> Wherefore, this is consecrated unto him whom he shall bring. And if it so be that they shall serve him according to the commandments which he hath given, it shall be a land of liberty unto them; wherefore, they shall never be brought down into captivity; if so, it shall be because of iniquity; for if iniquity shall abound cursed shall be the land for their sakes, but unto the righteous it shall be blessed forever. (2 Nephi 1:7.)

So what is it, my young friends, that you can best do for America? Commit yourselves to serve the God of this land by living according to the truths he has given. Knowing what we know, none of us should do less.

There is so much that you can do to help others and thereby live more fully. Have you walked the hospital corridors and seen the suffering—men and women so racked with pain that they can barely shuffle one foot in front of the other? Who will find the medicines to cure these ailments?

Have you seen the despondency in the eyes of those whose disease knows no stopping point? Who will find the cause?

Have you watched with a lump in your throat while someone you love inches courageously forward on an unsteady leg after extensive surgery and an amputation? The therapy is so long and so hard. Who will care enough to help guide him through the hours upon hours of struggle and heartbreak until new muscles take over unaccustomed tasks?

Who will prepare the children to receive knowledge through more effective teaching?

Have you wondered how to solve the difficult problems of air and land pollution? Somewhere there are answers. Someone will find them.

Have you a symphony or a hymn in your soul? Are you getting the knowledge and discipline so that the world may hear it someday?

Who will discover the perfect diets and serve the meals that will allow people to perform up to their full potential?

Have you seen the waste of human life in the slums of the world? Who is going to find a way to stop the deadly cycle that leads to such ruined, wasted human life?

How about the energy crisis? Or the overriding cynicism of a world caught up in existential philosophies? Who is going to make contact with morality and faith a reality? Are *you*?

Now is the time of your preparation. You will be better able to help our country if you come to your tomorrows having made the most of this precious time. You will be of less value if you try to build your life on expediency and false principles. We all have this responsibility.

Shakespeare said it this way:

> Be just, and fear not:
> Let all the ends thou aim'st at be thy country's,
> Thy God's, and truth's.

> *(King Henry VIII, 3.2.)*

As you explore that unknown country inside of yourself, look for the talents and dream the dreams that will make you aspire to great and noble things. Then what you leave behind will be a great country, a strong, stable family, a life of significance, a torch still burning bright like the one handed you by the founding fathers.

In our day, young women are encouraged to reach out and fulfill their potentials in many ways. It is important in so doing that they think carefully about the years ahead. In the light of the eternal perspectives the gospel provides, they need to use wisely these years of preparation and fill their minds and hearts with dreams and with learning. The Church cannot afford to waste any of its precious human resources; neither can our nation. Both must use the human resources in ways that will be in keeping with true values and divine approbation.

Women should approach their options and choices thoughtfully and prayerfully. When they choose to rear children and thereby build strong family units, they should realize that such a choice is filled with challenge and fulfillment. It cannot be merely a "spare-time" option if we are to give our nation strong, stable families that are our society's hope for continued existence. No society in the history of the world has survived the breakdown of the family.

Consequently, it must be with thoughtful hearts that we hear and heed the prophet's present-day counsel to strengthen family units. The choices made in planning any career, occupation, vocation, or avocation should be those that will have the strongest influence for good on family units.

As a leader of the nearly one million Latter-day Saint women in the Relief Society organization, I would use my full influence to persuade every young woman to accept with joy the opportunities of her divinely given role as a woman. Whether she is a student, homemaker, mother, wife, teacher, or whatever her chosen profession, she can exemplify womanhood at its best and have the faith to stand for high ideals that will be an inspiration to all about her, including the new and rising generation. She can be a guide to those who follow, and thereby help them build that high type of character that is necessary in citizens who would maintain a strong nation. While men and women are of equal worth in God's eyes, he has made it clear that they are not the same and are not intended to be. Because of the differences, there are some activities for which women are better suited and others for which men are better suited.

As an example, I would not encourage any young Latter-day Saint woman, especially one just out of high school, to enlist in the military. I say this despite the inviting brochures that are designed to persuade young women to enlist in the military services, some of which have lately come into my hands. I know that many factors, including the extremist views of the women's movement, have impelled the government not only to encourage but to actively recruit women into military ranks. Looking at the thrust of their approach, I see page after page of appeals that seek to entice young women to enlist. The blandishments employed come in very appealing packages. They emphasize personal opportunities, travel, challenges, training, and money.

The success of this strong recruitment effort for women is dramatically apparent in the statistics. In October 1975 the *Salt Lake Tribune* carried an article by Barry Rohan of the *Knight Newspaper* staff. He wrote, "This fall nearly half of the freshmen ROTC classes are women students." The Office of the Assistant Secretary of Defense reports that "great strides" have been made in increasing the number of women in uniform. The result of these efforts has been that the number of women serving in the military has increased from 55,000 in 1973 to 97,000 in 1975, and the goal is 120,000 women by 1977. (Unpublished Report, "Manpower Requirements Report for FY1976," prepared by Office of Assistant Secretary of Defense, Manpower and Reserve Affairs, 1975.) These statistics give some idea of the appeal of the recruitment program. A recent article in the *Deseret News* called it "The Latest Military Invasion—Women!"

I feel that the regimentation of military life places a great strain upon most women who enlist. It is difficult for them to live under the pressures that put their lives so completely into another's charge, resigning their actions to another's command.

A recent letter from some concerned parents is typical of others I have received. It illustrates some of the problems to which I refer:

Dear President Smith:

Some time ago we received a phone call from our daughter. She is in the army. She was crying over the phone; in fact, she was almost hysterical. She felt she had not one friend on earth. Those she thought were her friends had deserted her and were in fact persecuting her unmercifully, for one reason because she is a "Mormon." To say we were in despair is an understatement.

A second letter was enclosed with the letter from these parents. It read in part:

I am your daughter's Relief Society visiting teacher. My companion and I were at first unable to locate her. When we . . . did make contact, we found a . . . depressed and mixed-up young lady. . . . I'm not connected with the military and I soon had my eyes opened to the unfortunate circumstances in which girls in the military may find themselves. How very difficult it would be to keep gospel standards in mind when one was continually subject to the rowdy, cigarette-filled . . . barracks, the . . . regimentation of being dumped into a job for which one is neither suited nor trained.

Since that initial visit, and on following visits as she became aware of the Church here . . . a distinct change came over her. As far as her work would permit, she attended ward functions and everyone was aware of her friendly presence. One could almost measure the light that came back into her lovely eyes . . . she began to smile as she realized that people cared. . . . You're going to be welcoming home a very special daughter . . . I shall miss her because she is my friend. I shall always be grateful to her for showing me . . . the change that can come into one's life when they grasp firmly the iron rod.

I would hope that all Latter-day Saint women would think long and hard about the regimentation of enlistment in military service, for our experience shows women's involvement in the military to be very disappointing. A career military officer who is a good Latter-day Saint made the following observation:

> I have seen both sides of the story; clean, wholesome young ladies who have lived their religion and who have anxiously and effectively shared it with others, and then I have sadly witnessed some of these young ladies become engulfed in the mire and filth. . . . Unfortunately . . . the majority of the cases fall in the latter category.

Very little moral guidance is provided by the military. Each person sets his own values. The result is consistent with current trends in society.

As Latter-day Saints, however, we are committed to live according to a God-given set of values. Moral integrity is not just what *we* say is right. Moral cleanliness and integrity will always be that which God has revealed to be right. Whether we *live* these principles or not is a personal choice.

The special conditions of regimentation and assigned living quarters in the military make it difficult to remove oneself from unwholesome environments and their consequent pressures and temptations. We must do our best to keep ourselves free from situations that might cause us to compromise our standards.

As I voice my concerns for a young woman who chooses to enlist into the regular military ranks, I am at the same time in favor of the military service organizations such as those you have on campus. One of my daughters found great growth as she participated in and was commandant of Angel Flight here at Brigham Young University. She learned personal discipline. She found great pleasure in mingling with associates. The Angel Flight drill team was very successful that year, and she took pride in their accomplishment.

I raise my concern about service in the military, particularly for young women, because I want them to make knowledgeable choices. At the same time, I recognize the great good of the military.

I have personal knowledge of the good being accomplished throughout the world by Latter-day Saint military personnel, both men and women. I have seen their good influence as I have traveled through the Far East countries with the General Authorities for the area conferences. Many people have accepted the gospel because of the teachings and the good example set by many outstanding Latter-day Saint military men and women. I pay them high tribute. I know that we need such leaders who dedicate their lives to the protection of our country, who will keep alive the ideals of morality, Christian living, and freedom upon which our democracy is founded. They are a strength to our country and to our Church throughout the world.

I know that a dedicated, strong, technically trained, well-directed military segment is vital to maintaining the good life, the free society, and the American dream. Since its founding, however, this country's freedom has been won and maintained largely by a male military, which was and is supported by wives, mothers, sisters, and sweethearts equally dedicated to the principles of freedom but, in my judgment, making their contribution to its cause in ways best suited to women.

I hope women will do in the future as they have done over and over again in the past: save families! I remember with pride the women who have been willing to help when the need arose. In the Revolutionary period, most of the women maintained the homes and families while their men went to war. But some of them, like Molly Pitcher, fired cannons when the need arose. Pioneer women built great, strong homes, but they also fired guns when they had to.

In periods of national emergency, women have always been able to rise to the need. During World War II, for instance, many thousands of women gave valued service in the military. But even in times of war, the home front is at least as vital to victory as is the battlefront. Without it there can be no victories on any front, in wartime or in peacetime. So whatever else we do as women, we need to remember that God has given us the home front to defend against all assaults.

There are many options open to women today, and Latter-day Saint women are caught up in the challenge of this change in society. We cannot with conviction turn our backs on the divine counsel that women are the homemakers of the world. As we build a strong home front, we provide a supporting line of defense in times of war and peace that is critical and irre-placeable.

Even our national anthem reflects this thought, as in the last stanza we sing:

> Oh, thus be it ever, when free *men* shall stand
> Between their loved *homes* and the war's desolation.

> (Italics added.)

America is the great ongoing dream of liberty and democ-racy. American deserves the commitment of our lives to the maintenance of this dream. America's essential ingredients must continue to be morality and integrity if we are to pre-serve this land. America is a land of personal choices and re-sponsibility. America is a land where one can fulfill one's des-tiny.

Nobody can tell you what the years ahead will hold for you. You can be sure there will be happy and tender moments. You can be assured there will be exciting achievements. You can be certain there will be down days, and problems you can-not anticipate. That is the nature of mortality. Your real job is to meet whatever comes and refine your souls as you do so.

You can map out a general path. You can commit to living the truth as you see it. You can, through your actions, tell the world that you are not ashamed of the gospel of Jesus Christ. Then wherever you are, whatever you elect to do, you will be building his kingdom and preserving this great land for your children and your children's children.

What will the next two hundred years hold for our land, this land of promise? What do you promise to our great land of promise? If you promise a life of integrity and moral purity, you are for your part again giving our nation the fundamental building block of greatness and of liberty. Without such gifts you give only ashes, whose effect is to destroy this great, free land.

As I stand here today, I remember Deborah, a mother, a prophetess, a judge in Israel, who rallied her wavering and oppressed countrymen to battle to accomplish the work needed to deliver the Lord's people in her day. Deborah's greatness lay not in her physical strength but in her moral leadership, in the confidence she inspired that the Lord would aid those who fought for a righteous cause. May we all have that same greatness. May we have the vision our Founding Fathers had of a free nation. It is worth all the sacrifice it took to create it, and worth all the sacrifice it will take to maintain it. Thomas Jefferson can be an eloquent reminder. "The people," he said, "are the only sure reliance for the preservation of our liberty."

It is my prayer that as American citizens we will search our souls and, as George Washington counseled, rededicate ourselves and "Labour to keep alive . . . that little spark of celestial fire—conscience."

With that conscience and the Holy Spirit we, men and women, can accept the challenge of our time and contribute effectively to that which our nation needs most. We can give dreams for a future of growth, solutions to problems not yet solved, and hope for the future. We can build a foundation of moral virtue that gives strength and stability as our part in that final victory which will make it possible for the Lord's people to be safely gathered into his kingdom.

May this be our promise to this land of promise.

Life: The Essential

O n a former visit to the state of Washington I was greeted with "Welcome to the apple bowl of the world!" Those who met me were proud of this beautiful state. They were pleased to live in a state noted for its production of superior apples and were eager to tell me about this industry. I had received a big box of delicious Washington apples each Christmas for the past six years, so I listened with genuine interest to every claim they made.

As we rode toward Quincy, I enjoyed the discussion that continued about the apple industry, and I learned a lot. I came to know that quality apples don't just happen; producing them is an exact science. A great amount of money, time, and effort is expended in scientific research. Scientists teach the orchard owners how to make good use of the state's natural resources.

I was told of the important work orchard owners do during the winter months when they prune the trees by hand to eliminate branches that will not produce good fruit or branches that would keep out the sunlight or cause the apples to rub against each other. I learned about the sprays used against mil-

Address delivered in Graham, Washington, January 22, 1977.

dew, cutworms, leaf rollers, aphids, and insects. I saw the elaborate watering systems that had been installed. I was fascinated when I was told that the orchard owners knew exactly when the trees would blossom. They just add each degree of temperature above fifty degrees until a thousand degrees are counted, and the trees then burst into full bloom.

I could hardly comprehend importing thousands of beehives to ensure pollination or that there is a "king" blossom that can most easily withstand the forces of nature. The blossoms are protected, and it is planned that thirty or forty leaves will nourish each apple. I was told of the supports used to keep the branches from breaking under the weight of the fruit. I was told that professional pickers are hired to carefully yet swiftly pick the fruit so that it will be of top quality when it is delivered to the apple shed.

This multimillion-dollar business brings rich rewards to the orchard owners, pride and revenue to the state of Washington, and health to those who eat and enjoy the life-sustaining fruit. Tonight, I can't help but contrast the apple industry with another multimillion-dollar business that has developed in the United States since the court decision of four years ago today—January 22, 1973. It is one which will not bring rich rewards of beauty, of satisfaction, of health, and of life, but a harvest of a different sort. That decision states: "An unborn child is the property of the mother and . . . she may dispose of it for any reason during the first six months of pregnancy, and at any other time if, in the opinion of a single licensed physician, it is necessary to preserve her life or health."

In the name of "human rights" a multimillion-dollar business has grown up in America facilitating abortion to prevent the birth of the unwanted child, abortion to give men and women the right to participate in illicit relations without responsibility to a child conceived, and abortion to control the population and supposedly preserve life in the universe.

These are the rationalized terms used to describe abortions, terms under which thousands of conceptions are ended in the harsh, white light of a hospital while young interns marvel at the clean, deft touch of the doctors who sever the life-giving cords and destroy the forming child. These young students are thus acquiring attitudes of affirmation for a basically life-destroying skill. When they graduate, these young men and women will be trained in the healing arts, and yet far too many will enter into an industry which brings financial remuneration and controls population but which makes infinitely less of all those who participate in it.

The lucrative business of destroying life is becoming more and more acceptable in today's world. The legalizing of abortion has encouraged individuals to use their self-proclaimed "human rights" to destroy the life potential of others. No wonder immorality and irresponsibility are also becoming more and more accepted as a life-style today.

What are the fruits of this industry? Let us consider them. First, there are thousands of women now who will never know motherhood to the child they have aborted. What does it do to a woman not to bear that child?

Let me tell you about one young woman with whom I am personally acquainted. We worked together in an office, and we became friends. She was a beautiful young woman, and very capable. We spent our rest breaks and lunch hours together. One day she was absent from work. When she returned, she told me that she had missed work to have an abortion. She said her husband felt it was important for her to work for a few years before they had a family. So she submitted to the abortion to please him. She had no idea of the impact that abortion would have upon her future life and her mental health.

We never mentioned the subject again, even though our friendship continued through the years. We both had children at about the same time. I had seven and she had five. She was an exceptionally good mother. I loved to go to her home and watch her with her children. She prepared and served good meals. She was one with her children. They had every advantage; they were clean, happy, well cared for, and loved.

When she was in her forties she had a complete nervous breakdown. Her doctors told her it was a direct result of the abortion she had had many years before. After the birth of other children, feelings of guilt and remorse preyed upon her mind. She knew too late the significance of her acquiescence to the pressure that caused her to destroy a life. Women like my friend, women who are sensitive, thoughtful, and love life, will undoubtedly experience lifelong remorse over a destroyed life. They will carry the weight of that guilt and suffer so many unhappy moments that it will be like a millstone around their necks.

Second, there are the fathers who never really were, the men who, in these instances, might have become true fathers and learned the important responsibilities they should have assumed when they participated in the conception of life.

For many of such men the endless, meaningless chase after sexual gratification will continue without the tempering, shaping, growing which would have come as a man holds his newborn infant and begins to realize the blessing of his own life and his responsibility in the creation of new life. The maturity which would have come as he tried to provide food, clothing, and shelter for his loved ones will never come to the man who participates in conception and yet does not become a father. He will never know the strength received as a father develops the capacity to walk tall with a child or to have children follow in his footsteps.

Third, there are the unborn babies, the children who never will be able to experience the joys and challenges of mortality, of discovering their talents and making their contributions.

Carl Sandburg, the great American poet, declared, "Babies are God's opinion that life should go on."

Another writer, F. M. Bareham wrote:

A century ago (in 1809) men were following with bated breath the march of Napoleon and waiting with feverish impatience for news of the wars. And all the while in their homes babies were being born. But who could think about babies? Everybody was thinking about battles.

In one year, between Trafalgar and Waterloo, there stole into the world a host of heroes; Gladstone was born in Liverpool; Tennyson at Somersby Rectory; and Oliver Wendell Holmes in Massachusetts. Abraham Lincoln was born in Kentucky, and music was enriched by the advent of Felix Mendelssohn in Hamburg.

But nobody thought of babies; everybody was thinking of battles. Yet which of the battles of 1809 mattered more than the babies of 1809? We fancy God can manage his world only with great battalions, when all the time he is doing it with beautiful babies.

When a wrong wants righting, or a truth wants preaching, or a continent wants discovering, God sends a baby into the world to do it.

Fourth, there is the society and its impoverishment that results because the babies were not allowed to grow up. The leadership and potential of each child aborted is a denial to society at large. What a terrible waste, when we have so many problems yet unsolved!

A woman from your locality wrote her feelings about abortion from the viewpoint of an adopted person. Let me quote from her letter:

> Fortunately for me, abortion was hard to obtain when I was conceived. I was an illegitimate baby born just before World War II broke out. I was, therefore, not a person conceived due to a soldier marching off to war, or home on leave. The act of lovemaking was not an "I may never see you again" thing!
>
> I believe it was a thing that happened naturally between two young people in love, who were unable to control their emotions. I also believe an abortion was not sought because it was deeply frowned upon, as well as illegal. The majority of people's morals were very high, too high to allow them to seek out a "butcher," as the doctors who did perform illegal abortions were commonly referred to.
>
> If I were conceived today, I might not be illegitimate. I might be dead. I would never have been born. And, if I were dead, then my three lovely daughters would not be here either.
>
> You know something? I'm just glad I am here! I'm just as sure that my three daughters feel the same way.

As I think about her gratitude for life and about the evils of abortion, I am appalled at the ever-increasing statistics on abortion:

317 abortion for 1,000 births

1,007 abortions in Washington, D.C., for 1,000 births

80 percent of the abortions performed are on unmarried persons

1,000,000 abortions for 3,150,000 births in the United States last year

I am saddened, but not surprised, when I realize that, according to Lawrence Feinberg of the *Washington Post* staff, the numbers of lives aborted have continually increased each year since the legalization of this action.

I am concerned when I see the report of Dr. Matthew J. Bulfin to the convention of the American College of Obstetricians and Gynecologists in October, 1975, wherein he documents the complications which follow abortion, including hospitalization and even death. In his report he declares, "As the vast majority of abortions are done for social reasons, the deaths and near deaths that do occur from the operation are especially tragic."

I will not detail the processes or effects of abortion, for you and I are all too well acquainted with them. But I would like to make a few comments regarding some of the core arguments that bolster this practice and continue to win legal approval and public acceptance for it.

It is argued that this world of ours has insufficient food to care for the tremendous population explosion that would result from continued unplanned parenting. This argument carries no weight with members of The Church of Jesus Christ of Latter-day Saints, who believe in a divine destiny for mankind. It seems to us that the challenge and the solution lies not in preventing life but in developing the earth's resources and our distribution skills so as to support life at the highest possible levels. In modern revelation we read that "the earth is full, and there is enough and to spare" (D&C 104:17).

Elder Ezra Taft Benson, world-renowned agriculturalist and former Secretary of Agriculture, has said, "There isn't any question but what the resources of this earth, if developed as they are in the United States in our agriculture, could produce food sufficient to take care of several times our present world population."

If the energy going into population curtailment were being spent in these other challenging areas, we think there would be more satisfactory solutions to the problems, solutions at which we could all be justly proud—not grieved, as we should be at the abortion "solution."

In the matter of individual families, couples will have to make their own decisions regarding family size. But the only morally acceptable way to do so is before conception, not afterward.

It is often argued that only children who are wanted should be born. We counter that children should certainly be wanted and that adults must be taught in such a way that they grow to the point of accepting that each life is divine and that the challenge to bear and nurture children, helping them grow to maturity, is a gift from God. Parents also grow from the experience.

There are many challenges in the field of child abuse, challenges for which we must find solutions. Some of these solutions include teaching children more effectively so that they in turn may become effective parents; motivating men and women to genuinely improve their overall performance as parents; more effective schooling in the doctrine of responsibility; and encouraging more skill in family communication. But destroying life merely compounds problems. Abortion cannot be considered a solution; it is a contribution to social problems.

So we are against abortion, as we should be. However, consider also the fact that many will make the decision to have an abortion in panic, out of fear of severe familial and social reprisals, and because of ignorance. At the same time that we are working against abortion, then, we should be doubling our efforts to prevent the "need" for abortion. We should be educating parents and children on the need for chastity before marriage and fidelity after marriage.

In our Judeo-Christian world we are aware that the great Judeo-Christian prophets and leaders, and even Jesus Christ himself, taught that sexual impurity was to be avoided in all circumstances. As children of God we must do all we can to strengthen prevention of whatever causes lead to abortion. As people of compassion as well as of determination, however, we must also forgive the person who has erred and enclose them in our loving care and concern; we must help them to repent and forsake soul-destroying practices, and help them to know that forgiveness is available.

I am of the opinion that it really takes courage in today's world to give birth to a child, because so much is being said and done to arouse people's doubts and fears about the age-old tasks of parenthood. However, as I read in the pages of history the accounts of courageous men and women of the past, I realize that today we also have much going for us in comparison.

I am impressed by the life of Jochebed, a Levite woman of the Old Testament, whom you will recall lived as a slave in Egypt many years ago. She married a man who was of the house of Levi. In her day women could bear children, but the Pharaoh had the power of life and death over them. In Jochebed's time he decreed that if a newborn child was a female, she could remain alive; but if the child was a male, he must be cast into the river.

As I read these words from the book of Exodus, I have deep feelings for Jochebed, who bore a son. I too have borne a son. She looked at her newborn baby and saw that he was a goodly child; how he was saved from being thrown into the river to drown isn't explained; the scriptures say simply that "she hid him three months" (Exodus 2:2).

Her infant son grew and she couldn't hide him any longer. She must have felt with great pain the edict of death. The Pharaoh had decreed this infant son was to die, not because he had done anything wrong, simply because he was born male to an Israelite in the land of the Pharaohs. Jochebed had no rights; she was a slave. She couldn't take legal action; she couldn't flee out of the land with any hope of sustaining life. What was she to do? The scriptures say: "And when she could not longer hide him, she took for him an ark of bulrushes, and daubed it with slime and with pitch, and put the child therein; and she laid it in the flags by the river's brink. And his sister stood afar off, to wit what would be done to him." (Exodus 2:3–4.)

Here was a mother who defied the power of the monarch. Why? To give life to her son.

You know what happened. The princess, daughter of the Pharaoh, came down to the river to bathe. As she walked on the riverbank, she saw the ark of bulrushes. She sent her maid to fetch this curious thing. When it was opened, she discovered the baby, and the baby cried.

The princess took the baby and reared him as her son. She named him Moses. She asked for a nursemaid for the baby and the sister offered to fetch one. For this purpose she ran to get her mother.

Jochebed took the child and was its nursemaid. As the child grew, how she must have loved and cuddled him! She must have given him a developing sense of right and wrong. Then Moses went to live with the Pharaoh's daughter, and he became "her son." I do not believe Moses ever forgot the first strong influence of his mother's nurturing.

Of what value is one life in this world of ours? Who can say? One mother risked everthing to give life to her infant son, and he became the lawgiver of Israel, the Lord's anointed to lead the children of Israel from bondage. What baby might God send with a great mission in our time? He has told us that each human being is of infinite worth. There is no qualification as to worth being determined by sex, race, creed, or color. And yet, so many sanction the aborting of babies before the time for the birth to occur that a history of our time will probably record that millions of babies could have been saved by

mothers, when instead they were denied life and the fulfillment of earthly missions because some women did not have
the courage to face life in such a day as this.

I restate my belief that it takes courage to give birth to a
child. It takes faith and dedication to nurture that life. But it is
infinitely worthwhile.

Like the challenges which face the great apple industry of
this state, the challenges of rearing children are challenges
worth taking. If we care enough for our children, we can set
their feet upon a productive path. If we give careful attention
to details, we can probably see to it that they walk tall and
strong and are able to move forward with confidence. We
must provide food and clothing, give love and tender care, for
no infant arrives so helpless into this world as does the human
infant.

It will require hard work on the part of both fathers and
mothers to provide food, clothing, shelter, and education for
their children.

It will require the wise use of all our resources—both spiritual and material.

It will take a lifetime of commitment. But it is possible. We
can provide a climate of growth for our children. It is the only
hope for our generation. Now, as in the past, all parents hope
that their children may grow stronger and better than they are
themselves. And the children can be if we realize who we are
and why we are here. William Wordsworth's "Ode to Intima-
tions of Immortality" offers responses to these questions:

> Our birth is but a sleep and a forgetting:
> The soul that rises with us, our life's star,
> Hath had elsewhere its setting,
> And cometh from afar,
> Not in entire forgetfulness,
> And not in utter nakedness,
> But trailing clouds of glory do we come
> From God, who is our home.

My message is a reiteration of an ancient communication.
There is a God who is the father of us all and the author of a
divine plan of salvation for all his children. With this under-

standing the members of The Church of Jesus Christ of Latter-day Saints stand strong against unlimited abortions.

First, we teach the sanctity of life and the eternal nature of each soul. We further teach that each soul was created before the world came into being, and that it will continue its growth and development endlessly. It not only has a *right* to life in mortality, but we believe that, except in cases where the Lord takes an infant in death for reasons he understands, it also has a great *need* for this mortal experience. In fact, we teach that eternal progression is dependent upon mortality. As William Penn said, "Nothing but a good life here will prepare man for a better one hereafter."

Second, we teach a single high standard of morality for both men and women. A proper foundation for peace of mind, for personal satisfaction, and for the establishment of good homes and good parents lies in moral purity.

Third, we plan programs to help all Church members develop the skills and prepare themselves for marriage and then, through the institution of marriage, provide mortal bodies for eternal spirits.

Fourth, we teach the eternal nature of the marriage covenant.

Fifth, we help individuals understand that through the development of strong family units, a good society results for our benefit now and continues as a part of the eternal society forever.

It should be no surprise, then, to find us standing against abortion, actively working against it, and urging our members to support and join in the battle to preserve life.

We have produced a filmstrip on the subject of abortion entitled "Very Much Alive." Listen to some of the lines from that script:

> Life is precious.
> Each person is unique.
> Each person is important.

"Very Much Alive" helps those who see it recognize the fallacies behind many proabortionist claims. It helps those who see it realize that life is too precious to be taken from any infant at any state of its development.

The young woman in the film who had an abortion had these haunting words to say: "You think back on what happened. How old the baby would be. What kind of a person it would be . . ."

Wherever the film is shown, we invite parents and teenagers to participate in a discussion. The filmstrip has been very helpful in explaining the issue to both members and nonmembers of our Church.

For those who need professional help and consultation, our Church has a licensed Social Services Department that provides adoption services, foster care, professional consultation, and help for unwed parents.

In the rare cases where the life of the mother might be at stake were she to deliver a baby, there would be no hesitation in saving the mother; for we recognize that a strong and nurturing home is essential to the well-being of children. We also recognize that when conception results from forcible rape, there may be justification for abortion.

But never should we individually or collectively condemn the tender young beginnings of life to wanton destruction. Responsibility is the keystone of our understanding. Life must be preserved, enriched, and nurtured in order that each soul might have its full opportunity for growth in this mortal period of our existence.

Our vision of the true relationship between God and man is that there is a destiny for each soul, with the possibility of each soul growing, developing even to godhood.

I know and you know that there can be no justification for the wanton destruction of human life. We both know that happiness in mortality doesn't just happen, any more than delicious Washington apples just happen. Happiness in mortality requires selflessness and wise guidance. To have a good society we must become involved in the greatest business in the world, that of quality living.

Tonight we must rededicate ourselves to joint and individual action that will bring about that society. It will take time, money, and effort to grow and mature in such a way that we may produce responsible adults who will value human life.

The poet Edwin Markham clearly states for us the nature of life's dilemma:

> . . . in the beginning of the years
> God mixed in man the rapture and the tears,
> And scattered through his brain the starry stuff.
> He said, "Behold! Yet this is not enough,
> For I must test his spirit to make sure
> That he can dare the vision and endure.

> "I will withdraw my face,
> Veil me in shadow for a certain space,
> And leave behind only a broken clue,
> A crevice where the glory shimmers through,
> Some whisper from the sky
> Some footprints in the road to track me by.

> "I will leave man to make the fateful guess,
> Will leave him torn between the no and yes,
> Leave him unresting till he rests in me,
> Drawn upward by the choice that makes him free,
> Leave him in tragic loneliness to choose,
> With all in life to win or all to lose."

Yes, we are individually responsible for our actions. We must choose what we will do and how we will respond to each issue and concern of life. Often our sophisticated society would make those choices an enormous challenge.

By our individual efforts may we meet that challenge and bring about enlightenment in today's thinking. The Chinese record that their great sage Confucius said: "Do not curse the darkness; light one small candle."

Our one small candle can be the light to motivate someone to action. Elton Trueblood said, "We are just as responsible for the evils we allow as for the evils we commit."

Tonight, let us join the battle against abortion with the gentle, persistent tools of persuasion. Let's write to our legislator, attend legislative sessions, and encourage vigorous action to rescind the abortion legislation.

Life is a gift of God. It is not to be taken lightly. It is wrong to abort life's normal flow, except under the circumstances we have mentioned earlier.

We lived as individual souls before entering this existence. We will live in the eternities once more. This time in mortality is essential to our growth and development. We have the responsibility to protect life and not to allow it to be aborted.

Let us invest our time, talent, and energy in this worthy task.

Because *we live* and *know* life—the essential.

Index